Viva Texas Rivers!

THE WITTLIFF COLLECTIONS LITERARY SERIES
in partnership with

THE MEADOWS CENTER
FOR WATER AND THE ENVIRONMENT

TEXAS STATE UNIVERSITY

WITH GRATITUDE TO THE FOLLOWING FOR
SUPPORTING PUBLICATION OF THIS BOOK:

Texas State University
Susan Vaughan Foundation
Jacob and Terese Hershey Foundation
Texas Historical Foundation
Will and Pam Harte
Kathie and Ed Cox Jr.

Viva Texas Rivers!

*Adventures, Misadventures,
and Glimpses of Nirvana
along Our Storied Waterways*

**Edited by Steven L. Davis
and Sam L. Pfiester**

Texas A&M University Press
College Station

Maps copyright © 2021 Molly O'Halloran

Cover painting, *Viva Texas Rivers*, by Clemente Guzman. © 2020 Clemente Guzman

This paper meets the requirements of ANSI/NISO Z39.48-1992 (Permanence of Paper).
Binding materials have been chosen for durability.
Manufactured in the United States of America.
∞

The editors dedicate all royalties from this book to The Wittliff Collections
and The Meadows Center for Water and the Environment

Library of Congress Cataloging-in-Publication Data
Library of Congress Control Number: 2021942188

ISBN: 978-1-62349-980-8 (cloth)
ISBN: 978-1-62349-981-5 (ebook)

*Dedicated with gratitude to these running waters
and to everyone who has served as their guardians,
from the First Nations that began more than 20,000 years ago
to everyone today who loves a Texas River*

Contents

North Texas

Interlude

West Texas

The Lower Guadalupe River

The Nueces River

The Lower Río Grande

Benediction

In the half-light of the canyon all existence fades to a being with my soul and memories and the sound of the river. . . . Eventually all things merge into one and a river runs through it.

—Norman Maclean

We divide time into years. We divide years into seasons. We have different names for every river, a different name for every ocean on the earth. But the river does not know that we have named it "river"—it does not know that it is separate from the waters that call "Come."

—Benjamín Alire Sáenz

Introduction

With a push from the riverbank, we are off, steering our canoe into the main current of the Brazos. It's a cloudy spring day in early April, and we've put in just below Possum Kingdom Dam. Behind us, the highway bridge and telephone lines quickly recede. Soon the only sounds we hear are our paddles quietly dipping into water.

This section of the Brazos is officially designated The John Graves Scenic Riverway, named for the author of *Goodbye to a River*, one of the most beloved books ever written about Texas. We've launched at the very same place that Graves put in on a cold November morning in 1957 when he began the three-week, 150-mile journey chronicled in his classic book.

At the time Graves navigated these waters, plans were underway to dam the last remaining free-running stretches of the Brazos and turn the river into a series of lakes. Graves's solo voyage was his quiet way of paying homage to this historic and ecologically vital stream before it disappeared forever. Graves also understood that by trying to tame the Brazos, we would destroy it—and lose much of our own essence in the process. He was no environmental activist, merely a writer, but in telling his story of this river and why it matters, he helped change people's minds. Thanks in large part to *Goodbye to a River*, the Brazos was spared all but one of those new dams. This section of the river, named in Graves's honor, is a fitting tribute for the man who helped save it.

As we float through the river's broad valley, we note that the water is surprisingly clear, though stained a light amber, owing to the rich sediments the river is steadily transporting from the Texas heartland to thriving coastal estuaries in the Gulf of Mexico. The gentle river current carries us along while clouds overhead are pushed by their own invisible currents. We glide alongside the riverbanks past the spring-fresh lime green of newly leafing trees. Rising beyond the riverbank, the rolling Palo Pinto hills are draped in the darker forest green of mountain cedar. Up ahead, a great blue heron rises majestically on slow-motion wings and guides our way downriver.

We are out on the Brazos today "to follow in the paddle strokes of John Graves." The two of us met at the Wittliff Collections—the extraordinary archive at Texas State University that holds the literary papers of Graves and many other major writers from Texas. We have since become good friends and literary compadres. Steve Davis is the literary curator at the Wittliff, the author of four nonfiction books, and the editor of four others. Sam Pfiester is the chair of the Wittliff's Advisory Council and author of four novels.

Pfiester, sitting aft, guides the canoe. Born and raised in the Trans-Pecos, his affinity for rivers took root as a toddler on family trips to Big Bend National Park. He and his brothers began floating one-man rafts through the Río Grande's canyons in the early 1960s before any commercial trips were offered. Later, as a navy lieutenant in Vietnam, he was an advisor to Vietnamese sailors on old wooden junks that patrolled the rivers of the Cambodian border and Cà Mau Peninsula south of the Mekong. Shortly after the war, Pfiester gathered a group of Vietnam vets and fellow Texans to canoe the Río Grande through the entire Big Bend. At the end of their seventeen-day river journey, the sunburnt, mud-caked, unshaven, evil-smelling group attended a lecture on fauna of the Big Bend. At the end of the lecture, the park ranger announced to the audience, "We also have an indigenous subspecies here with us this evening," pointing to the ragged group. "May I introduce you to RRA, River Ratus Americanus."

For more than forty years now, Pfiester and his fellow RRAs have continued making river pilgrimages. They've rafted dozens of the great Rocky Mountain rivers, and they've floated through remote stretches of Alaska and Canada. On the western edge of the Yukon, they navigated the Firth, with its terminus through a maze of ice floes in the Arctic Ocean. From southern France to the far reaches of Patagonia, from the Cotswolds in England to the steppes of Mongolia, where it took ten days on horseback to reach the rivers, River Ratus Americanus has delighted in exploring many of the great rivers of the world.

Steve Davis, paddling at the front of the canoe and glancing back every now and then to make sure he's not the only one doing the work, is the novice on this Brazos River trip. Davis grew up in a suburb of Dallas, in a world of tract homes and chain stores bordered by interlocking expressways. His knowledge of water recreation was confined to swimming pools and canned amusement park rides. Then one day in 1973, when he was ten years old, a friend's parent drove him and his pal two hours southwest to a brand-new state park on the Paluxy River near Glen Rose. As he explored the clear, shallow waters, the world came alive for him in a new way. He saw the sun's reflection on the water sparkling like liquid diamonds. He listened to the flowing stream tumbling and splashing over rocks. To him, it seemed as though the pretty little river was laughing with delight.

Walking up the riverbed that day, he came across the fossilized tracks that gave this place its name: Dinosaur Valley State Park. Stepping into those giant footsteps from an ancient era, he suddenly realized how the past connects to the present. Years later, Davis moved to San Marcos to attend college at Texas State, where a beautiful spring-fed river runs through the campus. He fell in love with the San Marcos River and other Hill Country streams, seeking out swimming spots where the waters speak just as they did on the Paluxy back in 1973.

Davis may love rivers, but he is no canoeist. He jokes that he's spent more time swimming after capsized canoes than actually paddling one. Pfiester acknowledges that even for experts, canoes are capricious, and he has wisely stowed all their gear in waterproof bags.

The wide, gently sloping Brazos valley is narrowing now, and we are coming up on the first rapids. The river seems to disappear below the horizon even as the sound of rushing water swells. Pfiester steers into the most promising-looking channel, one with a fairly straight run. Suddenly we are moving rapidly, the Brazos propelling us forward. Up ahead, a massive limestone bluff looms. The river crashes against it and spills off to the left. Pfiester shouts, "Paddle right!" and we dig into the current, bearing left and shooting just past the overhanging trees, whose branches could have easily swept us off the canoe. Davis, relieved that they haven't tumped over, lets out a whoop.

We continue paddling downstream, taking note of turtles stacked on logs and deer flagging away through the forest. We slow in amazement at the sight of an osprey hovering in the air, ready to dive for a fish. Late in the afternoon, the clouds begin to break up, and the famously brilliant Texas sky reasserts itself. Now the water is a dazzling, rippling blue that soothes our spirits and sharpens our awareness of the magnificence of the natural world.

We spend three blissful days on the Brazos. One night we camp under the sheltering branches of an ancient cottonwood, and another night on a grassy bluff overlooking a set of rapids. We sleep to the sounds of flowing water and awaken to the serenade of coyotes. We follow the river's sinuous arc as it patiently winds its way through cedar-covered hills, past Garland Bend, Fortune Bend, Chick and Dalton Bends. We see little in the way of civilization, or even other people. Yet we are aware that over the decades, a steady stream of enthusiasts, among them many writers, have dipped their paddles into this same stream. We all do this as a way to pay homage to John Graves—and to perhaps gain a little bit of inspiration for ourselves.

Goodbye to a River did more than help spark environmental awareness in Texas. It also inspired a new kind of writing, creating a bond between rivers and writers that has flowed ever since. Since Graves's day, many more authors have brought to life "the spirit of place" for dozens of Texas rivers and streams, highlighting the distinctive qualities that make each waterway special. Our aim in *Viva Texas Rivers!* is to gather the best of these works into a single volume.

In assembling this anthology, we have explored hundreds of books, magazines, and archives. We have also asked individual authors to write something new for this anthology. We found so much wonderful material that we had to, regretfully, leave out several fine pieces. We also realize that we surely missed other worthy works that deserved inclusion. We apologize for the omissions.

Overall, however, we hope that by collecting so many sparkling literary works, *Viva Texas Rivers!* can contribute to what John Graves started all those years ago—educating and inspiring more of us to cherish and protect these beautiful, fragile, and essential rivers. These writings can help us learn how to look, and how to see in Texas rivers not just our present and past, but also our future.

Steven L. Davis and Sam L. Pfiester

Viva Texas Rivers!

Invocation

This River Here

by Carmen Tafolla

This river here
is full of me and mine.
This river here
is full of you and yours.

Right here
(or maybe a little farther down)
my great-grandmother washed the dirt
out of her family's clothes,
soaking them, scrubbing them,
bringing them up
clean.

Right here
(or maybe a little farther down)
my grampa washed the sins
out of his congregation's souls,
baptizing them, scrubbing them,
bringing them up
clean.

Right here
(or maybe a little farther down)
my great-great-grandma froze with fear
as she glimpsed,
between the lean, dark trees,
a lean, dark Indian peering at her.
She ran home screaming, "¡Ay, los Indios!

Carmen Tafolla is an internationally acclaimed Chicana writer from San Antonio and the author of more than thirty books. She was named San Antonio's first-ever Poet Laureate. She is a Professor Emerita of Bicultural Bilingual Studies at the University of Texas at San Antonio. From *This River Here: Poems of San Antonio* by Carmen Tafolla. Wings Press, 2014. Published by permission of Carmen Tafolla.

Ai vienen los I-i-indios!!"
as he threw pebbles at her,
laughing.
Till one day she got mad
and stayed
and threw pebbles
right back at him!

After they got married,
they built their house right here
(or maybe a little farther down.)

Right here,
my father gathered
mesquite beans and wild berries
working with a passion
during the Depression.
His eager sweat poured off
and mixed so easily
with the water of this river here.

Right here,
my mother cried in silence,
so far from her home,
sitting with her one brown suitcase,
a traveled trunk packed full with blessings,
and rolling tears of loneliness and longing
which mixed (again so easily)
with the currents of this river here.

Right here we'd pour out picnics,
and childhood's blood from
dirty scrapes on dirty knees,
and every generation's firsthand stories
of the weeping lady La Llorona
haunting the river every night,
crying "Ayyy, mis hi-i-i-ijos!"—
(It happened right here!)

The fear dripped off our skin
and the blood dripped off our scrapes
and they mixed with the river water,
right here.

Right here,
the stories and the stillness
of those gone before us
haunt us still,
now grown, our scrapes in different places,
the voices of those now dead
quieter,
but not too far away.

Right here we were married,
you and I,
and the music filled the air,
danced in,
dipped in,
mixed in
with the river water.

   dirt and sins,
   fear and anger,
   sweat and tears, love, music,
   Blood.
   And memories.
It was right here!

And right here we stand,
washing clean our memories,
baptizing our hearts,
gathering past and present,
dancing to the flow
we find
right here
or maybe—
a little farther
down.

East Texas

The Sabine River

"Where will Papa be when he's in the water?" Abigail says. "After he steps off the bank and ain't in Louisiana?"

"He'll be nowhere, Abby," I say to her as she hangs to the skirt of my dress and leans her head back to look up at me. "Your papa will be between two places, and he won't be anywhere then."

"Don't tell her such things as that," Amos is saying as the mule finally begins to move forward slowly, blowing its breath out through its nose as though something has got up inside its head and won't get out. A fly, maybe, or a wasp, or a piece of trash the wind has lifted up into its face. "You'll scare the child, telling her that."

"It's the truth," I say to him. "A little bit of it she needs to hear. Abby must get used to it, the truth, by drips and drabs."

"Oh," my husband says, "Carolina," and then his feet are wet, and he's knee-deep in the Sabine River, out of Louisiana into a moving stream, and Texas is over there waiting on the bank as solid as a green tree stump just after it's been cut.

—Gerald Duff, from *Blue Sabine*

East Texas native **Gerald Duff** has published several books of fiction, poetry, and nonfiction. His 2011 novel, *Blue Sabine*, won the Fiction Award from the Philosophical Society of Texas.

The Lost Sabine

by Wes Ferguson

*y*ou notice things when you come home after being gone too long: the way the pine trees sprout from the hills, or the curve of a narrow river as it winds through the forest.

One fall afternoon before Jacob and I had ever considered boating down the Sabine, I found myself driving into town when the pines gave way to the boggy floodplain. The Texas Highway 31 bridge approached where it straddles the river, just outside Longview. In no hurry to be anywhere, I eased off the gas and peered over the guardrail, down to the river below. From the bridge I could see tangles of brush and a few downed trees. Beer cans littered the muddy banks, and a ribbon of brown water disappeared around a bend. I had surely crossed the river here a thousand times and had never given it much thought. Today, as usual, the Sabine appeared stagnant and dirty, like an oversized drainage ditch.

But then I noticed something smaller. A twig in the water drifted by and was soon followed by another. The twigs bobbed in the current and were swept beyond the bend. This river was not stagnant at all. As I realized how swiftly the water was flowing, I began to wonder what lay beyond my field of vision. I was struck by a desire to follow those twigs around the bend and see where the current led.

I grew up near the Sabine River and graduated from Sabine High School, but no one I knew had ever talked of traveling the river. It seemed like such a novel idea that I could find a boat and set off to explore a section of my home where none of my friends or family had ever gone. Then I told my girlfriend about it. She crinkled her nose, not even trying to veil her disgust.

"Nothing but snakes and dead bodies in that river," she said.

Many East Texans dismiss the Sabine as a dump for dead bodies. They tell each other that snakes writhe across its waters and dangle from the branches of hardwood trees, where they have been known to fall into the laps

Wes Ferguson grew up in the Piney Woods outside Kilgore. An award-winning journalist and the author of two books on Texas rivers, he is a Senior Editor at *Texas Monthly*. Excerpted from *Running the River: Secrets of the Sabine* by Wes Ferguson. Texas A&M University Press, 2014. Published by permission of Wes Ferguson and Texas A&M University Press.

of unsuspecting fishermen. There had to be more to it than that, I thought. I pulled out my Texas road map and traced my finger along the wiggly blue line marking the Sabine's course. It rises in a soggy spot in a cow pasture in the blackland prairie about fifty miles northeast of Dallas, then meanders south-easterly through the Piney Woods of Northeast Texas before elbowing Louisiana and bending hard south into Toledo Bend, the largest human-made reservoir in the southern United States.

Over the next several days, I took alternative routes into town so I could scope out the Sabine from different bridges in the area. No matter where I looked, the little river offered only glimpses of itself before turning the bend and ducking out of sight. On those country drives, I also began to think of possible companions for the journey. In the end, I realized only one person would do: my buddy Jacob. He has a beard. He wears flannel and seems kind of outdoorsy, and he comports himself with a quiet earnestness that I respect. At the time he was working as a photographer at the *Longview News-Journal*, the same newspaper that put me on the payroll whenever I came home and needed money.

After leaving East Texas again for a winter job in another state, I sent Jacob an email suggesting that he and I take an "epic" boat trip down our stretch of river when I came home the following summer. "Why should anyone care about the Sabine? What purpose does it serve besides filling up Toledo Bend?" I posed the questions. Then I offered the best reasons for our trip that I could think of: "Because it's there, and I like to explore. Because it's muddy and slow and people take it for granted, but I know we can find some beauty there, or at least a few stories that have yet to be told. Because it's our river, and we should celebrate it. We should know it."

I hit send. Jacob never responded. A few days later, I passed a message to him through my girlfriend, who had stayed in East Texas when I left. "He says that's a terrible idea," she reported. "He says, 'What about mosquitoes?'"

A man shot at us our first day on the river. Of course he did. You expect that sort of thing to happen on the Sabine.

I met Jacob at his father's house early that morning. He hitched the boat to his truck, and we drove south and east into the border country where Texas blends into the forests and swamps of Louisiana. Jacob's father, Henry, rode shotgun. You could tell he was nervous the way he chattered against the quiet. The boat belonged to him, and he was loaning it to us, but Henry swore he didn't care about the aluminum sixteen-footer. He envisioned the gun-toting types who live along the river, the snags that capsize little boats, and the bewhiskered catfish lurking in underwater dens, and he couldn't help worrying about his adult son. For distraction, he told jokes.

"Y'all gonna do any noodling on your trip, Jake?" Henry asked.

"I doubt it, Pop," Jacob replied, his eyes fixed to the blacktop.

"You should; you really should," Henry said. "Reach down in that river with your bare hands and yank a forty-pound catfish in the boat, and rednecks up behind the bushes will see y'all and say, 'We've been watching y'all the past fifteen miles. Now you're one of us. We'll do anything you need.'" Henry was no fan of rednecks, though as I sat in the backseat watching the forests of longleaf pine trees blanket the East Texas hills, I suspected that more than a few people would classify us no more charitably.

We drove through heavy forest, where black creeks widened in the bottoms, their waters issuing imperceptibly toward the Sabine. The eighth-longest river in Texas, flowing almost entirely within the Piney Woods region on the far eastern edge of the state, the river swells to nearly four hundred yards wide near its mouth at Sabine Lake—no less than half the width of the mighty Mississippi at the Canal Street ferry in New Orleans. The Sabine appears less imposing upstream, however. Where I am from, the river is muddy and narrow and full of debris. In 1779, a Frenchman named Don Athanase de Mézières warned of its "frequent and dangerous turnings" and reported, via letter dated at the ferry crossing of the old Camino Real, "There is no other river that affords greater obstacles." What's more, from the earliest days of Anglo settlement in Texas, the Sabine has earned a reputation as a no-man's-land and a haven for outlaws fleeing justice on both sides of the state line.

Some say not much has changed . . .

The boat motor hummed. The wind cooled our faces, and sunlight danced on the river straight ahead. When the sun hit the water just right, we could see the fickle course of the narrow river channel, where the water flowed more swiftly and deeply than the rest. The channel appeared as a shadowy line below the surface, snaking from one side of the river to the other, a miniature version of the channels Mark Twain had navigated on the mighty Mississippi. It tended to hug the river's outer bends, carving away the steep banks. Sloping sandbars formed a string of private sandy beaches along the lower inside bends.

An anonymous green thicket crowded the riverbanks, which varied from high and clifflike to low and swampy. We saw no houses or other signs of civilization, only trees and brush. Taking in my surroundings, I chose to ignore the difficult time Jacob was having as he steered our boat through the shallow water. The rudder kept thumping the riverbed, and each time the boat lurched to a stop.

We were better off when we stayed in the deeper channel but often lost sight of it under the shade of willows or oaks, and we ran aground. Other times the channel fragmented into a braid of smaller channels, and we slammed into a sandy bed. On these occasions I climbed out and tugged the boat into deeper water, drenching my boots and filling them with silt.

Because there were so many twists and bends in the river, it did not take long to stop noticing them, until we came around one that was taller than the rest. The high, far-off bluff created a kind of balcony where four people were sitting in a row of lawn chairs overlooking the water, as though they had purchased tickets to a matinee show. Come to think of it, the Sabine River was probably the only show on that lazy afternoon at the western edge of Louisiana.

I swear I'm not making up what happened next. We waved, and they waved back, so we decided to stop and visit for a moment. But just as we were pulling onto the sandbar beneath their bluff, a burst of gunfire exploded in our ears. The river plop-plopped behind us. A warning shot! The gunfire echoed across the water.

"Was that aimed at us?" I asked.

We ducked in our boat and froze, not sure what to do. Soon we heard a shout from the tall bluff: "Sorry for shooting at y'all! I thought you was my brother."

Jacob shook his head and muttered, "I'm not sure that makes it any better." Then he yelled to the people just out of sight, "Can we come up there and talk to y'all?"

They didn't answer, so I hollered louder: "Hey! Can we come talk to y'all?"

"Sure!" they replied.

The voices sounded friendly. Not like the kind of people who would shoot a trespasser on sight. I scrambled up the loose dirt bank and introduced myself. To my surprise, they knew who I was, having read a series of stories I had written about the Sabine River for the newspaper in Longview, a three-hour drive to the northwest.

"I was wondering when we'd see you down here," said the shooter, a shirtless man named John Flack. Tattoos adorned his arms and chest, and his jeans were tucked into his boots. A .22 rifle lay across his lap. "Sorry for shooting at y'all," he repeated. "My brother has a boat just like yours."

"That's okay," I replied, not wishing to offend a trigger-happy stranger. "What have y'all been up to?"

"We was out here shooting turtles," said his wife, Kathy. "I got one." Then she gestured toward her husband. "He ain't got nothing."

"I shot three!"

Their children could be heard playing and laughing at a house that sat farther inland from the bluff.

"It's peaceful out here," John said.

"Till you decide to start shooting everything," his wife corrected.

Their friend Corey Ducote looked at me and chuckled. "I can't believe y'all got shot at your first damn day on the river," he said.

Where the River Flows

by Joe R. Lansdale

When I was a teenager, me and my friends went down in the deep woods and along the banks of the Sabine River on a regular basis. We went there to fish, to camp, to hang out, and in that special teenage boy way, be stupid. From time to time, as part of a Boy Scout excursion, or on our own, we cruised down that long, mud-brown river in boats, inner tubes, and rafts.

The Sabine is a long and narrow river, but it has a sense of mystery about it. Jack Kerouac called the river and its banks the Mansion of the Snake in his famous novel *On the Road*. He called it an "evil old river" and said, "We could almost hear the slither of a million copperheads."

Had he listened better, he would have heard the cottonmouth water moccasins as well, the snake that we as kids, and I admit as an adult, were most frightened of. I have heard snake experts say how they are not aggressive or particularly dangerous, and I take them at their study and salute their expertise, but from time to time we had them climb into our boats or rear up in surprise—the surprise belonging to the snakes and us—along the river banks where we treaded toting fishing gear and camping supplies.

Fortunately, we all had a spring in our step and the ability to temporarily levitate in a snake's presence, so therefore, none of us were bitten.

Certainly, there was nothing more disconcerting than to be floating along in an inner tube, legs dangling down through the hole in the tube, looking up to see several moccasin heads poking out of the water near us, swimming along on the muddy current with remarkable swiftness, causing us to wish we were in boats, or better yet, on shore, or perhaps home in our living rooms.

At night, the river and the woods were a crawling black velvet of sound. Things unseen moved along the river bank, slithered or crawled or pranced between the thick growths of trees that ran for miles. Sometimes the splashes were quite loud and you could hear the water ripple, and if the light was right,

Nacogdoches-based **Joe R. Lansdale** is the internationally acclaimed author of nearly fifty novels and a recipient of numerous literary awards. Film adaptations of Lansdale's work include *Bubba Ho-Tep* and *Cold in July*. The television show *Hap and Leonard* is based on his detective series. © Joe R. Lansdale, 2019. Published by permission of Joe R. Lansdale.

you might see those ripples in the moonlight, but rarely the instigator. Alligators maybe, though I never saw any back then, except for a dead one in the back of a pickup at a feed store. Still, I knew they were out there and heard splashes that had to be attributed to lizards of the economy size. Alligators were a rarity at that time, due to overhunting, but since those days, they have gained considerable ground and can now be seen in ponds and lakes and crawling along the shores of the Sabine, dipping into the water like scaly submarines.

Other animals moved through the woods as well. Possums and coons, wild hogs, bobcats and such, maybe even panthers, though that's a much-debated topic. There were those who believed Bigfoot prowled the river bottoms, and even some suggested something more sinister, a companion of the Devil himself, the goat man. The goat man supposedly lived near what was called the Swinging Bridge, which was a dilapidated cable bridge that had formerly been used by the oil companies before the oil played out and towns along the river went from being overnight boom towns to being overnight mud holes or sleepy bergs inhabited by a lingering collection of oil field workers, prostitutes, and poor people, black and white and lost all over.

Creatures like the goat man seemed to always have some sort of mischief in mind, lingering like one of the Billy Goat Gruff family under the swinging bridge, seemingly on an endless mission to grab someone and drag them to hell.

He was supposedly ripe with a stunning stench that was due to his habit of bending over to pee on his beard. He caught you, you were doomed, because he would kill you slowly and horribly and drag your soul off to hell, said soul reeking of goat urine.

In short time, I learned that the mythical goat man couldn't match the cruelty of human beings. Bad things happened down there in the bottoms and along the river from time to time. There were people who lived on or near the banks of the Sabine who were fine folk, and there were others who were not. That old river could carry blood just as easily as hope.

But sometimes, just the night and what naturally lived there were enough to send a thrill up your spine. I remember going with friends down into the dark depths of the woods, alongside the river, and the mystery that I felt is as fresh in memory as the aroma of baked bread. We were teenagers with first-time car licenses and nothing much to do but ride the roads and explore, talk about girls and how tough we were. Once, cruising a blacktop road and later a road made of red clay and scattered gravel, we parked in a clearing where lightning or a careless camper had caused a fire and blackened the earth.

From there we walked through a growth of trees to an old cemetery that one amongst us knew about, had discovered while hunting, perhaps. Through the trees, you could hear the nearby river gurgle and flow, splash at the banks, wandering on down to the Gulf of Mexico.

I remember us using flashlights to look at the dates on the tombstones. They were old, and a number of the mossy stones leaned out from their graves or were tumbled onto the earth, grass having grown up around them like pesky nose hairs.

Many of the graves had caved in. Some had fragments of wood inside them that may have been the remains of ancient coffins. I remember flashing my light into the open graves, expecting to see bones, but I did not. I know it was then that the idea of being buried went out of my head. I would rather be cremated. My ashes carried away by the wind, or washed away by the rolling river, carried all over the world by the tides. I found it far more appealing than being a plug for a hole in the ground. My corpse withering, my coffin dissolved by rust, worms growing fat on my flesh, animals happily gnawing my bones.

One of the times we came to the cemetery, one of our group brought a recorder. A device that would be crude by modern standards, with a spinning tape and heavy buttons that required determination and strong fingers to activate and stop.

Recorded on the tape was the heart-wrenching sound of a dying rabbit, or at least an imitation of one. The noise a dying or injured rabbit made was of the sort that could cause the backbone to shift and the contents of your stomach to curdle.

We turned out all the flashlights, and then the recording was turned on. The plaintive cry of a suffering rabbit filled the air, and as we sat there, bright eyes gradually appeared around the perimeter of the cemetery. The owners of those eyes were unseen, and I can't honestly tell you what sort of critters they belonged to. I could imagine slinking coyotes or red wolves—or at least their dog-mixed descendants—licking their lips. Hot little eyes like golden cigarette tips burning holes through black velvet. Gradually the eyes came closer, and when we could stand it no longer, flashlights were flicked on. It was as if the owners of those eyes were made of shadows. They disappeared into the trees and undergrowth so fast, there was only a slight rustle and a sensation of having imagined it all. Our lights couldn't find them.

On one occasion when we were there, planning to camp but soon forgoing the idea due to the eeriness of the location, we left so quickly I forgot my transistor radio. Turned out the woods were too deep for radio waves anyway. Only static buzzed in my transistor. I placed it next to a tombstone, and it wasn't until I was home, woke up late in the day, that I realized the radio had been forgotten.

I saddled up my '64 Chevy Impala and drove out there, bringing a cane fishing pole, weights and sinkers, hooks and worms I dug from the backyard. I had an aluminum chair with me, a cheap thing my mother had rescued from a dump somewhere, cleaned up and put on the front porch for a while, but eventually for some reason, it ended up folded and leaned against a tree in the backyard, along with an old washing machine and a fire pit for trash.

I thought if I had to go out there and look for my radio, I might as well fish a bit, maybe bring something home large enough to eat.

When I arrived at the cemetery, I located the radio immediately. Where at night the cemetery was mysterious and scary, in the day it was merely sad. I knew without consciously considering it that I would never go back, and I knew too I never wanted anyone to play that dying rabbit tape for me again. Imitated or not, it gave me the willies and made me feel a bit less than human.

I placed the little radio in my car and drove down the road a short distance, parked, grabbed my fishing business, draped the lawn chair over my arm, walked to where the river widened and so did the bank. I had fished there a few times before with some success, and I liked the spot. You could sit and look out at a sandbar that was more of a small island. I made up stories in my head about being on that sandbar, unable to reach the shore, trapped there by raging waters.

I sat for a long time, not really worrying about catching a fish but enjoying having time alone with my thoughts.

Sunset on the river, the big orange orb swelling like a paint spill, tumbling its dying light onto the river, was a beautiful sight. Purple stains streaked the sky above the descending orange sun, and shadows clung to the trees like black crepe paper.

And then I saw something strange.

Across the narrow river, backed by the dying sunlight, a great black cloud rose from the trees and climbed high to the sky like a flying ink blot.

The cloud moved through the trees, headed in my direction. It was more disturbing than the cemetery at night, with the eyes all around and that horrid rabbit sound. It wasn't until too late that I realized what it was.

It was a great wad of mosquitoes, rising into the night sky in search of prey. That would be me. The cloud moved across the river. I hastily gathered up my stuff and headed out. The cloud moved faster and there was a buzzing sound and I began to move more swiftly. Then the buzzing sound was louder than before, and I began to run. I couldn't hang onto the chair or the fishing goods. I let it all go, sped through the dying light toward my car.

Instantly, I was being poked and blood-sucked by an endless number of miniature winged vampires. That cloud was so thick, it was as if a dark bag had been pulled over my head. I swatted at them. I could feel them go wet in my hands, but when one was squished, another took its place. They seemed like an infinity of insects.

It was so bad, I veered toward the river, stepped off the bank and into the water. I went up to my waist, but still they came, swarming around me, biting my face, neck, the top of my head. They buzzed in my ears. They slipped up my nose and into my mouth.

I held my breath and ducked down into the water, washed the ones on me away, but when I came up, their comrades were there. I ducked again and came up with handfuls of mud that I slapped on my face, the top of my head. I waded back toward shore. I had lost a shoe. I started to run, the lack of one shoe giving me a feeling that I was running with one muddy, socked foot in a trench. The other shoe squeaked and squirted water.

The mosquitoes came with me. They continued to attack my face, but now they were biting me through my shirt. I could feel them moving under my hair. The way I was leaping and running and slapping, I must have looked like a clown act at the circus.

I made it to my Impala, jerked open the door, and slipped inside, splashing water and mud across my seats, dripping the same from my sock and single shoe onto the floorboard.

That wall of mosquitoes covered the windshield, and soon all the windows were darkened, and then the night came down full and moonless, and it was darker yet. I think the night and the car finally deterred them.

I had itchy bumps forming all over me from the mosquitoes. I turned on my lights and turned around and drove out of there, alongside the river for a while, until the road widened and drifted through a split in the trees. The road was red clay there, hard and polished by heat and time, and finally I broke out of the bottom land and onto a blacktop, greasy looking in the pale starlight.

I remember those roads and those mosquito bites like it was yesterday. My face bumped up and was red, and my eyes nearly swelled closed. I remember too that I never went back for my fishing goods, or that lawn chair.

At least I went home with my transistor radio.

The Neches River

We would tell about the Neches and the people who have walked its banks, fished its waters, and harvested its bounty. We would tell about the animals that come to the river to drink and about the birds, big and small, that wade along the water's edge seeking bugs, reptiles, and small fish for food. We would give people a mental picture of eagles sitting on broken treetop snags and help them hear the sounds of night. We would share the rewards of silence and solitude and of becoming an unobtrusive part of the world around us. The Neches would tell our message for us if we would only listen and watch.

—Richard M. Donovan, from *Paddling the Wild Neches*

Daddy always said that his greatest desire was to retire and become a river rat. In my younger days, I deplored Daddy's lack of ambition and appreciation of a "better" life, but as time has passed and I often grow weary and disillusioned with the world and everybody in it, I finally understand . . . The Neches River, by its floods and shifting, filling and cutting, has erased all evidence that it was once an important route of commerce and transportation, so one can still see there a bit of this world as God made it and find refuge as Daddy did and as I have done.

—Geraldine Ellis Watson, from *Reflections on the Neches*

Richard M. Donovan grew up along the Neches River. When he learned of plans to build three new dams that would destroy the river's free flow, he helped rally opposition. As part of the campaign, he canoed the upper Neches, writing about his experiences in his 2006 book, *Paddling the Wild Neches.*

Geraldine Ellis Watson (1925–2012) became a renowned botanist and a legendary environmental activist who helped lead the fight to establish the Big Thicket National Preserve. Her best-known book is *Reflections on the Neches: A Naturalist's Odyssey along the Big Thicket's Snow River.*

The Flow of the Neches

by Francis Edward Abernethy

*D*eep East Texas, the *real* East Texas, lies between the Trinity River and the Sabine. Some of East Texas might splash across these rivers onto Madison County in the west and Louisiana in the east, but the heart of it is that red-land, pine-forest region between those two river boundaries. And flowing through the heart of East Texas is the Neches River and all the smaller waters that pay it homage and tribute. They all give their all to the big Neches that gives its all back to the oceans of the world.

There are places in its northern beginnings where the river meanders through pastures and a small boy could hop across it. Farther down it stops to rest in ponds and lakes. Then it spills down a steep slope in Cherokee County, cutting a trench so narrow that the water shoots through a tunnel of cut banks and oak trees that shake hands and hug each other while the river passes beneath.

Farther south the river bottoms widen out, and huge gum and pin oaks and white oaks join their crowns together and shade out all growth below. In some places you can see several hundred yards through the bottoms, and the waters flow through on the big rises to feed the roots of the old giants and fill the oxbows.

The Neches River rises about one mile south of Colfax in eastern Van Zandt County in Doyle Dove's cow pasture. The coordinates are N 32 29′ 58.1″ by W 095 44′ 28.4″, and the elevation is 545 feet, in case you are taking notes. We ran that baby down to his hole! Armed with detailed area maps, three of us—Pat Barton, Bill Clark, and I—cut its trail every time it crossed a road. We had given up on finding its ultimate beginning when we saw this hillside pasture where, according to the map, it ought to begin. I knocked on the door at this house, and when this fellow came to the door, I told him we were looking for the source of the Neches. He said, "Let me get my shoes on." He was Doyle Dove, and he gave us the grand tour of the Neches springs—and a slab of beef when we left, by the way.

Francis Edward Abernethy (1925–2015) was a longtime leader of the Texas Folklore Society and the author and editor of dozens of books on Texas culture. Adapted from "The Flow of the Neches," originally published in *East Texas Historical Journal* 46, no. 1, article 6 (2008). Published by permission of Francis Edward Abernethy's family.

The Neches comes out of the ground in a white, sandy trickle about six inches wide. Some hundred feet away, on the side of the same sandy hill, more water seeps out of cow tracks in the black mud. It all goes down the hill, and by the time these seeps and springs get to the bottom of the hill, you have a respectable spring branch that could provide several families with water.

It flows southeast for 416 miles to its mouth on Sabine Lake, serving as a boundary stream and forming the county lines for most of the counties in Deep East Texas. Two major reservoirs are located on the Neches: Lake Palestine, near Tyler, and Dam B (Lake B.A. Steinhagen), near Woodville.

The Neches has a drainage area estimated at 10,000 square miles. Abundant rainfall in the basin results in a flow of some six million acre-feet per year.

Those are the *statistics* on the Flow of the Neches.

To really *feel* the Flow of the Neches, "ye must be baptized" in it, totally immersed!—like a Baptist, not splashed like a Methodist. You wade off a sandbar until it lifts you up into its current, you glide like an alligator with just your eyes and nose and the top of your head showing, then you sink and roll like an otter till you have thoroughly purged yourself of all your sinful city ways and become a part of the woods and the water.

Or you can feel the Flow of the Neches if you float fifty miles of it with no motor and one paddle, as Hubert Mott and I did for six days in Easter of 1947 and found that for all its beauty, it can test your endurance. The river was on a rise, and the third day out, we drifted off into an oxbow and spent the entire day going around in a circle. At sundown we recognized a big downed cypress that we had passed that morning, and we recognized our predicament and frantically started looking for any piece of dry ground we could find in those flooded bottoms.

Right at dark we finally located an island of mud about the size of a blanket. It was six inches out of the water at its highest, topped with squishy, ankle-deep gumbo, and it harbored a prosperous snake population that peckishly and with many a backward glance gave up their territory at our insistence. We set up camp, such as it was. We had no firewood, so we ate a can of pork and beans cold, except that Hubert cut up an onion in his and had indigestion.

It was a long night because we went to bed early, thinking it was better to lie in the mud than sit in it. We slept on two ponchos and under two blankets, and every time one of us touched the other, we popped awake, certain that snakes were creeping in amongst us. That was one of the longest nights I ever spent. We were off that island by the first gray light of dawn and eventually found the channel and a dry riverbank. We scrambled and ate every last egg we had. We saw one other person that whole trip.

Or another way that you can feel the Flow of the Neches is if you live on it like Old Man Ben Ramer did, who lived on the neatest river houseboat you ever saw. His territory was from Weiss Bluff downriver to Pine Island Bayou. He frequently tied up where Village Creek runs into the Neches. During the late 1950s and early 1960s, I fished Village twice a week, and when Mr. Ramer was there, we always visited a few minutes, not that he was all that sociable. He lived off the bounty of the Neches. He had trotlines, throw lines, and limb lines out all the time. He had traps set for 'coons, 'possums, and otters—whatever he could sell the hide and eat the meat. He had a feisty dog that helped him get squirrel stew whenever the mood hit him, and he took a hog or deer off the bank any time he needed the meat. I visited him one afternoon right after he had pulled one of his own teeth with a pair of pliers. He was a real backwoodsman—one of the river bottom strain.

The Flow of the Neches, however, is more than the water that glides between its banks or the backwoodsmen and buck deer that live off its bounty. The Flow of the Neches is also its history that reaches back to its beginnings over 12,000 years ago at the end of the Time of Ice, the Pleistocene, and during the Time of the Great Melting and the Time of the Making of Rivers, when the ice and snows thawed and ran down the sides of what we now call America.

We are all of one faith, totally immersed in the magic and romance of the big woods and the river bottoms, and of the Neches River that is the heart of the land that we love to our deep heart's core—that we suffer with in a scorching drought and glory in during a crimson fall and are resurrected by when the dogwoods bloom white in the spring. The Neches is our river.

The Enduring Neches

by Thad Sitton

The Neches River of East Texas takes its name from the Neche Indians, a tribal group of the Hasinai Caddo who lived beside it. The Hasinai themselves called the river "Nachawi," "osage orange," naming it for the tree from which they made their excellent bows.

The name makes sense. On a swift rise, heavy with the alluvial soils of the Texas redlands, the upper river assumes a color reminiscent of the orangish inner bark of the bois d'arc tree.

One morning in April, following the watery tracks of Hasinai dugouts of a thousand years before, several of us launched our canoes at Highway 21 ("El Camino Real") on the upper Neches. Plans were open-ended and indeterminate. We knew we would spend our first night on the river at Big Slough Wilderness ten miles below. Beyond that, things depended on the flow of the river, the number of log jams encountered, the turn of weather, and the way this particular trip evolved. Maybe we would stay out for days and go 150 miles to the watery maze above the confluence of the Neches and Angelina, the place old rivermen called "Forks of the River." On this spring day, the river ran fast and high, and anything seemed possible. Beneath our canoes, the Nachawi/Neches slid silently toward the Gulf, and the big bottomland woods were bright with new foliage. The twitter of warblers filled the air.

Sounds of the highway traffic disappeared after the first bend, and before us the Neches ran deserted through the big woods, the latter twentieth century left behind with only a few strokes of the paddle. The Neches is included in all the Texas river guides, but—except for the Big Thicket stretch on the lower river—it's still a semi-secret. I rarely see canoeists when I go out, although the Neches easily is the best float stream in East Texas and one of the best in the American South.

The Neches never has looked like a Colorado trout stream. When northeasterner Frederick Law Olmsted crossed it during his travels through Texas in the

Thad Sitton, a native East Texan, is the author of several award-winning books, including *Backwoodsmen: Stockmen and Hunters along a Big Thicket River Valley* and *Freedom Colonies: Independent Black Texans in the Time of Jim Crow*. "The Enduring Neches" was originally published in *Texas Parks & Wildlife* magazine, March 1995. Published by permission of Thad Sitton.

1840s, he wrote in his journal, "Like all the eastern rivers of Texas it is thick with mud." The Neches above B.A. Steinhagen Reservoir, the last of the more or less natural and free-flowing rivers of East Texas, still is thick with mud, but the silt it carries is the lifeblood of the bottomland ecosystems. Old-stand hardwood forest still borders the upper Neches for most of its length. It flows through two wilderness areas, two national forests, several wildlife areas, and the Big Thicket National Preserve. The last free-ranging East Texas jaguar was killed in the Neches River bottoms near Jasper in 1902. Although wildlife biologists tell me this is an impossible dream, I still hope to see a live one out there sometime.

Several flood seasons have come and gone since I canoed this stretch of the river, and I note many changes. The Neches and the valley through which it flows are really a single process—a world of constant change, dominated by the power of the river. For 20,000 years the Neches has meandered back and forth across its shallow flood plain. Whatever particle of sand the river drops at an accumulating point bar to become part of the forest floor under great oaks and gums, it may pick up and move again one hundred or one thousand years hence. The constituent elements that make up a giant black gum tree are in temporary residence only. In time, the tree will fall and decay, and the river will move its elements farther downstream.

The Neches is both creator and destroyer of its bottomland universe, and at every river bend both forces can be observed in action. On the cut bank, the outside of the bend, a mature forest of oaks, gums, and other hardwoods is toppled and destroyed as the river undercuts its bank. At the same time, on the inside of the bend, a point bar (sandbar) builds up from sediments carried down from cut banks destroyed farther upstream. Soon, this new ground created by the river is colonized by black willow and river birch. Across every sharp bend, a world coming into being faces a world coming to an end.

Eventually, the meander bend is cut off from the natural flow and left behind as a slough or oxbow lake, while the Neches takes a more direct course. The Neches River valley, at the time of high water, becomes a maze of channels as the river works at cutting new passages and flows through old ones that it is in process of abandoning. By the power of each flood, the river's floodplain ecosystems are sustained.

Big reservoirs halt floods, trap the life-giving sediments, and destroy the natural ecology of the river for many miles below them. But on this spring day, no lakes blocked our way for 150 miles downstream: a free-flowing river with no towns, few fishing camps, infrequent road crossings, and large areas of old-growth bottomland forest.

As early settlers along the Neches soon found out, spring floods made permanent settlement near the river all but impossible. Because the river periodically reclaims its miles-wide valley, that valley has been left for the most part in heavy woods, large portions of which are located within the Davy Crockett and Angelina National Forests. A maze of sloughs and side channels twist through the Neches valley, and perhaps because of these obstacles, some stretches of forest in proximity to the river appear never to have been cut. The Big Slough Wilderness area shelters enormous hardwoods and a loblolly pine fourteen feet in circumference. Some one hundred river miles downstream, the Upland Island Wilderness Area protects what perhaps is the tallest tree east of the California redwoods, a cherry-bark oak 165 feet high.

At a time when vast acreages of Southern bottomlands have been converted to pine plantations or soybean fields, the Neches has become a rarity: a nearly pristine Southern river bottom ecosystem.

How long the Neches bottoms will remain "intact" is an open question. Plans for the huge Rockland Reservoir, which would drown all of the middle valley, surfaced again during the 1980s and once again were defeated. In time, they will rise again. Currently, major timber companies intend to clear-cut large areas of the Neches bottoms for wood chips and paper pulp.

Until the clear-cutters come, the canoeist still may find at Big Slough, Devil's Bayou, Alabama Creek, Upland Island, and other places along the Neches scattered remnants of the great virgin hardwood forests that once covered southern lowlands from East Texas to South Carolina. Step out into the deep woods in these areas along the river to get a sense of what it all was like at one time. Beneath the huge cherry-bark oaks, water oaks, and sweet gums, there is little understory. You can see for hundreds of yards across an undulating ground surface sculpted by river floods sweeping across the bend. In the open woods, an occasional muscadine grapevine climbs into the high canopy to bear fruit in the sunlight somewhere out of sight, eighty to one hundred feet up.

The impression is that of an almost rain forest fecundity, and it is not mistaken. Biologists inventorying the Neches bottoms above Dam B reported 189 species of trees and shrubs, 800 herbaceous plants, 42 woody vines, and 75 grasses. Along the river, no fewer than 13 species of oaks and 7 species of hickories yearly drop a tremendous amount of mast to feed the large populations of squirrels, deer, wood ducks, feral hogs, and many other animals.

Wildlife abounds along the Neches. By evening of our first day on the river, the lead canoeist had spotted two beavers, an otter, a herd of feral hogs scavenging the river bank, and assorted kerplunks into the river by creatures large and small that saw him first. Deer are common, as are wild hogs left behind from the closing of the East Texas free range during the 1940s and 1950s. From time to time, pileated woodpeckers cross the river before us in undulating flight, laughing their crazy Woody Woodpecker laugh. To Neches valley stockmen and hunters, the pileated was a bird of many names: "Indian Hen," "Lord God," "Good Gracious," and "Johnny Good God," among other things. During the 1960s, old-timers still remembered and imitated the cry of the extinct ivorybill woodpecker, a sound some compared to the raucous tooting of a child's tin horn.

No ivorybill shattered the windless quiet of this first day on the river; only the pileateds and the barred owls (the "Old Eight-Hooter") broke the silence. In camp that night, some of us rediscovered that barred owls and coyotes can make so much noise, they keep you awake. Both species specialize in dawn and dusk serenades, and old-time woodsmen sometimes depended on the owls for reveille.

Anticipating a long run, we broke camp early the next morning, launched our canoes, and startled an otter into the river around the first bend. Minks and otters are common along the Neches, often seen at dawn and dusk. And in one of the few unambiguous signs of progress, beavers and alligators have returned to the river in large numbers. Along certain stretches of the Neches, beaver sign is everywhere: bank dens, trampled sandbars, peeled willow wands floating in eddies, vestigial dams on side sloughs, and big gum trees with the bark stripped up as high as the animal can reach. Beavers all but disappeared from the Neches for decades. Men in their eighties and nineties remembered beavers from the old days, but younger rivermen were unfamiliar with them. When one of my interviewees found one drowned in his hoop net twenty-five years ago, at first he did not know what it was. He showed it to an older riverman, who said, "That's a beaver. You ain't supposed to have that!"

Judging from their bankside destructions, current populations of beavers along the Neches might be too much of a good thing. On a trip last fall above Highway 94, I saw several beavers in broad daylight. One belly flopped into the river from a grassy sandbar right in front of my canoe; another slid stoically down a bank covered with fallen leaves, braking himself with his tail.

Perhaps the ever-increasing ranks of Neches alligators will keep the beavers under control? On the Neches, the biggest and toothiest of river predators are the various "alligators." Besides the American alligator (a 13-foot 1,040-pounder was killed at Forks of the River around 1960), the alligator gars and alligator snapping turtles (known locally as "loggerheads") rule the river. Stories about these formidable creatures abound along the Neches. Several old stockmen claimed to have witnessed alligator predation on their hogs or stock dogs. One elderly man I interviewed told me that many years ago he had practiced the old southern skill of "grabbling" barehanded to catch flathead catfish from under logs and in bank holes (often preceded by a nerve-calming dose of "pinetop whiskey"), until the day he viewed, dead upon the bank, a 150-pound alligator snapping turtle with a head larger than his own. After that he quit grabbling, drunk or sober, having belatedly converted to the opinion, expressed by another man, that "I ain't going to put my hand into no place I can't see."

Even in the old days, most country people regarded grabbling as a practice of the rural lunatic fringe, and snapping turtles were the reason. One inexperienced fisherman became so overwrought at the sight, smell, and sound of his first loggerhead, caught in a hoop net, that he shot a large hole in the bottom of his boat trying to kill it. Today, alligator snapping turtles are protected as a threatened species in the state and grabbling for fish is prohibited.

Although rare in recent years, alligator gars haunted stretches of the river, and some were so large and so regular in their habits that they became well known to local fishermen. For example, the big gar ("long as a sixteen-foot johnboat") haunting the Neches downstream from the Highway 7 crossing came to be known as "Felix." Gars often lurk motionless in plain sight at the surface, and rivermen shot at Felix for a decade, with no visible effect. Periodically, he entered their nets after fish captured inside and "tore the hell out of 'em on his way out."

On the third day, we passed through the former haunts of Felix the giant gar and drifted on downstream toward the New River-Old River split around Pine Island and a maze of sloughs where Cochino Bayou reaches the Neches. Once upon a time, timber thieves eked out a Robin Hood–like existence in this watery jungle, stealing prime white oak stave trees from the lands of both the 4-C and Southern Pine lumber companies and drifting them downstream to market. But that's another story, and a long one. The Neches country is thick in such stories, seldom recorded, dying out with the last old rivermen. On this fine spring day, we floated on, bound for Forks of the River.

Village Creek

Village Creek

by Gordon Baxter

In the Beginning

Village Creek, ten thousand years old and how I love her. Sweet Sister Creek, where my father brought me as an infant in his arms. That was back before too much of man, and we would huddle to hear the panther scream in the night. Village Creek, where I brought my sons and daughters in turn and let them learn the lessons of beauty and of courage and to hear God's peace.

As a teenager I built a canvas canoe and strapped it to the top of the Model A Ford and drove up from Port Arthur to where the old iron bridge crossed the creek. There was a favorite place a few hours downstream that I called my secret sandbar. This distance was far enough, paddling down from the bridge to have earned a rest, a cool swim and drink from the creek. I would belly flop on the untracked crescent of sand in the shade of the small willows and squint across the white glare to the wall of the forest.

With my mind I would try to penetrate the gloom of oak and pine and try to picture what it would be like to live here all the time. The vision was so hallowed that I could not give me permission to cross the hot sandbar, actually go inside there, and turn round and look out. I knew that someone must own this place, but it was beyond me to imagine such. And the fantasy of finding such a man and asking him if I could buy this land seemed as farfetched as speaking to the queen of England. And yet as I lay there, daring not to dream it, I was equally

Gordon Baxter (1923–2005) was a well-known radio personality from Port Arthur. He was also a journalist and writer with eleven books to his credit. Adapted from *Village Creek: The First and Only Eyewitness Account of the Second Life of Gordon Baxter by Himself* by Gordon Baxter. Summit Books / Simon & Schuster, 1979. Published by permission of Gordon Baxter's family.

certain that someday I would own this place and would be sitting in my house back there, looking out through the cool trees and remembering me as a kid dreaming of it. And that I would always tell it that way.

The years had rolled me along smooth and tumbled me as a slick river rock in the stream bed, and now l knew from some inner timetable that it was time to go and ask.

The land belonged to the Barry family and good ole Doc Dudley English. Some of them still lived around here. Good and decent people, they had settled this part of the creek in the early twenties. The last time they sold off a parcel of creek front was twenty-five years ago.

Now there are customs in deep East Texas. You don't just walk up to a man and offer him money for his land or his dogs. First you get to know him a little. You visit and hang around now and then and talk about other stuff. He knows well enough what you're there for. You never had showed up before, had you?

I got in touch with ole Huck and Wallace Barry and the doc. Got permission to camp out on the sandbar. Met them in town now and then. They got used to seeing me and my kids on their part of Village Creek. One day I told them I sure would like to homestead that place. They solemnly agreed that sure would be nice. Said they would think about it.

Ten years rolled by. Whenever I saw the Barrys, I would indicate that I was still thinking about it. And they would acknowledge, without so many words. And then one day, me and Wallace Barry and old Dr. Dudley English were stepping out of a boat and pushing our way back into that very forest and pacing off the yards and acres. It was floodtime, and the sandbar was underwater, but we knew where we were. And I was so dazed that when they named the price for this tract that they held in common that I was not sure if they were talking about all of it or that much per acre, and I wasn't sure how to phrase the question. I would have given all my treasure for this.

And later in the office, with the surveys and plats curling up on the table and the lawyer's papers signed and the solemn ceremony of standing up to shake hands all around, I asked them, "Why the ten years?"

"We wanted to wait a little and find out what kind of feller you are."

On a Wooden Island

This time it rained for forty days and forty nights. Man, I never saw so much water in all my life. I picked up the phone, and water ran out of it. The catfish are up and running through the woods again, catching baby rabbits. The copperhead snakes have all moved out of my woodpile and taken to the trees, and the owls are flying off with them. Sunday I saw two washed-out and starving spiders get together and weave a seine and start after minnows. Tilley and Norma Jo came down and helped us move a lot of stuff upstairs, then we went down to their place. Their ridge is about four feet higher than ours and seldom floods, but their cabin is built flat on the ground. Fresh, clear, golden creek water was running about a foot deep across Norma Jo's clean waxed floors. With sawhorses and boards, we built scaffolds in the house and raised the bed and dresser and freezer. When we left they were sitting on the couch eating fresh roasted peanuts, feet propped up on the coffee table and watching the color TV. All of it on scaffolds and planks, life passing as before, with Village Creek running in and out the door.

We got support for the "hell, no, we won't go" from watching Tilley and Norma Jo. He's a machinist; she works downtown in the catalog department at Sears. They shove off at daybreak each morning, Norma Jo dressed to the nines with her yaller hair all piled up on top of her head, setting proud up in the bow of the boat, riding for the bridge.

The Tilleys will be back, even though their garden is scattered again and will be sprouting up all over the place if it ever dries out again. It's the chances you take for the beauty you get.

Village Creek Will Heal You

The waters of Village Creek will heal you. Not surprising that little has been said of this in the scientific community. What do they know of the tangle tongue elm that will cure toothache? Or why ole Archer wears a red rag on his shoulder when he's got bursitis? Or why does a dog roll in dung, or about snow snakes, or revelation among the frogs?

The waters of Village Creek will heal you. Aches and wounds get better right away. I taught Diane this when she first came here, to wade the creek and make the awful red welts of mosquito bites go away. Mosquitoes do not bite me. They circle and sing but never sting. I have a natural immunity. Diane says it is the awful load of tobacco and whiskey fumes I carry in my bloodstream. That, plus my natural venom.

Everything in the Holy Ghost Thicket is God's work. Man cannot create nature; he can only change things. When we look out our windows, we see only the works of God, and in His works, we find His word.

In the dark baygall, the tall cypress is blasted by lightning. She grieves, then the stump heals and sends forth tender shoots to fight for life and to be whole again. In the stillness of the night before a thunderstorm, we hear a forest giant crash. We go there the next day and look upon the thrashings of that death. What we see are new seedlings sprouting. New life to be nourished from the body of the parent who is returning to earth.

If the bright hot days are too constant, then wait. God is sending an infinite variety of wind and cloud and rain. If all the familiar stars in the sky are shifting in a bewildering pattern of summer and winter, then look, there is Polaris, always constant.

And all of the creatures of the forest live and die in the same delicate balance of the wheeling of the stars of the universe. Did God make the delicate organs of the lunar moth any less intricate than those of the fox? Or less wondrous than the motions of the stars? All things set in balance and in a harmony of life. Life springs out of death in the fecund forest floor. The young sapling trees bend before whatever forces confound them but reach ever upward toward the light.

In the long twilight, Diane and I walked in silence down by the water's edge. There was dead calm, not a ripple of wind. The tall pines stood at the reflected painting of themselves.

We waded in the shallows, seeing our bare feet on the clear white sand bottom, standing naked. The full summer moon rose into the pine tops like pale music. With infinite care I leaned her head back, washing her hair. It flowed dark from her trusting face.

We stayed until the Eastern star rose bright over our sand-floored cathedral. And the other day, a fellow asked me if we went to church.

The Trinity River

Driving east from Dallas to Ennis to Kaufman,
I cross the Trinity River,
marking the end of the West,
and travel back into East Texas,
more primordial, lush, and ancient
than the spare, dry edge of the Texas plains . . .

The Trinity as was its wont,
regularly overflowed its banks and flooded the river bottom
sending the coons, possums, bobcats, swamp rabbits, stray cows,
and snakes searching for higher ground.

—Mark Busby, from *The Trinity, a Memory, Spring 1930*

That dirty Trinity River sure have done me wrong
It came in my windows and doors, now all my things are gone
Trinity River Blues keeps me bothered all the time
I lose all my clothes, baby, believe I'm going to lose my mind

—T-Bone Walker, from "Trinity River Blues," 1929

Mark Busby, a native of Ennis, Texas, is a Distinguished Professor of English Emeritus at Texas State University and the author/editor of several books of fiction, nonfiction, and poetry.

T-Bone Walker (1910–1975), born Aaron Thibeaux Walker in Linden, Texas, is considered the godfather of the modern electric blues guitar. He was inducted into the Rock and Roll Hall of Fame in 1987.

Holy Trinity

by Gary Cartwright

When I was growing up in Arlington, the upper Trinity River was a dirty joke. No one wrote love songs about the Trinity, much less ate its fish or canoed its rank and odoriferous waters. Our town dumped its sewage directly into the river. Our big-city neighbors, Fort Worth and Dallas, at least treated their sewage before sending it down river, though not so the fish could tell. In the 1960s, the US Public Health Service described the one hundred miles of river below Dallas as "septic." As recently as the 1980s, sewage from Dallas was killing fish downstream in historic numbers. Alarmed by fish kills and what they called "black-water rises"—the welling up from the river bottom of masses of oil, grease, copper, chlorine, pesticides, and toxic industrial and agricultural wastes—citizens in Anderson and Freestone Counties filed a lawsuit in 1985. The suit thwarted Dallas's plan to dump tens of millions of gallons of raw sewage in the Trinity, and more than that, it called statewide attention to this outrage.

Indignant Dallas officials denied that their sewage harmed fish; the water commissioner noted cavalierly that the Trinity was never meant to be "a trout stream." A guy from the Trinity River Authority had the gall to insist that the fish kill proved that the quality of the Trinity was getting better. "We wouldn't have had a fish kill this year if we hadn't made the improvements in water quality in 1970," he declared, "because there wouldn't have been any fish [left to kill]."

To this day, citizens of the Metroplex largely deal with the Trinity by ignoring it—with a few happy exceptions. True, nobody writes poetry about this river, yet the upper Trinity is far cleaner and more attractive than it used to be. Rivers are getting to be trendy. An eight-mile jogging and bike trail now connects Arlington's River Legacy Park to Fort Worth and Grand Prairie. After all these years of indifference, the city of Dallas has officially discovered the Great Trinity Forest, a 7,000-acre swamp where for decades, old toilets, tires, truck

Gary Cartwright (1934–2017) was a legendary Texas journalist renowned for his gonzo style. He was a longtime writer at *Texas Monthly*, a screenwriter, and the author of several books. Adapted from "Holy Trinity," originally published in *Texas Monthly*, October 2003, and "Contemplating the Trinity," originally published in *Texas Parks & Wildlife* magazine, July 2004. Published by permission of *Texas Monthly* and *Texas Parks & Wildlife* magazine.

axles, and slabs of asphalt collected. The seven-mile-long section of river that slogs through downtown Dallas, a rerouted ditch constructed in the 1920s, may someday be transformed into a landscape of lakes, wetlands, nature trails, and designer bridges; it's part of the proposed $1 billion Trinity Corridor Project.

For all its neglect and mismanagement, the Trinity is one of the great rivers of Texas. Half of the state's population lives along its course. It runs 550 river miles, and it drains an incredible 17,969 square miles, from Cooke County on the northern border of Texas to Trinity Bay, where it becomes the main source of nourishment for Galveston Bay. The river's curse is that it essentially begins and ends in the state's two great urban areas, Dallas-Fort Worth and Houston.

From the end of the Civil War to as late as the 1970s, civic boosters in the Metroplex clung to the delusion that the Trinity might be refashioned into a 370-mile ship channel connecting Dallas and Fort Worth to the Gulf of Mexico, creating an ersatz Port Metroplex rivaling the Port of Houston. That never happened and never will, but that didn't stop them from constructing several locks along the river.

When the Trinity River Authority impounded Lake Livingston in 1969, it created 450 miles of shoreline and flooded 90,000 acres of hardwood bottomland. The dam also arrested the flooding and silt that would have nourished estuaries and hundreds of thousands of acres of Texas coastal wetlands. A remnant of the bottomland hardwood ecosystem remains twenty-five years later, protected by the creation of the Trinity River National Wildlife Refuge near Liberty.

Where I grew up along the upper part of the Trinity remains a metaphor for mismanagement and neglect, cited among the top ten most endangered rivers in America. So you can imagine my surprise upon discovering that the lower Trinity, that stretch of the river just north of Galveston Bay, is a place so magical and exotic that it seems right out of the pages of Tolkien. My education began last winter, while I was researching a story on Galveston Bay. My friend Shannon Tompkins, a biologist and outdoors writer for the *Houston Chronicle*, had taken me to a rookery just east of the bridge where Interstate 10 crosses the river. To my amazement, the rookery turned out to be part of an incredibly beautiful and mysterious cypress swamp, so unlike the Trinity of my boyhood that it was hard to believe this was the same body of water. Shannon grew up in Baytown, has lived near the river since he was in grade school, and knows every oxbow, slough, and bayou. The rookery is only a small piece of the vast swamp, he informed me, one of the last of its kind in Texas. Unfortunately, the Trinity was so swollen from winter rains that a trip upriver would have been foolhardy, so Shannon suggested that I come back in the spring.

Early on the Friday of Memorial Day weekend, I again found myself at the rookery with Shannon. The first soft light of morning broke above the ground fog, twinkling off the shocking pink of a pair of roseate spoonbills gliding overhead. Crossing a footbridge, I stood at the edge of a shimmering world of electric-green water plants, giant cypress trees, Spanish moss, and so many snowy egrets, great blue herons, and other nesting birds that the trees appeared to be doing a fan dance. Without my noticing it, the rumble of eighteen-wheelers had given way to a chorus of birds and bullfrogs. A small alligator rustling through a cluster of water hyacinths watched us with patient yellow eyes. "We seem to have dropped off the edge of Texas and landed in some Louisiana swamp," I observed.

"Thousands of cars a day pass over the I-10 bridge, yet nobody notices what's down here," Shannon said. "'Rivers and the inhabitants of the watery element were made for wise men to contemplate and fools to pass by.' Izaak Walton wrote those words in the 1600s." Shannon is that rarest of men, a college-educated swamp creature who spends most of his life outdoors and can quote Thoreau, Faulkner, and any number of Greek philosophers and make it sound like casual conversation.

Once we had launched his sixteen-foot aluminum boat and passed under the bridge, I learned that it is the official demarcation dividing salt- and freshwater. Crab traps infest the river on one side of the bridge but are illegal on the other. Shannon comes here nearly every Friday, usually alone. The river and the swamp are his touchstones of reality. "I have clinical depression," he told me as we moved upriver. "This is the only place I don't feel bad."

The river is surprisingly wide and deep, sheltered on both banks by dense forests of cottonwoods and elms. Hundreds of nests of red wasps hang from the ends of branches, low over the water. I watched as an anhinga (or snakebird) plunged from the sky, vanished underwater, then reappeared with a small fish in its long bill. There are few snakes in this part of the river. "Snakes are mobile sausages for feral hogs, gators, and birds," Shannon explained. Thanks to the lack of rain (and standing water), there aren't many mosquitoes, either—at least there weren't that day. In another few weeks, the river would be alive with insects and unbearably hot and humid, but at that moment, conditions were perfect, and a deep sense of peace settled over me.

Somewhere south of Liberty, we exited the main body of the river into an old barge canal that cuts through the heart of the cypress swamp. Fifty years ago the canal was used to transport timber and molten sulfur from a now-long-abandoned mine to the ports of Galveston and Houston. You can still see the pilings of Texas Gulf Sulphur's loading docks, towering like ancient skeletons from the thick green water. Shannon pointed to a small rise where a single long-leaf pine stood sentinel. "Twenty-five years ago, that rise was covered with one-hundred-fifty-year-old longleaf pine," he told me. "Then one day they were all gone." Most of the old-growth cypress is gone too, cut down a century ago, when there were two sawmills in the town of Wallisville.

Shannon shut off the outboard motor, and the music of the swamp rushed around us. A gar splashed nearby. A brilliant yellow prothonotary warbler perched atop a piling, fluffing his feathers and whistling his reedy mating call. From the dark forest of cypress, tupelo, and pignut hickory, we heard the squall of a wood duck and the staccato scream of a pileated woodpecker. A barred owl barked, and Shannon answered: *Hoohoo-hoohooaw!* The swamp pulsed with life. In places, the water's surface boiled with clouds of tiny shad—"nervous water," Shannon called it. A black-crowned night heron stood poised to strike. What I assumed were two eight-foot logs unexpectedly flicked enormous tails, revealing themselves to be alligators. Shannon couldn't resist pulling out his fishing tackle. He hooked several nice-sized bass, which he comforted with cooing sounds as he plucked the jigs from their jaws and returned them to the river. "I bet I've caught every fish in this river twice," he said.

Back in the river channel, we searched out a bayou that leads to Lake Charlotte, one of several remote, shallow, and nearly inaccessible natural bodies of water in this river system. A squadron of great blue herons and great egrets, flying at eye level, escorted us deeper into the swamp. Knees of long-dead cypress lined the banks like pickets in a fence. The swamp is a shadowland of submerged stumps, tangled branches, and fallen trees, so forbidding and otherworldly that I half expected to see hobbits frolicking among the foliage. In the early 1800s, when hurricanes threatened Galveston Island, Jean Lafitte and his pirates hauled their ships along this bayou to the shelter of Lake Charlotte. (One or two of Lafitte's ships are said to be buried on the lake bottom, under so many feet of mud that retrieving them would be impractical.) The lake is so shallow now that our small boat couldn't cross it, much less explore an adjacent marsh of cypress trees that rose out of the shifting shadows like a cathedral.

Later, we stopped to investigate an Indian midden, a steep bank filled to a depth of four or five feet with clam shells, fish and alligator bones, shards of pottery, and God knows what else. Hundreds of years ago, this was a garbage dump for the nomadic Akokisa tribe. Despite the abundance of fish and fowl, life here must have been terribly difficult. In the absence of rocks, the Akokisa fashioned arrowheads from gar scales. Hardly a trace of paint or decoration enhances their pottery. "Art is a manifestation of the thought process," Shannon explained. "The Akokisa must have needed all their energy just to stay alive." The Spanish constructed a mission and fort near Lake Charlotte in 1756, but the friars complained of biting insects, extreme heat and cold, and the thick, stinking water of the lake. By 1771, the Spanish were gone.

As magical as it appeared to my novice eyes, the swamp is only a token of what the lower Trinity was before man had his way. The last two ivory-billed woodpeckers in Texas were shot near here in 1904 by a "naturalist" named Vernon Bailey. In a ten-year period in the late 1800s, a hog farmer named Ab Carter killed all the bears in Liberty County—182 of them—then shot his bear hound because the dog was no longer of use. Lake Charlotte was scheduled to be flooded out of existence in the seventies—so that Liberty could be a seaport—but was spared by the discovery of a bald eagle's nest. Had the proposed Wallisville dam been completed, it would have flooded 13,000 acres of marsh, cypress swamp, and marine nursery—and turned Galveston Bay into a sterile pond. Ironically, the dam was a key element in the moronic dream of Port Metroplex.

As we ended our excursion, exhausted and happy, Shannon remarked, "'You can't step twice into the same river.' Heraclitus said that." It's a truth I need to remember. There is no permanent reality except the reality of change. The only real state is the transitional one of becoming.

Buffalo Bayou

*A*bout noon we entered Buffalo Bayou, at the mouth of the San Jacinto River and opposite the famous battleground of the same name. Proceeding smoothly up the bayou, we saw an abundance of game . . . This bayou is usually sluggish, deep, and bordered on both sides with a strip of woods not exceeding a mile in depth. The banks have a gentle slope, and the soil on its shores is good, but the prairies in the rear are cold and generally wet, bored by innumerable crayfish, destitute of clover, but covered with coarse grass and weeds, with a sight here and there of a grove of timber, rising from a bed of cold, wet clay.

—John James Audubon, 1837

Jay looks out across the bayou before him. It is little more than a narrow, muddy strip of water flowing some thirty feet below street level; it snakes through the underbelly of the city, starting to the west and going through downtown, all the way out to the Ship Channel and the Port of Houston, where it eventually spills out into the Gulf of Mexico. There's been talk for years about the "Bayou City" needing a river walk of its own, like the one in San Antonio, but bigger, of course, and therefore better.

—Attica Locke, from *Black Water Rising*

John James Audubon (1785–1851) was an American ornithologist, naturalist, and painter. The Audubon Society is named in his honor.

Attica Locke, born in Houston, is a celebrated novelist and a Los Angeles–based screenwriter and producer. Her bestselling fiction, set in East Texas, has won wide acclaim and received numerous literary awards.

Buffalo Bayou
The Soul of a City

by Michael Berryhill

A few years ago, I came to live in a second-floor apartment overlooking Buffalo Bayou. The complex was situated on the bayou's flood plain and probably shouldn't have been built there at all. But the view of the water was beautiful. Healing from a personal crisis, I would sit on a bench in the parklike setting and watch the slant of morning light on the white sycamores and cascading willows that lined the bank and be soothed by the brown water flowing gently past.

I had a canoe chained up in a storage area, but I seldom took it into the water. And for good reason: for years, the city's overburdened sewage system had discharged into the bayou, with the River Oaks outflow being one of the worst. The result was that in some places the bayou smelled like an open treatment facility, but with no treatment. The canoe race along the bayou each spring had been given the name "Reeking Regatta," and my impression of the bayou's water quality, like the impression of many Houstonians, was not good. The bayou was picturesque. It was something to look at. But it was not something to enter into. A few months after I moved away, a heavy rainfall caused the bayou to rise and inundate the apartment complex where I'd been living. I was glad to have escaped.

I moved to west Houston, and living there my contact with the bayou was reduced to glimpses as I drove over its bridges: the green crowns of trees, a brown triangle of water, and then it would be gone. Like a repressed thought, the city's foremost geological feature lived in a recess. It was powerful, alluring, but out of consciousness.

But recently, I began to wonder if such a distanced connection was still called for. I'd heard that the water was getting better; the Buffalo Bayou Coalition had even dropped the word "reeking" from its annual race. This spring, the coalition announced that the water quality was the best it has been in many years.

Michael Berryhill is a Houston-based writer and editor and is a Professor of Journalism at Texas Southern University. Originally published as "Born on the Bayou." *Houston Press*, May 25, 1995. Published by permission of the *Houston Press* and Michael Berryhill. Today, Buffalo Bayou's restoration and revitalization stands as one of Houston's proudest civic achievements.

I was skeptical, as were friends of mine who, when I mentioned the possibility of actually going to the bayou and seeing it again for myself, wondered why I'd want to immerse myself in something so unpleasant.

The reaction was quintessentially Houstonian: Don't concern yourself with what was. Look to the future. Let Buffalo Bayou be. But I couldn't. I decided it was time to quit turning my back on the bayou.

So on a sultry morning not long ago, I slipped out of Houston's noise and bustle to paddle most of the bayou's serene western length. For a couple of weeks before, the bayou's technicians, protectors, historians, and lovers had been explaining the waterway's problems to me. They tossed around riverine terms such as natural repose, riparian fringes, and fluvial geomorphology. They retold the story of the successful battle to keep flood-control engineers from cutting the trees from Buffalo Bayou's banks, straightening its curves, and lining it with concrete.

They all claimed to have good news about Buffalo Bayou. After decades of neglect, they told me, it was gradually coming to be seen as an urban amenity instead of a stormwater- and sewage-effluent discharge system. Downtown and in the East End, the shores of the bayou were being turned into urban greenbelts, with wildflowers, tree plantings, hike-and-bike trails, and historical markers. Under the pressure of fines from the Environmental Protection Agency, the city of Houston had cleaned up its sewage discharges, and the water has been declared safe for "contact recreation"—a rather bureaucratic designation meaning that it was safe to let the bayou touch you again.

There would be plenty of touching in the open green kayak I had borrowed for my trip. I packed sandwiches and fruit, a jug of drinking water, binoculars with which to watch wildlife, and a camera that was supposed to be watertight. I planned to cover a stretch from the Barker reservoir near Highway 6 to the 610 bridge at Memorial Drive, a distance of a dozen miles or so by road, and longer on the meandering course of the bayou.

The experts had told me that everything was going just fine. But Houston has been notorious in the past for putting a good face on things, for trying to make the best of bad situations. I had listened long enough to the experts insisting that Buffalo Bayou was a treasure, not a nuisance. Now it was time, as one of them had said, to listen to the resource.

The early visitors to Houston had no such qualms about Buffalo Bayou. The bayou was the entryway to the new city, and visitors admired the stately magnolias adorned with huge lemon-scented blossoms and the live oaks bearded with moss that lined its banks. Traveling by steamboat from Galveston, the great naturalist and wildlife painter John James Audubon visited Houston shortly after it had been founded and Texas had won its independence, sharing a cup of grog with the new republic's president, Sam Houston. Only a few miles east on the bayou, Houston had defeated a Mexican army. Audubon was likely impressed by that, but he was more impressed by the birds he saw taking advantage of the bayou's water and foliage. Some of the birds that Audubon painted, such as the great blue heron, the wood duck, the anhinga, the green heron, and the kingfisher, still live along the bayou's green, secluded banks.

The Allen brothers had founded Houston because the bayou offered access both to the cotton, timber, and produce of inland farmers and planters and, via Galveston Bay, to the sea. Before railways and hard-topped roads dominated transportation, the bayou served personal as well as commercial transportation. When the city's roads were mired in mud deep enough to drown a mule, Houstonians who wanted to shop in nearby Harrisburg went there by boat. In an 1891 bird's-eye map of Houston, an artist drew the bayou as the most prominent geological feature of this flat coastal city. He found the bayou far more complex and interesting than the grid of streets lining its south bank.

Industry and business grew along the shores of the bayou. From its banks near the center of town, nineteenth-century brick companies mined red clay used to construct Houston's first buildings; timber companies floated logs down it, and sawmills used its water power to cut the logs into lumber. The most important street in town was Commerce, which ran closest to the wharves from which planters shipped their cotton to manufacturers in England.

Not all this attention, though, was benign. Some of the businesses polluted the bayou. A slaughterhouse situated just west of town had to be ordered to move east and dump its offal downstream from the city. The sawmills were forbidden to unload sawdust in the stream. Erosion from the cut-down forests and small farms to the west silted the bayou and muddied its waters. But as jobs were created in the eastern end of the city, the western banks of the bayou were abandoned to forests again, and the waters ran clear.

The natural beauty of the bayou was not lost on Will and Ima Hogg, who helped foster Houston's westward expansion. In 1929 "Miss Ima" built the Bayou Bend mansion to house her collection of American antiques, and in 1930 her brother developed the River Oaks neighborhood and established its country club on the south bank. Farther west, Memorial Drive ran parallel to the curves of the bayou and brought more development and erosion with it. But as more homes were built, the city failed to keep pace with the demands on its sewage treatment plants, which backed up during heavy rains. Eager to hold down taxes, politicians failed to add sewage treatment capacity as the city grew. By the 1960s, the western part of Buffalo Bayou stank of sewage from its wealthiest neighborhoods, and the Ship Channel into which it fed consisted of a poisonous soup of petrochemicals from the industries that lined its banks.

After being born on the bayou, it looked like Houston had decided on a little patricide. It was killing its own parent.

On the morning that I settled into the bayou's western reaches, the flow of water was particularly good because the Army Corps of Engineers was releasing water from the Barker Dam. The water was greenish brown in color with visibility of less than a foot. But it smelled fine, and it was cool as it lapped into the bottom of the kayak and drenched my shorts. Within seconds, the corporate parking lot from which I had launched dropped from view, and the green canopy of trees embraced the little craft. A dragonfly settled on the bow to hitchhike for a ways. A hundred yards downstream, I heard a splashing on the bank and pulled over to investigate. A pair of copulating frogs sat on the mud, the smaller male on top of the bigger female, making an almost seamless, clumsy, unified animal. Then I saw another pair, and another. I had stumbled into a frog rut. I left them in peace.

The western end of Buffalo Bayou runs for about three miles through a greenbelt county park that's lined with footpaths and jogging trails. The park occupies at least part of the floodplain and helps prevent erosion caused by encroaching development. It's named for the mother protector of Buffalo Bayou, Texas Parks and Wildlife Commissioner Terry Hershey.

In 1966, Hershey was headed to a party with some friends, and she was seething with anger. The Harris County Flood Control District was clearing all the trees from a nine-acre tract of land near the bayou at Chimney Rock. This was in preparation for straightening the channel and paving it with concrete. One of Hershey's friends said that he and a few other prominent Houston businessmen had formed an association to fight such plans. They had watched as the Army Corps of Engineers already turned Brays and White Oaks bayous into concrete-lined ditches, and they didn't want to stand by passively while the same thing happened to Buffalo Bayou. Well, Hershey told her friend, it was happening, and wasn't it time for the Buffalo Bayou Preservation Association to have another meeting?

The Corps had not decided to channelize the bayous all on its own. After disastrous downtown floods in 1929 and 1935, the city and county leadership had assembled a dramatic pictorial of the flood damage called "Wild River" and petitioned the Texas legislature and the U.S. Congress for help. In 1937, the legislature authorized the creation of the Harris County Flood Control District and gave it permission to levy property taxes through the commissioners court. The main purpose of the district was to leverage federal money through the Army Corps of Engineers. During World War II, the Corps built the Addicks and Barker Reservoirs, which were designed to impound enough water upstream to prevent flooding downtown.

The reservoirs were merely the first phase of flood prevention. The Corps intended to increase the speed of the flow of floodwater by removing meandering bends from Buffalo Bayou, clearing trees on either side, deepening the bayou bed, and finally lining it with concrete at the bottom. It was a simple mathematical solution to a complex organic problem. Construction companies liked it because it put people and equipment to work. And since the Corps worked on a long-term schedule that stretched out fifteen to thirty years, people were slow to realize the implications of what it was doing.

And there were implications, as Hershey discovered when she began investigating the Corps's plans. The "rectification" they were planning had the potential to do a number of bad things. One might be called a problem pass-along: instead of holding water upstream and stopping a flood, such systems are designed to rush water downstream, which can result in simply moving a flood from one spot to another.

"The sediment is rushed into the receiving stream," Hershey says, "which narrows its capacity, and then it goes downstream into the Ship Channel. Back then the Corps was charging us $2 million a year to dredge the Ship Channel. I would have thought that our preeminent engineers that started out to change the whole riverine system of our county would have known something about fluvial geomorphology or riverine hydrology, however you want to say it. Because what they were doing was absolutely wrong."

Hershey wasn't content to keep this to herself; she took her concerns to her congressman, a promising young Republican from Tanglewood named George Bush.

"His reaction," Hershey recalled, "was, 'That's a terrible thing to do to a river.' He just looked at it and instinctively knew it was stupid."

When the male leaders of the Buffalo Bayou Preservation Association all proved too busy to testify before a subcommittee of the House Appropriations Committee in Washington, Hershey volunteered to go. Bush took Hershey's request to his congressional colleagues, who were astonished to hear someone from Texas ask the government not to spend money in his district. But that's exactly what he was doing, and Congress shrugged and agreed. The result even decades later is that there's no more talk of lining the bayou with concrete. The Corps is learning that rivers are powerful natural systems that can't be tinkered with lightly. The preferred solution today is to build detention ponds to hold back runoff, giving the bayou time to empty.

Floating under a sylvan canopy, I was almost glad that so few people use the bayou. If it were completely cleaned up, it might be full of yahoos in inner tubes drinking beer and playing radios, and who knows what would happen to the wildlife? A sparrow perches on the bank with a moth quivering in its beak. A turtle with a shell as big as a hubcap scrambles down the bank and belly flops into the water. A great blue heron, big as a small human being, lifts languidly on six-foot-long wings and glides around the bend. It is hard to believe that I am surrounded by suburban homes on either side and that everywhere people are rushing to work and school.

Once the bayou clears the Beltway 8 bridge, expensive homes spring up on either side of it, and so do visible attempts to stop the erosion of backyards. Having already paid a premium for their land, homeowners then spend tens of thousands of dollars trying to resist the force of the water that drew them there. All manner of erosion controls have been fixed to the bayou's banks: steel bulkheads, stacked sacks of concrete, interlocking bricks, rocks the size of computer monitors, concrete rubble. Almost invariably, they fail. A gallon of water weighs eight pounds, and when thousands of gallons of it are moving at a high rate of speed, something has got to give. That includes the Corps's vaunted concrete linings, which began to break up in some places only a few years after they were installed.

I received my instruction on the bayou's liquid forces from the city's premier paddler of rivers, Don Greene. A shaggy, humorous man who left corporate marketing twenty-five years ago, Greene has led rafting and canoeing expeditions all over the world. He has trained as a gondolier in Venice and is the guide of choice when politicians want to raft the Río Grande in Big Bend National Park. Greene keeps a trailer full of rental canoes at the headquarters of Whitewater Experience in southwest Houston, and he has a special love of Buffalo Bayou. Excepting Bob Lanier, Greene has taken every Houston mayor since Fred Hofheinz on a trip down the bayou. And on occasions when the water rises, Greene and one of his guides go out on the bayou to videotape the bayou's condition, recording the hydrology for future study.

On a rainy Sunday afternoon a few weeks ago, nineteen people turned out for a trip on the bayou from the 610 bridge through Memorial Park to the Shepherd Drive bridge. Greene stopped the canoes carrying the group before a wilting steel bulkhead to give a brief lesson in geomorphology.

Rivers have an occupation, he said, and that is to move turbidity, or suspended particles. On the outside of a bend, the river erodes the bank. On the inside of the curve, it deposits sand, often creating a system of natural terraces that engineers, Greene noted, would do well to imitate. Engineers who don't take the subtle nature of these forces into account can find their retaining walls buckling.

Greene led the group downstream and pointed to a steep yard covered with a burlap matting, through which small black willows had been planted. Willows bend flat with a flood and hold the soil with their roots. Unlike conventional erosional controls that deteriorate with time, as the willows age, their root systems grow stronger and deeper. This is an erosion-control method that gets better with time. "It's an ancient form that dates back to the biblical times," said Greene. "It's less expensive, stronger, and more effective."

At noon on my solo trip down the bayou, I stopped for a sandwich on a pink clay bank. A raccoon had left its distinct hand-like prints in the clay where it had washed its food the night before. Through my binoculars I watched a diamondback water snake wend upstream on the opposite shore.

As I sat there, thoughts of A.V. "Army" Emmott, the grandfather of Houston's conservation movement, kept coming to mind. Army's mother was the person who wrote the letter that led to the creation of Memorial Park. With his late wife, Sarah, Army worked in the 1950s and 1960s for the Texas Open Beaches Act and fought the rapacious dredging of oyster shell from Galveston Bay.

Eighty years ago, after a few minutes of instruction in the dog paddle, Army's older brother threw him into a crystal-clear Buffalo Bayou millpond near the Shepherd Drive bridge. Army came up swimming, and he has been a lover and an advocate of the bayou ever since. When he was fourteen, he built a small canoe from wooden barrel hoops and canvas. He would toss a few cans of pork and beans and a blanket into the makeshift boat and paddle upstream from town for a weekend camping trip. "We didn't have to worry about drinking water," he recalls, "because as you went along, you could scoop out a place in the sand and wait a few minutes, and fresh spring water would bubble up."

It's easy to see why Army Emmott became such a supporter of the bayou. Like the city itself, he was practically conceived in it. But while Army Emmott's concern with the bayou may be in part nostalgic, a look backward to his halcyon boyhood days, that's not all there is to it. Even for those in whom the bayou stirs no memories, there may be substantial reasons for caring about the resource, reasons beyond simple flood control. Caring for the bayou may be more than a simple act of nostalgia. It may be a necessity.

In recent years, a growing number of scientists have argued that the human species, genetically shaped by tens of millions of years of hunting and gathering, is innately sensitive to all other forms of life, including plants. The Harvard naturalist and writer Edward O. Wilson calls this instinct "biophilia," or, literally, love of life. We can see this instinct at work in the way we teach our children through stories about animals and take them to zoos. Advocates of urban parks point out that the 1992 Los Angeles rioters destroyed businesses but left communal gardens and parks untouched. And when community leaders asked urban gangs what was needed to heal their neighborhoods, their response was unequivocal: more parks and more green space.

So there are plenty of reasons to treat the bayou kindly. Lined with trees, Buffalo Bayou acts as the city's lungs and circulatory system. It is a wildlife corridor, harboring birds, fish, reptiles, and amphibians. There are even beavers in it. It is a vibrant, living place through which flows Houston's past and much of its future possibilities. Buffalo Bayou, it could be argued, embodies the soul of the city. And how we care for our collective soul will affect the health of the city.

Somewhere, somehow, we lost track of that vision. But in my time on the bayou's waters, I discovered that what I had been told was in fact true: the bayou is coming back. I had a tough time completing the final leg of my paddle. Trees had fallen across the water, and I had to pick my way around the edges and hump the kayak over low clearances. I grew careless, and a snag caught my shirt and ripped a hole in it. Then I broadsided a tree and tumbled out into the bayou's flow. When I emerged, my watertight camera no longer worked, and my binoculars were clouded and useless. When I finished the trip, I was wet and tired and wished I had taken it a little easier. As I hauled my boat out of the water on the north side of Woodway, a woman pulled into traffic a little slowly, and a blonde woman in a red convertible Mercedes came roaring up behind her, her horn blaring.

"Welcome back to the city," I thought. Waiting for my ride, I thought back to the bayou, where I had drifted with a pair of wood ducks, the male easily identifiable by his shaggy head. When I floated past a dead tree, I spotted a downy woodpecker at the top. His bill was half open as though he had something in it. Then I heard a high-pitched scree, scree, scree, the sound of its young calling for food.

I wished Army Emmott could have been there with me. I wished life were simpler and the water in the bayou was as clear as it had been in his day. But that, I assumed, would never be. I couldn't imagine scooping a hollow out in the bayou's sand banks and drinking spring water. I couldn't imagine seeing bass in schools at the bottom of deep pools in Buffalo Bayou.

But following my trip, I had a long talk with Janet Wagner, a landscape architect who's researched the history of the bayou for the flood control district's new erosion study. Wagner knows where the bayou was mined for clay and knows the names of the brick companies that mined it and in which buildings you can still see the bayou-bred brick. She knows where the fords used by the Indians were situated on rocky bottoms and can show you how the early Anglo settlers damaged them by cutting deep ramps in the banks for their wagons.

When I wondered aloud to her if the bayou's water could ever be as clear again as it was in Army Emmott's day, she surprised me. Oh yes, she said. Buffalo Bayou is still fed by clear springs. And if we could control Houston's urban and suburban erosion and discharges, the bayou would carry the sediment that now discolors it out to the bay, and the water would again run crystal clear over its hard, blue-clay bottom.

We could have it back. We could have it all back if each of us took care of our own piece of the problem. If we kept our grass clippings and our soap suds and automobile oil out of the gutter. If we cleaned up our construction sites and our gas stations. It would take an effort, but I'd already seen how far we'd already come. And I knew now it wasn't impossible. If we took care of the moment—the only time in which any of us ever had a chance to really make a difference—Houston could have its bayou back.

Central Texas

Along the River

by Elroy Bode

I want to spend, once again, a day along a river. I want to take cold fried chicken and potato salad and pork-and-beans and buns and an ice chest with drinks and go in midmorning to a river place in Central Texas. I want to get an old quilt from the trunk of the car and spread it beneath a sycamore tree and stay there near the river for the rest of the day.

I want to lie on the quilt, reading, and then put a marker in the book and close my eyes and hear, once more, the leaves of the sycamores and oaks and willows moving in the breeze and the sound of water running somewhere over rocks. I want to walk along the river through weeds and clumps of grass. I want to stand in the deep river shade, feeling the sense of the river, its large open silence, the all-enveloping heat of the summer afternoon.

I want to take an old coffee can that is half-filled with moist dirt and fishing worms and bait my hook and edge out onto a mounded rock along the bank and, sitting beneath the overhang of trees, fish throughout the rest of the afternoon. I want to watch the ripples begin to circle and then spread away from my cork as small unseen perch nibble at my bait, but mainly I just want to continue being where I am. I want to sit and lose track of time—letting four and five and six o'clock blend into the flow of the river and the muted, random call of birds. I want to become the reflection of the trees on the water, and the idle swarming of gnats in the shafts of the setting sun, and the periodic surfacing of turtles.

And then, after the sun goes down and the river settles into its deep twilight mood, I want to walk back to my car—slowly, deliberately, as if each step is giving something back to the riverbank, as if the river and the gathering night can know, somehow, that I am offering a thanks.

Elroy Bode (1931–2017) was a longtime resident of El Paso and the author of ten books. "Along the River" first appeared in *Home Country: An Elroy Bode Reader.* Texas Western Press, 1997. Published by permission of Phoebe Bode.

The Brazos River

Warm skies, the stars are listening
Country night sings her song
Fireflies light the distance
Making me want to sing along . . .

Dusty small towns and big families
Cooling my memory like a summer rain
Cold well water and dewberry pie
Brazos River running through my veins.

—Ruthie Foster, from "Home"

Ruthie Foster, a singer-songwriter of blues and folk music, was born near the confluence of the Little and Brazos Rivers. She has received three Grammy nominations along with numerous awards for her music. "Home," lyrics © Ruthie Foster, from the album *Runaway Soul*, 2002. Published by permission of Ruthie Foster and Blue Corn Music.

Drifting Down the Brazos

by John Graves

Fall is usually the good time to go to the Brazos in North Central Texas. Snakes and mosquitoes are torpid then, nights are cool and days blue and yellow and soft, and in autumn's abundance, the shooting and fishing are both likely to be good. Scores of birds pause in migration before the later northers push many of them farther south. Men and women are scarce. Most autumns, the river is low from the long dry summer and from time to time you have to lead or drag your boat through trickling shallows from one pool to another long, twisted pool below. October is the good month, in a normal year, though some people doubt that normality exists in southwestern weather.

It didn't that year. In October rain fell all month long. But with luck November can be good, and I needed to say good-by to the stretch of the river I'd always known, the hundred and seventy miles of it that wind from the Possum Kingdom Dam between the low rough mountains of the Palo Pinto country into sandy peanut and post oak land and end in the limestone hills above Lake Whitney. Few highways cross that stretch; it is harsh country for the most part, and even to get into it is work. The river's shoals shear propeller pins, and quicksands or whirlpools occasionally swallow folks down, so that generally visitors go to the lakes, leaving the Brazos to the hard-bitten countrymen scattered along it and to those others of us for whom it has some sort of meaning. For the most part it runs wild and neglected, and when you paddle along it, the things you see are much the same things the Comanches and the Kiowas used to see, riding ponies down it a hundred years ago to raid the new settlements in its valley.

Five new lakes were scheduled for impoundment along that stretch. In booming Texas, where floods and droughts alternate, electrical power and flood control and moisture conservation and water skiing are praiseworthy matters; we river-minded ones cannot say much against dams, nor do we usually. But I had been living out of the state and knew that it might be years before I came home again with time enough on my hands to make a last float trip along the

John Graves (1920–2013) was author of the classic *Goodbye to a River*, an account of his canoe trip along the Brazos before a series of proposed dams threatened to change the river forever. "Drifting Down the Brazos," adapted from *Goodbye to a River*, originally appeared in *Holiday* magazine's November 1959 issue. Published by permission of Jane Graves, Helen Graves, and Sally Graves Jackson.

Brazos. I wanted to do it before what I and the Comanches and Old Man Charlie Goodnight had known ended up under all the big outboards.

Below the dam, the river cuts beneath high sandstone cliffs, yellow, gray, and red and stratified like laid brick, with dark cedar along the top. But on the gray afternoon when I started out, I had to take the yellow and red for granted, remembering them from times of sunshine. Standing at the low bridge, I doubted the dark sky, and the bite of the wind and its ruffle on the water, and under that grayness, the swollen rapids below looked dangerous.

A friend named Hale had brought me out. We had grown up together, hunting and fishing and poking into places where we didn't belong. Until business got in the way, he had been planning to come with me.

"Call from Route One Eighty," he said. "I'll drive out."

"I'll call. You won't come," I said.

Collaring my pup to keep him from scrambling ashore, I pushed off into the rapids. The current carried me smoothly the mile and a half down to the sharp turn of the Flint Bend and around it under the cliffs. Sandpipers flushed, and a kingfisher and a great blue heron and chickadees buzzed in the brush. By the time I pulled out below a narrow flat that lay between the river and a mountain, the wind carried flecks of cold rain. I set up the tent under a mesquite, threw my bedroll in it, chopped dead limbs into firewood, and then carried up the gun and the rods and the boxes and sacks from the boat.

As evening's light failed, the wind dropped. The rain kept on, a steady soft autumn drizzle. But the fire was roaring between two sandstone blocks, with a potato in it, and I sat smoking a cigarette in the tent, savoring aloneness. I would have liked to have Hale along, but not many other people I knew.

The pup, a six-month-old dachshund, edged against me. Even after he was grown, he wouldn't be a very practical dog, but he was company—more concrete, maybe, than memories and feelings.

"Passenger, you watch," I told him. "It's going to be a good trip." In the firelight he registered disbelief.

It rained for three nights and intermittently during the days. I knew that if it kept up, I'd finally get so soggy, I'd have to pull out at one of the bridges below and telephone for a ride, quitting for the year. But meanwhile I inched along, letting the days' journeys find their own length. When the wood got too wet, I cooked on a little alcohol stove and in the mornings lay under canvas until the rain let up. We made only five or six miles a day, but the sandstone mountains are good country, and even with damp feet, there were things to see—rotten log corrals and the nostalgic ruins of cabins, hillside sumac, frost-red, above old fields choked with briars and oak brush where cardinals and titmice and towhees and a dozen other kinds of birds fed . . . I paddled a half mile up Ioni Creek one foggy morning for a last look at the crossing where, one day in 1873, young Jesse Veale's horse went to bucking instead of running when the Comanches jumped Jesse and a friend. They found him later sitting, dead but unscalped, against a double elm tree with Indian blood on the ground around him, and there was a fine fight on cedar-shrouded Crawford Mountain across the creek.

For twenty years or so of the last century, that section of the Brazos was frontier, so that hardly a twist in it or a hill along its shores does not have some old bloodiness attached to it. In my childhood wrinkled women still lived who remembered how the owl cries and turkey gobbles had sounded in the moonlit nights of the raids, and who had seen Indians eating roasted horses beside trails in the cedar brakes.

I passed Eagle Creek, with huge rocks fallen into the river and the big oaks gone red and the ashes yellow under the cliff, and Kyle Mountain, with the Boy Scout ranch, deserted now in fall, and Dalton Bend above the country where Parson Slaughter preached and fought and founded a range dynasty. The cottonwoods were golden but the willows still green, and there were deer tracks and coon signs and herons yelling their protest in the dawn when the owls left off, skunks and possums, woodpeckers and sparrows, doves by the hundreds, wild-calling canyon wrens in the rocks, Carolinas, Bewicks. . . . One afternoon a bald eagle flew past me upstream and lit in a dead tree, a rare, clean sight.

But we got damper day by day, shivering at night even with a fire. The likely bet, it seemed, was that the good-bye trip would be short.

Except that suddenly, one noon, while we were drifting in the flat, even-flowing stretch that bears down on the Dark Valley bridge, a big southwest wind swept up and cleaned the sky, and when the last cloud tatters dropped north of the sun, they left that blue that you never see at other times of year, and the country lay washed, bright with two dozen shades of green and frost-bitten leaves.

Grateful, I shot the big twisted rapids under the bridge and stopped on a gravel bar a mile below to make a sandwich and coffee, and to watch the sun-revived passenger dig great soggy holes, yelping down them after imaginary badgers. Across the way, a gap showed in the cottonwoods where Elm Creek comes to the river from a hollow called the Indian Hole. Here, in 1858, an inoffensive old type named Choctaw Tom and his ragged followers found out what a bitter thing it was to be red men. Unwarlike Indians, most of them scraps of tribes who had fled there as white men advanced in the east and the south, lived all along that piece of the Brazos when settlers first came in the 1850s. Innocuously, they raised pumpkins and squash and corn in the bends and the valleys, but land-hungry frontiersmen did not differentiate much between them and the nomadic, deadly, thieving Comanches and Kiowas. Choctaw Tom's little party was unlucky enough to camp in the path of a bloody-eyed bunch who rode out under a bravo named Garland to avenge horse thefts. Garland hit them at dawn while they slept, shooting women and children along with the decrepit braves. Later he said, "We have opened the ball, and others can dance to the music."

Others did. The fierce nomads piled into the uproar with satisfaction, and shortly all Indians of whatever breed were marched across the Red River and planted in Oklahoma. But the Comanches and Kiowas kept raiding along the Texas frontier for fifteen or more bitter years, and practically froze it on one line during the Civil War and Reconstruction.

That antique violence, though, seemed to have little to do with a drifting, sparkling, sunlit afternoon between the mountains, past Little Keechi Creek and the Harris Bend, and down the slick fast water into Post Oak, where redbirds sang from both shores. Running too late in the bright evening, I made a hasty camp among sand burrs; they stuck fast to the passenger and he went in the tent and sulked, picking them off onto my bedding.

The good weather held. I saw deer in the mornings, tame now before the big rifles had begun to crack; they stood drinking and watched the canoe float down toward them with only curiosity until they caught my smell and flagged away into the brush. Poking, I found the tumbled sandstone foundation of the cabin old Henry Welty rode away from one evening, to look for his milk calves, and never came back to alive, and on a high flat east of the mouth of Big Keechi, where the Old Painted Campground lies, I dug the toe of my boot into the midden of Indian centuries and kicked up flint chips and potsherds and hearthstones.

Up Big Keechi, Mr. Charlie Goodnight grazed his herds in the 1850s and '60s before he headed farther west to become one of the legendary cattlemen of the high plains. He was a tough and honorable man in tough, not usually honorable times, though old people still say he took credit for blazing cattle trails his partner Oliver Loving had explored before him. But the Comanches got Loving on the Pecos, and Mr. Charlie lived to spin stories. The Indians called him "Buenas Noches." He lived a long time and at ninety-one married a second wife in her twenties.

The trip had found its shape; I eased into the rhythm of paddling and making camp and breaking it, cooking and cleaning up, grubbing about at Indian sites and the scenes of old murders, field-glassing animals and mountains and birds, seeing no one for days on end. At the Highway 180 bridge, to call Hale, I hitchhiked to a crossroads store labeled, like all its ilk in our country, SER

STA GRO and found that I had so adjusted to being alone that automobiles and people had acquired strangeness. I felt shy and unwilling to deal with them.

Hale was still ensnarled. I told him he'd be sorry he hadn't come later.

He said he already was.

I told him a yellow catfish that had looked to weigh forty pounds had nearly torn the paddle out of my hands that morning, feeding in a fast clear chute. Though they run twice that big in the Brazos sometimes, few are caught on hooks. Some are wrestled ashore by the "grabblers," sturdy rural sportsmen who tread water while they probe the recesses of the undercut banks with their hands, disregarding water moccasins and game wardens and other dangers. Others succumb to the magnetos of the less sporting "telephoners," who crank electricity into the still, deep pools.

Four hundred creaking, whistling sandhill cranes in a flock flapped in ahead of a high norther that caught us in the Village Bend and brought fine loud thunderstorms all night long. Geese, too, were flying high toward the south in the hard-frosted clear morning that followed.

Looming over the outer edge of a bend called Poke Stalk is a line of high bluffs where the mountain country falls abruptly away to farming land. I camped beneath them at a spot where, in an October years before, Hale and I had stopped and eaten fat bluebills out of season. This night, when ducks would have been legal if I'd had any, I ate chipped beef and brown rice and slept hard with screech owls, rare now after the big drought years, quavering in the flats across the river. In the glass-clear early morning, the rancher who owned that land came picking his way among the boulders of the shore, and after I'd convinced him that my purpose was not to poach deer, he had coffee with me, and we talked. He was one of the quiet, tough, unprofane people that this country still produces occasionally, close in type to the best of the old ones; he told me of Indian corn-pounding holes along a high ledge, and a field with arrowheads and metates, and animals he'd watched, and a cave where he'd once let a hermit live for five years, bringing him coffee and flour and beans. He said he'd always thought he'd like to do some floating himself.

"Come on," I said.

"Dang if I wouldn't," he said, smiling, but then shook his head and went on along the bank. . . .

On down alone, then, drifting with the brown-swollen river through the low country's tangled bottoms. More clear cold weather, the whitethroats suddenly in and whistling, hound packs and owls at night, cabins and battlefields and gullied wagon crossings, biscuit bread and beans and squirrels and catfish and an armadillo and finally a couple of mallards to roast.

And there were, finally, five days of winding among the low limestone hills, from above Thorp Spring, down the forty-five bridgeless miles below Granbury, past flat Comanche Peak, into the lands where the moonshine whiskey still drips from copper worms. It is cedar and live oak country for the most part, the dark foliage on the hills untouched by the winter change that during the time of my float had stripped the deciduous trees of the bottom.

Like all limestone country, it has a cleanness; day by day the river subsided from its brown spate, scouring itself clear in the sands, and the tributary streams of Hood County—Robinson and Stroud and Walnut and Fall Creeks and the others—ran crystalline, jammed with bass that were gorging without caution on hickory shad, against the winter's cold torpor.

As I resumed my paddling down in the long, bright afternoons, widgeons and mallards and teal and bluebills and pintails would swim out, not much alarmed, from the banks and would keep ahead of me downstream, accumulating until at times I'd be herding maybe a hundred. Then a sunflash from my paddle or a rapids below or some other small spur would flush them scattering into the sky, and maybe a few would cut back to give me a shot, if I wanted it.

Most often I didn't. The sporting attitude has little application when you're only feeding yourself with a gun and a rod. A mallard or a brace of teal make a good supper, and if I felt like eating ducks, I usually had them shot by noon. Bass scrambled to hook themselves on a quarter-ounce spoon with pork rind. Glutted on squirrels, fried or roasted or stewed, I let them play in the live oaks and wished them well. On Thanksgiving I camped at the mouth of Fall Creek and for supper, overdoing things a little because of the holiday, ate fish and beans and steamed brown rice and a roasted widgeon stuffed with prunes and saw no reason to envy anyone in town.

Carolina wrens and chickadees visited me there in the morning, and a Mexican woodpecker and a squirrel, and finally sixteen picnicking Camp Fire Girls herded by counselors and parents who looked sidewise at my two days' beard. The girls romped with the passenger and fed him sick on sandwiches and candy, and one of them named Karen did not like me when she found out what I ate. She said, "Oh, you're the reason there are only five ducks by the bridge now."

I said what ducks by what bridge?

She said angrily, "You know. Oh, you. . . ." But she was friendlier when I gave her a bass off the stringer and backed her loud claim that she had caught it.

One afternoon in the Mitchell Bend, I dropped around a little turn, and five green-winged teal were asleep in the sun on the caved-away slope of a sandbank, just above the water. They sat squatted back on their tails, cinnamon heads down against white breasts. I drifted almost on them, then rapped the side of the canoe. One by one they came awake, comically, straightening their necks and staring, and took off in confusion.

With a twinge, I swung the gun on the last one as he went, to fill out supper, but he was flying fast or maybe the twinge threw me off; I only speckled the water behind him with both barrels.

More and more of the hermit feel comes into that kind of travel, after a time. You get it in the evenings by the fire and in the clear mornings, when your muscles have toned themselves and the paddling and camping have become routine. It is clean, and most people who go alone into the country for more than a few days must experience it—a feeling of balance, of rightness, a knowledge that you could go on forever were there river and time enough.

But there never are, and the feeling is an illusion, anyhow, based most likely on a certainty that things end.

Where I pulled out finally, three weeks below Possum Kingdom, a road goes down to the river past a shack with a sign saying "Minnows" nailed slantingly to a big sycamore. I had seen it before while driving around but had not stopped there. As I climbed the hill, a bloated old man rose out of a cane chair under the sycamore and demanded to know what the hell I was up to.

I told him.

He said, discernibly rosy from white cedar country whisky, that I looked like I might be able to read sign, and dragged me down to other sycamores where lovers, probably, had once cut their initials. He said they were Comanche treasure maps, if he could only read them. I said I wasn't expert in such matters. Disgustedly, he said he could see that, now.

It was a queer place, with springs flowing out of the hillside over humps of soft travertine and volcanic rocks strewn about. He said they weren't volcanic.

"Why not?"

"Because, neighbor," he said with patience, belching, "hit don't say nothing in Scripture about no volcanoes in the United States."

"Didn't you get lonesome?" someone's wife asked in town.

"Well . . ." I said, but thought then about the complications of trying to say no.

"It wasn't so bad," I said. "I had a dog."

Double Mountain Fork of the Brazos

by Walter McDonald

Living on stones and runoff from rain
that rarely comes, this fork in forty miles
drains dust, dry mouth swearing
all it owns to the Brazos.

Whoever named it liked romance,
mountains two hundred miles away,
nothing where it begins
but a sudden drop-off in a field,

a sinkhole twenty feet across.
I've stood there, seen
a mighty river start, if I believed
in names. I've backpacked forty miles

and never found a stream so deep
I couldn't step across on stones.
I slept under train trestles so low
I almost bumped my head.

I named creatures living on nothing
but each other, coyotes and skunks,
owls, a thousand diamondbacks, rabbits
with wide eyes and rapidly beating hearts.

Walter McDonald, born in Lubbock, served during the Vietnam War and became one of Texas's leading poets, publishing many award-winning books. "Double Mountain Fork of the Brazos" first appeared in *All That Matters: The Texas Plains in Photographs and Poems*. Texas Tech University Press, 1992. Published by permission of Walter McDonald.

November

by James Hoggard

For John Graves

Shimmering spreads of golden fire,
Oak leaves fan Comanche Bluff
Where the Brazos de Dios turns deep
Against a cliff, high limestone wall,
Current speeding up at the curve
Hard toward a white water roar:
Shouts of giants trapped in rock,

And a russet granite boulder,
Monolithic in the river's wide rush,
Organizes the water slapping at it:
Whirlpools drilling into sinkholes,
And down them cold November purls
When fierce blue northern winds
Come beating the brilliance off limbs.

James Hoggard (1941–2021) was a Distinguished Professor of English at Midwestern State University, a Fellow of the Texas Institute of Letters, and the author of twenty-six books, including poetry, novels, essays, short stories, and plays. © James Hoggard, 1991. Published by permission of James and Lynn Hoggard.

The Cruise of the Red Turtle
A Brazos River Sketchbook

by Gardner Smith with Robert Reitz

I can't give you three unanswerably good reasons why one should care a damn
about what the land is, but if one does, one does, and rivers thread through it
and are still public domain . . . canoes, too, are unobtrusive; they don't storm
the natural world or ride over it but drift in upon it as a part of its own silence.
As you either care about what the land is or not, so do you like or dislike quiet
things—sailboats, or rainy green mornings in foreign places, or a grazing herd,
or the ruins of old monasteries in mountains.

—John Graves, *Goodbye to a River*

Dalton Bend

Often in our river voyage, we are impressed with the metaphorical
nature of it. On a river in a canoe, one floats downstream with the
current. And while it is possible to have some control over where
and in what channel one goes, there is no going back. You live the moment, and
then it is gone. From time to time, we stopped paddling and let the wind or the
current swing us around, and we gazed back from whence we came, knowing
that we shall never see it again. Or if we are fortunate to come this way again,
we may see it, but not like this.

With the eyes of men
becoming children again
exploring new places.

Gardner Smith and **Robert Reitz**, fellow Vietnam veterans, made dozens of trips throughout Texas and the Southwest from the 1990s to the 2000s. Influenced by early Texas
landscape painter Frank Reaugh and Japanese haiku poet Bashō, they published their
observations in a series of handmade books. Excerpted from *The Cruise of the Red Turtle:
A Brazos River Sketchbook* by Gardner Smith with Robert Reitz. Sun and Shadow Press,
1992. Published by permission of Gardner Smith and Robert Reitz.

The Brazos River in this stretch of the river flows through the beautiful Palo Pinto Mountains. They are not large mountains, but in a state as flat as this, they are certainly worthy of notice. The Palo Pintos are roughly comparable to the Blue Ridge Mountains of Virginia in the vicinity of the Potomac River around Harpers Ferry. The highest peak in the Palo Pintos is Crawford Mountain at 1,470 feet above sea level; Sugarloaf is 1,462 feet, and Antelope Mountain is 1,321 feet. The range runs about 15 miles from southwest to northeast in Palo Pinto County. The Brazos River picks its way through them like a rattlesnake, taking its own sweet time, and that is fine with us, in no hurry to end this journey.

We paddle our canoe
through the heart of the Palo Pintos
going seven miles for every one.

Backwards Falls

Rich or poor, it's all mostly a matter of chance, but in deep water or shallow, everyone paddles his own boat.

—Li Shan-fu (ca. 874)

There are some rapids above Spanish Walls where we totally lost it and let the river spin us around and shove us down a narrow chute backwards, and we had no choice but to do it the way the river wanted.

We could hear the laughter
of the water in the rocks
as we went down there
looking back.

Going backwards we didn't see the cow
standing with all four feet in the stream
drinking from that good old salty water
with an astonished expression
on her placid black face.

Dark Valley Revisited

The metaphor of the canoe trip for the voyage through life comes repeatedly to us as we paddle down the Brazos, passing to one side or the other of some island. Hearing the sound of a rapids up ahead, we scan the scene and pick the channel. Sometimes there's just one channel and the decision is easy; other times there are two or three from which to choose and the choosing is more difficult. At first we chose the wrong one and had to get out and pull the boat over the sand and gravel. In one place we had to beat back out of a cove and around the long gravel bar in front of an island.

But as we learned to read the river, we correctly picked the deepest part and sailed right through, picking our way through the rocks and snags and down into the quiet water below. Which is to say, we learned from our mistakes and made fewer of them. . . .

Of course we did choose a shallow channel now and again just for the adventure of it, knowing the danger and accepting it. In life, as on the river, one really does choose the channel in which to float one's boat.

Just before you reach Rochelle's, you pass below the Dark Valley bridge. As bridges go, it is not much to look at. From the perspective of a canoe, I guess all bridges are plug ugly. This bridge was built between August 1955 and June 1957. It replaced an earlier bridge at this location, actually slightly upstream. You can still see the approaches to the old bridge, which was a suspension bridge hanging free and clear of piers. The new bridge is 70 feet above the water, 880 feet long, and with a 26-foot roadway width. To accommodate the modern automobile, two miles of approaches had to be graded to the bridge. Modern drivers can speed by at a mile a minute and hardly know the Brazos River even exists, but we know, for we have canoed it.

One of Rochelle's good old boys comes over to say howdy. He's been sparking a couple of Dallas ladies camped on the riverbank with not much success. "Come down from PK?" [Possum Kingdom Dam] he asks, slightly impressed. "The boat still floats," we assure him. He's got the look of a former rodeo man, probably is, and would druther shoot hisself in the foot than go to Dallas. He doesn't need to prove anything to us, and with twenty miles of the Brazos behind us, we don't need to prove anything either.

He wades a little way out into the river, stoops down, and takes a drink. "Delicious!" he says, spitting it out and looking over at the ladies again. "Delicious!" he reiterates and walks away.

> Clearly impressed,
> we exchange glances—
> we know what that river tastes like!

B.C. Harris Bend

I can't say we much liked B.C. Harris Bend. For one thing there's a grand palace perched up there on top of the bluffs that is owned by a man who made his fortune in the pawn-shop trade over in Dallas. "I've got mine," that house says. He's got the view of the river, and we've got the view of the house. Then on the right bank, we come across a bunch of people in powerboats making camp, leveling the terrain with chainsaws. Though it's late in the day, we paddle seriously the hell out of there!

> One shore of the river in sun,
> the other in shadow—
> we paddle down the middle.
> Deep and smooth the river flows,
> round white stones clearly seen below;
> at end of day cattle low somewhere out of sight
> as ever so slowly an island appears . . .

Trifles and oddities, in these our hearts find simple joys.

—Li Shan-fu (ca. 874)

> Deep blue of evening falls
> slowly across the water.
> Softly the water drips off our paddles
> as we drift along with cicada calls.
>
> Golden orange the color glows
> from the windows of someone's home
> sweet home on the Brazos.
>
> Crows cawing in the trees
> are unable to stop
> this life from flowing away.
>
> No one is spared the sorrow
> of growing old, so hold
> your paddle and dip it in the river.

The Brazos was the artist Frank Reaugh's favorite painting place. We were well versed in Brazos River scenes from grazing through the four hundred and some Reaugh paintings up at Panhandle-Plains Historical Museum.

> Nevertheless we saw
> colors even Reaugh
> was unable to create.

Now there's a Reaugh painting, we thought, letting the boat go wherever her little heart desired while we gazed thoughtfully up at a sugarloaf mountain of gray stone with the sunset colors of evening shining there.

> Colors indescribable
> on canvas or in
> haiku poetry.

> Our haiku are just bookmarks
> on a long and pleasant journey.

We came through B.C. Harris Bend late in the day looking for a campsite. It was a Saturday, and the river was a little crowded, the best campsites already occupied. Scott Canyon looked like a good place on the map, but in the flesh, so to speak, it was dark and thickly overgrown. The left bank of the Brazos past the tip of the bend was richly lit with the golden sun of an autumn evening, but the banks were high and unapproachable. The right bank was dark and gloomy. We investigated two or three campsites and reluctantly paddled on. There's just something a river campsite has to have, and lacking it is unacceptable. First, there needs to be a sandy beach. The gelatinous goo that the Brazos throws up is as slippery as sin and clings to one's boots. The site needs to be fairly high, but you've got to be able to get to it. We saw a fair number of good campsites, but lacking a place to haul out the boat or a tree to tie it to, we passed by. There were a goodly number of places where cattle had made a trail down to the river to drink, but there were often lots of cattle hanging around. True, they would obligingly move away, but well, they left a lot of cattle-dharma behind.

I think mostly what we looked for were friendly trees, and seeing them, we invariably paddled over to have a look-see. Mesquite seem to be best, for they tend to be twisted and bent over and afford places on which to sit, although the thorns can be troublesome. Post Oak groves are pretty good and so are pecans. Best of all is some combination of sand and short grass and trees and limestone ledges. Unfortunately, these ideal campsites tend to appear when you least need them. When you really need a campsite, having paddled overlong into the twilight, they seem always just around the bend. We are not alone in our campsite aesthetics, for every good one we discovered had been previously discovered, to judge from the fire rings. Down near the foot of Post Oak Bend, we spotted a grove of live oaks up on the second terrace and a convenient gravel bar on which to ground the boat, so we did. Unfortunately that terrace was so heavily infested with sandburs, we retreated back to the first terrace, which was awfully stony but free of burs and with patches of that short grass that makes for good bedding places.

"Bob," I said, "it's not much, but we've run out of options." So we resigned ourselves to our fate for this closing day of our lives and unloaded the boat and hauled it up above the high water mark and made supper in the purple afterglow. When it got good and dark, we built a fire from the abundant driftwood the Brazos affords and settled down with a bottle of Springtown Mist. Bob has had the foresight, as he so often does, to bring along something special, and it's a tape recording of John Graves reading from his book *From a Limestone Ledge*.

And so even a poor campsite, having little or none of the glamour of some we've known, was transformed into an unforgettable occasion, transmuted by a long friendship, a bottle of wine, and a good book into something that will draw tears from our eyes in not so many years when we think back to these few days when we put our boat in the Brazos and paddled off into adventure.

Drinking from the River

by Chip Dameron

Whether it's a torrent or a trickle
it's where you have to go

when you're thirsty and you
dip your cup and draw out

the clear tang and sip it first
and then take one long swallow.

An aftertaste of sky and stones
tree bark and feathered shadows

carves their names into logs
that you stack up one by one

against the failing light and let
the heat soak into your skin

and when you wake you can smell
the river beyond the scattered ashes.

Chip Dameron is a Professor Emeritus at the University of Texas Río Grande Valley, the recipient of a Dobie-Paisano Fellowship, and the author of ten books of poetry. From *Drinking from the River: New & Selected Poems* by Chip Dameron. Wings Press, 2015. Published by permission of Chip Dameron.

The Leon River

The Bluff

by Leon Hale

O ut in the Texas West Cross Timbers where I spent most of my early times, there's a high place on a bend of the Leon River that we used to call the Bluff. The last time I went back to visit that river, in what I still think of as my home country, I wanted to locate the Bluff and sit on the edge of it one more time and try to see what I could see there when I was fourteen years old. Because I once witnessed some most extraordinary scenes from the top of that Bluff.

Along with a flock of country cousins and friends who had plenty of time to waste, I left many a footprint on the banks of the Leon River. All rural Texans have a river in their background, one that had a part in shaping their lives. That river, for me, is the Leon.

Close to a hundred miles west of Fort Worth in Eastland County, the various forks of the Leon run together and try to become a major stream, without much success. The water ends up eventually in the Brazos.

Long ago we wrote notes and stuffed them in stoppered bottles that we pitched in this river and dreamed that the bottles would reach the Brazos and the Gulf of Mexico and be found on the beaches of foreign lands. Fat chance. Probably they all sank fifty yards downstream.

Leon Hale (1921–2021) worked more than sixty years as a newspaper columnist for the *Houston Post* and then the *Houston Chronicle*. He was the author of eleven books, including two novels. "The Bluff" originally appeared as "Lazy Days Spent on the Bluff" in the *Houston Chronicle*, January 10, 2010. Published by permission of the *Houston Chronicle*.

When I was supposed to be studying arithmetic and geography out in that country, every time I got a new teacher he/she would ask if I had been named for the river. No, my mother's name was Leona, and I got the shortened version of it.

My mother was a God-fearing, rule-abiding, Bible-reading woman, and I still wonder what she could have done to get saddled with that name. She hated it. Wouldn't answer to it. My father hated it. My older sisters hated it.

So when I came along, they knocked a vowel off the end of the thing and gave it to me, thinking, I suppose, that I wouldn't recognize it. I did, though, and I've never liked it any better than they did. But let's move on.

The Bluff was a high rocky ledge that made a sweet spot to sit and look down at what the river was doing. At this point the stream was no more than thirty feet wide and the color of a mud puddle, but it was my river, and I loved it and wanted it to be important.

On dreamy days I'd sit alone on the lip of that ledge and face downstream and squint my eyes and make the river wide as the Mississippi. If chunks of mesquite or post oak floated by, I could turn them into boats and barges, and on good days when my system was working right I could produce a paddle-wheel steamboat coming around the bend a quarter of a mile below the Bluff.

Once, I created a submarine, right there on the Leon River.

I said I was alone. No, my old dog Jiggs was always with me. This was the dog that couldn't swim, until I taught him how. He was a great lover but timid in a fight and he was afraid of heights. When I sat with my legs dangling off the ledge, he would stay behind me and look over my shoulder.

On these magic days, though, Jiggs became a wonder. At my hand signal he'd leap off the rim of the Bluff and sail about, above the river. Jiggs the Flying Dog. He'd do swoops and loops and make a perfect landing at his spot just behind me.

He could see everything I saw, all the marvels taking place on our river, and he was interested. We saw huge fish jumping. Great sharks never before seen in those waters, and sometimes a whale the size of a six-room house.

We saw sailing ships from the previous century and sea monsters with several heads. We saw mountains rising on the far bank, the only mountains ever known in that part of Texas, and we saw a volcano erupt and spill its lava into the river and produce great clouds of steam.

We watched Indians make a camp just below us and shoot fish with bows and arrows, and we saw buffalo, and bears, and mountain lions come to the river to drink.

All these things we saw, me and my dog Jiggs, there on our river.

But when I went back not long ago, the pastures I once walked through to reach the river had "No Trespassing" signs on the fences, and I couldn't get to the Bluff.

The Leon

by W.K. Stratton

I lived along the Leon River in Belton.
Sometimes I smelled floodwater
    from my back porch.
Once a great horned owl flew past low
A full-grown cat in its talons.
A year later, a heron of some sort
Built a nest in the woods,
A five-gallon bucket of sticks and mud.
Someone murdered the owner of a café
A few blocks down the street.
Six shots to the head at midnight:
No money went missing.
I knew the crime would go unsolved.
I had lived in Texas forever.
My wife moved to a different bedroom.
I didn't care.
I'd drive to a beer joint called He's Not Here
And listen to the Georges on the jukebox,
Strait and Jones.
I played golf on the municipal course
That hugged the river. I paid green fees
To an old drunk who wore overalls.
A blind dog sat on his lap.
I never really cured my shank.
One January morning my mother called
To say my brother was dead in Fort Worth.
I couldn't tell if she was crying.

W.K. Stratton is the author of eight books, including *The Wild Bunch: Sam Peckinpah, a Revolution in Hollywood, and the Making of a Legendary Film*. Born in Guthrie, Oklahoma, he has lived much of his life in Texas. He is a Fellow of the Texas Institute of Letters.
© W.K. Stratton, 2019. Published by permission of W.K. Stratton.

The Leon was little more than a creek
    that season.
A hundred bluebirds and more
Descended on the winter kill grass
Just as my mother hung up.
I took a six pack of Pearl
Down to the river for first rites.

The San Gabriel River

Walking the San Gabriel during the Drought

by Alan Birkelbach

We walk this dry riverbed as if we had sense.
We've seen rainwater rise up faster
than calves could scramble,
watched them bawl and be swept away,
their mothers knee then chest deep,
as helpless as we were just watching.

We've seen seasons so wet
the water flowed from the riverbank,
cool from the folds of the earth,
streams called by Aaron's rod,
flavored by mint, wild berries,
sweet enough to bless our face in.

Today we stop at the bottom of the swimming hole
we've splashed a thousand times,
replaying the summer days
when we touched bottom on a dare,
bringing up rocks from the bottom
just to prove we could.

Alan Birkelbach, born in Central Texas, is the author of several books of poetry and was the 2005 Texas Poet Laureate. In 2016, he and poet Karla K. Morton launched a three-year project to visit all sixty-one US National Parks, documenting their journeys through poetry and photography. © Alan Birkelbach, 2020. Published by permission of Alan Birkelbach.

We were certain then
the water would flow forever,
knowing we would always dive here,
like pale angels into the mossy green,
our arms holding us in place,
our cheeks puffy with wide-eyed, holy breath.

The Colorado River

The 21st we reached the Colorado River. This stream is very large and full of water; its banks and margins and meadows are very pleasant, with much foliage of many trees, willows, cottonwoods, elms, sabines, walnuts, cedars, pin oaks, post oaks, black walnuts, and many others as well as vines which twine around the trees; it has many fish, pilmontes, barbos, pullon, haddock, and many others. On the bank of this river dwell many barbarous Indians of the Coco nation.

—Fray Gaspar José de Solís, 1768

This range is not so high as it is sudden and aberrant, a disorder in the even westerly roll of the land. One could not call it mountain, but it is a considerable hill, or set of hills, and here again the country is transformed. The land rises steeply beyond the first escarpment and everything is changed: texture, configuration, blistered facade, all of it warped and ruptured and bruise-colored. The few rivers run deep, like old wounds, boiling round the fractures and revealing folds of slate and shell and glittering blue limestone, spilling back and across and out of the hills toward the lower country.

—Billy Lee Brammer, from *The Gay Place*

Fray Gaspar José de Solís traveled through Texas from 1767 to 1768 and kept a diary recording his impressions. His account was translated by Margaret Kenney Kress and Mattie Austin Hatcher and published in the *Southwestern Historical Quarterly* 35, no. 1 (July 1931).

Billy Lee Brammer (1929–1978) was a journalist who joined Lyndon Johnson's senatorial staff. In 1961, he published a celebrated political novel based on his experiences with LBJ, *The Gay Place*.

Colorado Bend

by Margie Crisp

We launch the boats in early morning quiet. The Boy Scouts are all asleep. White-eyed vireos call back and forth across the river. Canyon wrens drench us in liquid cascades of song. Spotted sandpipers bob along the shore, squeal plaintively, and fly downstream whenever we draw too close. The riverbed is rocky, and there is enough water and current to form small rapids. Within the first five minutes of being on the river, I get distracted from maneuvering through boulders by an eastern phoebe dancing over the water, snagging insects. The current pins the kayak sideways on a rock, and I'm almost dumped out of the boat.

The anglers are soon out in force. Every rapid has an angler or two working the pools below. We glide past dozens of people fishing in the river and from the banks. For most, a Texas nod is enough. Some, we are compelled to ask one of the infinite variations of the fisherman's greeting, "Catching anything?" A few ask us if anyone upstream is having any luck. This time of year, most are trying for the last of the white bass run.

The Colorado River above Lake Buchanan has one of the strongest white bass runs in Central Texas. As early as February, schools of males migrate upstream to locate running water with a gravel or rock substrate for spawning. April and May—when the redbuds are blooming—are good months for fishing; spawning is over, and hungry fish are migrating downstream to the reservoirs. Some fishermen swear by flies; others insist that small jigs are the only lure to use. As far as I can tell, when the fish are schooling and hungry, they will bite just about anything.

The canyons are flat-out gorgeous. Sulphur Springs and a hundred other springs seep through the karst limestone to flow pure and clear into the river. The swift current spills over rocks, riffles, and small rapids. The river's voice is ringing through the canyon: laughing, sparkling, vivacious, and compelling.

Margie Crisp is a nationally exhibited artist and writer who lives in Elgin, Texas, with her husband and fellow artist, William Montgomery. Her first book, *River of Contrasts: The Texas Colorado*, which she also illustrated, won the Texas Institute of Letters Award for Best Nonfiction. Excerpted from *River of Contrasts: The Texas Colorado* by Margie Crisp. Texas A&M University Press, 2012. Published by permission of Margie Crisp and Texas A&M University Press.

Bill and I arrive at Gorman Falls just before noon. We tie the kayaks to a rock and scramble up the steep, bare dirt riverbank to the falls. Hot, sweaty people stand behind the fence and the "Do Not Enter" signs. They stare at the cool, dripping water of the seventy-five-foot falls with unabashed lust and a solemn reverence. We take photos and admire the moss and fern-covered cliff glistening with spring water that flows over stone, plants, and travertine deposits down to the river. A breeze swifts across the face of the waterfall, and a cool mist wafts over the crowd. The people around me groan and are visibly weak-kneed. Hikers ask over and over, in whispers, if we rented our kayaks or know where to rent canoes.

From the falls, Bill and I skid down the steep bank back to the kayaks. In the river are huge chunks of limestone karst, once part of Gorman Falls. I look into the rotten heart of the stone, into the fissures connected by fragile-looking, slender ribs of stone and tenuous bridges. It reminds me of images of the interior of bones. Because rainfall is normally slightly acidic, it naturally dissolves the limestone as it seeps through fractures and clefts in the rock. The steady drip of water through the limestones and dolomites of Colorado Bend State Park has created an extraordinary variety of karst features, including sinkholes, caves, underground streams, and fractures.

The last mile or two of the river slows with still water backing up from Lake Buchanan. The rapids, riffles, and boulders are submerged.

We end our paddle at a Texas Parks and Wildlife boat ramp. Behind a rim of thick grass lining the shores, the broad sweep of campground is jammed with people, brightly colored tents, kayaks, canoes, and picnic tables covered with food, stoves, and lanterns. Kids are running around, and anglers of all ages troll the banks. The murmur of many voices and the smell of grilling meat fill the air. While I prefer to be a little more secluded, the sight of so many families enjoying the river is a profound pleasure.

I watch the kids running and playing games while others attend to the serious business of fishing. I think of the many people I have met who live along the river. An ancient Chinese proverb speaks of a silken red thread of destiny, which connects one person to another. The magical thread may tangle or stretch but never break. For me, the Colorado River is a magical green thread that winds its way through the heart of Texas, binding the lives of people together.

The Texas River
That Masquerades as a Lake

by Carol Flake Chapman

I think it must have been the Colorado
Masquerading as a slow-moving lake
That drew us to the old hippie neighborhood
Where you could still hear bands trying out
Some new songs on old drum sets in garages

We loved living just a stone's throw away
From our so-called lake which was actually
One of the series of big bulges in the coils
Of the snake that was the Colorado before
The dams tamed it into widened reservoirs

We would launch our kayaks from the little park
Where Bob the harbormaster would make wisecracks
About our dogs in their bright orange life vests
As he sat in his folding chair and cast a line
For the occasional perch that he always threw back

We'd paddle upstream to the narrow inlet
We pretended was a tributary of the Amazon
As we ducked under branches while turtles plopped
Into the murky water and great blue herons squawked
As they soared reluctantly from their wading spots

Carol Flake Chapman is a journalist, a poet, and a founding editor of *Vanity Fair.* Her latest book is *Written in Water: A Memoir of Love, Death and Mystery*, which tells of her pilgrimage from grief to consolation after the sudden death of her husband on a wild river in Guatemala. © Carol Flake Chapman, 2019. Published by permission of Carol Flake Chapman.

I never held it against the Colorado that another river
That rushed through a narrow jungle canyon in Guatemala
Claimed my husband as he spun from his red kayak
Into the rocky depths not far from the ruins of Tikal
As rivers don't pick and choose or play favorites

It was beside the Colorado aka Lake Austin that
The neighborhood musicians joined Marcia Ball
Who had brought her own portable piano to play
For a jazz funeral as we danced with parasols down
To the river and released rose petals into the current

And now every morning I walk down to the river that
Masquerades as a lake and I sit on the new fishing pier
To watch the sunrise as my little dog barks at the swan
I call Sweetie that swims up to me to say hello
While the great blue herons soar up from the opposite bank

Going with the Flow

by Brad Tyer

It was not my fight. That was not even my part of the country anymore; I had been living out of the state for years. I knew, though, that it might be years again before I got back with time enough on my hands to make the trip, and what I wanted to do was wrap it up, the river . . .

—John Graves, *Goodbye to a River*

I have a piece of river. It's the Colorado Rivèr, in and around Columbus, Texas. It's mine because I claimed it. Not by any birthright—I grew up in suburban Houston near an unnamed and channelized "bayou"—but because it found me.

I hadn't been looking. I was driving home from Austin in the early 1990s, and I ended up on the Hwy. 71 business route through Columbus, which led me across the old truss bridge over the Colorado. I hadn't seen that view before and I liked it. It was hot, so I stopped and stripped to my shorts and waded in. The water was sluggish and green and just barely cooler than the air.

Later I called the Chamber of Commerce and asked if anyone in town rented inner tubes, which confused the lady on the line. She connected me with Frank Howell, who ran a tire-and-wheel shop on the edge of town.

So began a long series of summers during which a group of friends and I would gather on selected Saturday mornings and caravan out Interstate 10. We'd stop at the local grocery to beer up and float the 6.5-mile loop from that truss bridge to Beason's Park, less than a mile away by road.

It was always perfect. Nobody else was out there. The river was a skilled hostess, slowly swirling the ten or fifteen or twenty of us into shifting configurations that could seem almost ordained. The beer and the sunstroke helped.

Brad Tyer is a seventh-generation Texan who grew up in Houston. He's an award-winning journalist and former managing editor of the *Texas Observer*. He is currently editor of the *Montana Free Press*. "Going with the Flow" originally appeared in the *Texas Observer*, August 19, 2009. Published by permission of Brad Tyer and the *Texas Observer*.

One day we got squatted on by a heavy-duty lightning storm. We couldn't figure out whether to ride it out in the river (the low spot) on the rubber tubes, or under the trees at bank's edge (don't trees get hit all the time?), or beyond the trees in open pasture, where we'd be the tallest targets around. We ended up at the tree line, huddling under the tubes in the slapping rain. People cried.

Then there was the time a buddy showed up late and we launched without him. He swam the first stretch to catch up with us, emerging naked from the deep water like a mirage, his shorts in one hand, two Lone Star tallboys in the other. He hung on to the side of a cooler tube the rest of the way down.

When I pulled into Columbus last weekend, Frank Howell and his wife, Evelyn, were sitting on the porch of their boat barn watching the river. Frank no longer owns the tire center. He bought a piece of property on the Colorado's south bank a few years back and set up his livery there, just downstream from the truss bridge. He still rents tubes, now covered in red cloth, with bottom buckets and his name printed on the side. He's added canoes and kayaks to his stable. We spent a while catching up—we don't see each other often, but we're becoming old friends over the years. Then I loaded my canoe and dragged it down the wooden steps of the launch he's built at the bank and slipped it into the water. Which was low. Seems like it's almost always low. The float takes about four hours in a tube when the water is optimal, but I've meandered my way through plenty of five-hour floats on this stretch. Frank says it's taking about six hours today.

It takes about two in a canoe, which hardly seems long enough.

It's not much of a river, but I've gotten attached to it. It's green and wide and murky even when the mud's not up, and there's nothing you'd call a rapid, just a few brief riffles. The first landmark is a low, scrubby island where we used to beach the tubes and have a smoke and look around. The banks on both sides alternate between tree-lined jungle and low sand bluffs topped with bald pastureland. The wildlife tends toward the pedestrian: egrets and kingfishers and herons and the occasional eagle. Sometimes a gar will roll; sometimes a water snake undulates alongside for a while. Frank swears that last month some of his tubers floated up on a five-and-a-half-foot blue catfish trying to eat an egret in the shallows. I would like to have seen that.

This time I saw a deer browsing on the bank, uncharacteristically unconcerned with a flashing red paddle. I don't usually see them here. She must have been as hungry as Frank's catfish.

There are scattered houses backed up to the river and some swooping sandy beaches. There are a few more commercial-looking picnic areas scooped out of the private undergrowth than I remember from my last trip.

About a third of the way down, there's a long, graceful bend to the right. To the left the bank is bluffed, and the bluff is fronted with thick stands of bamboo. This, I'm pretty sure, is the place I remember from a spring trip close to ten years ago. I was on the river after midnight under a quarter moon when I drifted around this arc facing the outer bank, like a huge, curved projection screen, watching I don't know how many thousands of fireflies dancing against the deep-black backdrop.

I've been reading *The Last River: The Tragic Race for Shangri La*. It's about a 1998 kayaking expedition on Tibet's waterfall-studded Yarlung Tsangpo through the uncharted Tsangpo Gorge—a trip on which one of the four boaters drowned.

That story is about as unfamiliar to the world of *Goodbye to a River*, or to any river experience of mine, as an egret is to a catfish. The expedition pursuing the first descent of the gorge was sponsored by *National Geographic* and took place in a highly pressurized environment of competition and stress. After the aborted trip, the Chinese government shut down access to outsiders.

The river itself is huge, the charismatic megafauna of the whitewater world, inspiring suitors and advocates. It's too wild to run and too remote to ruin.

The Colorado is a hard-used and semi-scenic stream at best. It's not the kind of river that gets people worked up about saving it, but that doesn't mean it's not threatened. It's water, after all, and water is under siege. We're running out of water in its usable forms much faster than we're curbing consumption or replenishing dwindling sources. Water issues are multilayered and deeply complex, but in another sense, they amount to simple math: more and more people struggling for access to less and less water, a seemingly inevitable diminishment calling for sober management.

But management and math are foreign to me. Naturalist Loren Eiseley wrote, "If there is magic on this planet, it is contained in water," and it's magic that claims me on a river.

On Sunday, I drove through periodically heavy rains to get to the river and put in under grumbling clouds. As so many times before on that looping stretch, those clouds left open a pocket of sunshine, rimmed by heavy blue, that followed me downstream. Only once, on a broad, windy stretch near the end, did I drift beneath a gray wisp, and it rained on me lightly in bright sunshine, drops hitting the water at an angle, backlit and glistening. It was as magical in that moment as anything on the mighty Yarlung Tsangpo, or John Graves's history-soaked Brazos, or any river anywhere.

Paddling in that rain, simple math began to seem like fuzzy abstraction, and magic—for the moment anyway—the natural state.

The Llano River

The Llano River

by Bill Minutaglio

Struggling over twisted tangles of tree limbs and damp muck, I could feel my absurdly clunky city shoes being clutched and sucked into the deepening mud. It was August 2, 1978, and the outer bands of Tropical Storm Amelia were dumping rain in the Hill Country and North Central Texas. A haggard-looking state highway worker was watching me try to stand up, maybe measuring any panic, and then his eyes were darting over my shoulder to the usually tame Bear Creek as it barreled into the Llano River.

He had been out in the storm, studying the movement of the rising waters and trying to warn people to stay away. He had the slightly eerie, taciturn demeanor of someone who had seen some things over the years and was expecting more. In a low, flat voice, he said we should leave and that floodwaters would drown Interstate 10.

I was with a good photographer friend and we raced in a car back to Junction, where the north and south forks of the Llano merge. I was a cub reporter for the newspaper in Abilene and we had been sent out to track the storms. We pulled to the side of a road and scrambled to an overlook.

The Llano was heaving, and splintered logs were popping up in the middle of it, as if they were gasping for air before being yanked under again. Big plastic cattle-feed buckets were spinning by like the teacup ride gone dizzy mad at the State Fair. People had told us that cowboys on horseback had tried to ford rivers around the state—the Nueces, the Medina, the Guadalupe—and some had disappeared.

Bill Minutaglio, born in Brooklyn and educated at Columbia University, moved to Texas in the 1970s to become a reporter. His writing has appeared in many publications in Texas and around the world. He is the author of eleven books and has received numerous honors, including a PEN Center Award for Research Nonfiction. © Bill Minutaglio, 2020. Published by permission of Bill Minutaglio.

I had only been in Texas for two months. I had treated myself to my ridiculous shoes after somehow graduating a university in my hometown of New York City. I had never heard of the Llano before, and I had never known a river to emit a relentless rumble that rose from the far distance. I was fixed on the Llano, mesmerized, and then there was something bobbing in the dead center. Rushing from the west. A cow was struggling to keep its head above the water. You could see its painted face and its wide eyes and nothing else, as the Llano carried it to the gunmetal gray horizon.

A few years later, Maury Maverick Jr., one of the great men of Texas (hell, anywhere), invited me to his family's old lodge on the river. The Mavericks were iconoclasts and gave the word "maverick" to our language. Maury's father stood up for the ordinary people when he was mayor of San Antonio. Maury did the same, representing conscientious objectors during the Vietnam War and fighting a righteous fight as a state lawmaker.

He preferred underdogs, including a three-legged one he had rescued from the streets—and a massive, gently noble Irish wolfhound he named Llano. One time, I visited Maury and found him asleep on his bed and covered by a pile of stray dogs he had accumulated. On another day, he demanded I meet him at a hidden field in San Antonio, where Maury showed me a mutt huddling with its puppies. He was angry I didn't take one home.

Maury said to take the highway into Marble Falls, veer through Burnet, and follow a narrow, winding road to the west. He added, mysteriously, that I should look for a red cloth tied to a cedar fence post. I found the ribbon of sheet and turned south onto a dirt path. Maury was waiting at a weathered stone cottage. He pointed to some rock steps, lined by live oaks and cedar trees, leading down a gently sloping hill.

It was the second time I had seen the Llano.

Giant maroon-and-pink-hued hunks of granite emerging from translucent pools. Even bigger, quartz-flecked outcroppings, some of the oldest on Earth, forming a Hill Country Stonehenge in mid-river. The water's surface as clear as a freshly cleaned pane of glass. I stripped down and dove in. The palms of my hands glided along the soft, sandy bottom. I wondered if I could drink the water. Muddy Waters used to sing about a river being whiskey and Muddy being a diving duck. I floated off, losing sight of the lodge and Maury.

I stood up, with the Llano up to my waist, and an abrupt spasm of wariness gripped me. I looked over my shoulder, wondering if there was a surge of water ready to rush from beyond the bend to the west, from beyond the somber gatherings of billion-year-old sentinels. But there was no droning monotone.

No rumble. Just the steady chattering of the river as it swirled into channels on either side of the boulders, or as it rolled over the shoals, or as it settled into shimmering pockets close to the riverbank.

It was one thing to know Maury Maverick in the heart of the city, to walk with him in Brackenridge Park in San Antonio, and to see his family's name on the buildings downtown. It was another thing entirely to be at the Llano River at his invitation, wading among stones birthed from the same geological uplift as Enchanted Rock. Maury was sturdy, unyielding and stubborn. He was a flinty but benign Diogenes trudging relentlessly across Texas in search of anything, anyone, pure and at least honest. As long as I knew him, Maury often seemed to be judging me, and I'm quite sure he was studying me hard as I came back to the lodge.

Maury used to write stories about the times he went out looking for big truths in Texas and how he often sought out ghosts for answers. He wrote about strolling with Davy Crockett and talking to him about why some things in Texas were the way they were, both then and now. Maury no doubt talked to the phantoms and memories along the Llano—maybe the ones from a billion years ago. From the days before the wandering, pilgrim tributaries—Hickory Creek, Six Mile Creek, Vasterling Creek—were sucked dry by the conquerors that claimed the water for their own purposes. Before the bears disappeared from alongside Bear Creek. Before the beavers were mostly gone from along Bauer Shoals. Before the black willow trees were cut down in Sandy Creek. Before the last wolf was hunted at the hem of Babyhead Mountain.

In the 1980s, I faked editors into doing a story other con artist writers have done—"the top swimming holes in Texas" article. In one of them, I named a little spot off River Road in San Antonio as one of the best in the state. It was near a highway and a municipal golf course. It was a nostalgic inclusion, a nod to when some of us would jump into that part of the San Antonio River after rounds of tequila and bottles of "Solo Estrella" late night at the Esquire bar downtown. The first time I went in and touched the bottom, my fingers wrapped around a bullet. After my article came out, a friend reminded me churlishly about the time he was jogging and stopped to splash water from the "swimming hole" on his face—and a bloated, dead dog came floating by.

I left the Llano off my list, perhaps for selfish reasons. In the 1990s I visited it for the third time.

I drove past the looming Llano County courthouse, near the Llantex Theater, and then north over the two-lane metal bridge spanning the river. I parked on a patch of dirt and grass just west of the bridge and jumped into the water, again reaching for the bottom: it must be some kind of way of connecting an insignificant self to land and sky and water.

Scooping up fistfuls of the riverbed, I came to the surface and saw my fingers coated with gold and silver flecks. I dove down again and touched more sand and came up with the same glimmering dots. Prospectors had once tried to get gold from the river and the lacy network of creeks. The air was warm, and it was good to dream.

I spent the afternoon lolling in the Llano, listening to it as it thundered over the spillway. I watched it flow from what was left of its children—Flag Creek, Oatman Creek, Buttery Creek, Byrnes Creek, Wrights Creek, and the Little Llano River. I watched it head toward where I had waded into the water for the first time at Maury's lodge.

Back in Austin, I met the ex-wife of Billy Lee Brammer, the doomed writer famous for his novel *The Gay Place*—the thinly veiled chronicle of the perditions inside Texas politics. She was pushing seventy, and it was a lot like visiting Maury; she seemed to see right through me, and she certainly knew things about Texas far beyond my ability to comprehend. I told her how much I liked the Llano River. She asked, almost conspiratorially, if I had ever heard of the riverside town of Castell.

As soon as I could, I headed toward the edge of the Hill Country on an undulating road that follows the river to the west. Leaving the city of Llano, you can see the pregnant rise of Enchanted Rock to the south, just beyond miles of loping ranchland. To the north is Iron Mountain, maybe where the ancient nomads had gone to find chunks of blood-colored hematite they would use to draw the pictographs at Paint Rock—their final meditations on the rivers, the wildlife, in Texas. This was the lair of the Comanche, the people hunted ceaselessly just like the deer and the bear. The people who retaliated by abducting the white settlers' children and raising them as their own.

Almost twenty miles later, I found Castell. It was one of a series of small German communities—Bettina, Leiningen, Meerholz, and Schoenburg—that traced to the mid-nineteenth century. There were a dozen beat-up wood buildings, including the faded-yellow Sunshine General Store and a one-room post office. Castell felt empty, abandoned, like a movie set imagined for Horton Foote. There was a low-water crossing over the Llano, and I stopped to peer into the shallows. There were plump Guadalupe bass. Long-nosed garfish. Turtles sunning, mossy shell to mossy shell, on a granite orb in the middle of a channel. It was desultory, a wistful kind of alone.

I headed back through the village—there was a small sign that said, "Population 25," which seemed exceedingly optimistic. And for the next several months,

I kept returning to that stretch of the river, to the curling roads on both sides of the water.

From south of the Llano, you were on the same plane as the water, moving alongside it. From the high road on the north, you looked down toward the furrows and the dancing bends, the way the river had decided to split into deep ponds, or the way it would ring and chime against the rocks.

One day my wife and I drove to Castell, and there was an older woman out on the porch of a small country house. We had slowed to look at her place, under centuries-old oaks, and she waved for us to stop. She and her husband had run the Sunshine General Store in Castell, but he had died not long ago. She had laid him to rest alongside a tiny church down the road, in a cemetery filled with the German settlers and their descendants. She said that it was time for her to leave the homestead, to go somewhere else.

It was near the end of 2000, and my wife's grandfather—a hearty man of the earth, a water-well digger in the hard outback of Eastern Oregon—had also just passed away. He had left us a very small sum of money. We had two small children, a drowning mortgage in the big city, a car headed to 200,000 miles, and shaky jobs. I told my wife we should use her tiny inheritance to take out another mortgage, this one for a place hugging the Llano River. For reasons I'm not sure of, she agreed.

A writer friend told me how when he moved to the Hill Country, the thing that staggered him, maybe scared him, was the yawning vastness of the night. The way you step into the deep evening and you know that something enormous is alive beyond what you can see and touch. Being more often near the river multiplied my need for humility. All night there was the constant sound of the Llano burnishing the igneous mounds. In the dead of the dark, it would rise up alive, beyond the tall trees. Steadier than the coyote howls, the hoot owls, the animal rustlings in the brush.

The children learned to swim in the gin-clear water, and they caught catfish until we all agreed that taking more things from the river wasn't what we wanted to do. I stood on the bank one day and saw a water snake swimming in one direction, a garfish gliding in the opposite direction, and then a turtle going the way of the snake. Strolling the bank, I spotted a log that had been gnawed by an animal. My wife, raised in Oregon, said it was the work of a beaver. Not long later she and I were standing on the water's edge. Her ritual was to go to a particular spot and look for "her" alligator gar. As she said hello to him, there was a sudden splash from submerged reeds—and a golden beaver zoomed into deeper water, his paddle tail clearly visible.

As time went on, I thought I knew the river well enough, or got from it what I believed I needed. That changed six years later: we had a new dog, a flat-coated retriever named Augie (in honor of the musician Augie Meyers). I took him down to the river for his baptism. I watched his feet instinctively begin paddling as I held him above the water. He quickly learned to dash by himself from the house to the Llano, to disappear for a good spell, and to finally return soaking wet and deliriously weary.

The flat-coated retriever is often described as the "Peter Pan" of dogs, never seeming to grow old. He could spend all day in the river, and sometimes I'd join him, both of us swimming into the deepening swirls or clambering across Bauer Shoals—named after the family we had bought our land from.

Sometimes, Augie would let me embrace his midsection, and then he would paddle hard, guiding me for yards through the water. I'd hug his muscled body and listen to his panting. I'd listen to his heartbeat as he pulled me through the Llano, as if he was trying to save me.

I had felt guilty for years after reading the writer Rick Bass's theories that many of our dogs are denied their innate nature. That we turned off something pure, honest when we steered them from their connections to the natural order, from the call of the wild, I suppose. On the Llano, there were no second thoughts, no doubts. Augie and I moved together in the clear, clear water. I held him as close as he would let me, and then I let him take me where he thought best.

When I climbed out of the river, I would sit and watch him frolic by himself. Sometimes he would fly off a tall bankside, and his paws would brush the powdery bottom. And then I would see him begin to sway through the river, searching for what he wanted. I liked to fix on his eager face, his pure exultation. Maury Maverick would have found the honesty in Augie's eyes.

We went together to the river for many years. I once saw Augie chase a jackrabbit for over one hundred yards—and then throw himself merrily into the Llano as if to cap off a really, really fine day. I would watch him glide in the river and then later, I would watch him sleep like never before, his legs paddling through a dream that should never end.

One morning we went to the Llano in the wake of some hard rains. The river was up and moving fast. Augie was much older by then, but he scrambled and swam to his usual place in the Bauer Shoals.

I watched from the bank as the river gusted him suddenly into an area of choppy water. I called him, and he turned—but for the first time, he didn't dance and hop over the rocks and white water like he always had. He seemed surprised to be struggling to hold his own against the churning flow. I stumbled quickly across the shoals, half crawling, half swimming, cutting my knees and hands on the granite. I picked him up and somehow carried him to the shore.

Augie died, very suddenly, in 2016. It broke my heart, of course, but his quick death made some sort of sense. He had brought me the kind of zooming, rocketing joy that comes without hesitation or complication. And then he was, well, just gone.

It was an easy decision to release his ashes in the river, at Bauer Shoals. Augie had his own great joy by becoming one with the river, by swimming under the herons and the occasional eagle that fished and brought their catch back to a huge, complex nest atop a dead tree to the east near the Little Llano River.

I assembled my wife, son and daughter, and we lowered fistfuls of Augie's ashes into the chilly, fast-moving water. I fumbled my way through some grand statement about Augie never being good on a leash, and that he was always a bit wild, and how the Llano River was a "wild river." It rang hollow, thin, and I knew it was probably better to leave things unspoken—or that some things at the river didn't need to be drawn out or ever explained.

My family headed up the hill and back to the house, but I stood for a bit longer, watching the Llano and the ashes of my best friend flow away. The first time I had ever seen the river, it had ferried a frantic, living being to somewhere else. Now the Llano and Augie's ashes were headed in the direction of Maury's old lodge. That place where I assumed Maury had talked to the ghosts of Texas. The conquerors, the natives, the settlers, and anyone or anything else ever drawn to the river.

Forty years after I had first seen it flood, the Llano rose again.

There was a devastating surge that came from the west that thundered from Junction, just like it had in 1978. Fifty-foot-tall pecan trees along the riverbank were toppled. Logs were hurtled onto forty-foot-high blocks of granite. Century-old cedar post fences built by the Germans were ripped from the ground and tossed away. Mounds of beaten-up cactus were flung into the remaining treetops. Fish were thrown onto land, not far from the house, which somehow escaped damage.

The Llano had been furious, and it had completely surrounded Castell. It had broken homes and even destroyed a bridge in Kingsland. Some people had also been taken by the river—a woman's body was carried miles from Junction and right past our property, right by the shoals, right by where we had seen a beaver making a home, right by where Augie and I rescued each other.

When the river calmed, the parks and wildlife experts announced that nature had taken its course. That the Llano was purging itself, perhaps cleansing itself. Some of the more poetic said the river was reminding people of its primacy.

For days, weeks, and months, I went to the river to stare at the tangled, impossibly complicated piles of wood and vines and limbs, trying to understand what the flood had meant. I learned that, more than ever, there were still people along the length of the Llano trying to conquer it. Who had new tools, new weapons. They had been busy erasing the riparian systems, those delicately complex areas where land meets water, and where pecan trees, the black willows, and a hundred other native plants worked for ages with the river to provide rich, enduring homes for the fat freshwater mussels, the beaver, and the parade of other animals—the red foxes, road runners, and wild turkeys. Some people were scalping the riverbanks of trees, brushes, and native grasses, and installing lawns and sprinkler systems fed by long pipes jutting into the river. Some put in swimming pools alongside the river. Some poured pesticides, the kind that drive away the jackrabbits and kill the harvester ants that the vanishing horned lizards feed on.

Several months after the great flood, I also learned about a tall, weathered-looking cowboy from San Angelo. Steve Nelle was a multi-generational Texan who had begun traveling the state and basically atoning for the way his and other ranchers' ancestors had diverted the rivers, drained away the springs and creeks, because . . . they didn't know any better. Now he was on a mission, holding "river repair" workshops and telling people how to heal the creeks and rivers, how to make them resemble something like the way they once were. How turning the Llano River into a "backyard setting" was to deny its very nature. He was a legend in certain Texas circles, including some state agencies, and he was, some said, a river whisperer.

We met one day in the bone-dry bed of Sandy Creek, and he told me that the black willow tree was a particular life-saving part of the Llano's extended system. That it needed to be reintroduced and that it could slow the floods. He said that you could carefully cut off long stems of the black willow, stick them in the riverbank, and that the river would nurture the cuttings and protect the roots through droughts.

I told him that the Llano had toppled almost everything that grew on my land. That it had knocked down the dizzingly fragrant catclaw mimosa and the fruit-laden tasajillo cactus—what we had come to call Christmas cactus. The Llano River had taken away cattle, homes . . . people. He said it reminded him of a truth that those who had lived longer than me with the Llano River already knew: *"The river giveth and the river taketh away."*

When I had first gone to the river to study the flood damage, I could see clearly that there was one very tall black willow tree that had bent to the ground by the flood. It had been denuded by the power of the water, turned into a fallen pole, and it was bowing, even prostrate, to the east.

The cowboy river whisperer had said that you shouldn't clean natural debris after a flood. That fallen things will return to the earth as part of the system binding land and water. That they will serve as new bulwarks against erosion, and that they will eventually become places where life renews itself. He said leaving fallen nature alone was the most important counterpoint to those scraped acres of earth, those places stripped bare by the people who wanted to drain the river, who wanted the Llano to be something it shouldn't be.

As months went by, I trudged down to the water, still missing Augie, still wondering if it was a good thing to leave the ungodly mess of wounded trees and broken limbs alone.

One day, I noticed that the black willow, still on its side, seemed to be leafing out. Then, as each week passed, it began to very slowly straighten. For months, it continued to emerge from the disheveled mounds of fractured logs, driftwood, and jumbled vines. I stared, amazed, and vowed to take cuttings from the black willow. To try to add them to the riverbank. Maybe they'd grow, maybe someday someone would see sturdy, tall trees shading the river—shading the bass, the turtles, the gar, the beaver.

I also vowed to bring more of Augie's ashes—I still had some in a little wooden box—back to Bauer Shoals and right next to the black willow tree. Perhaps I'd do it on a day when the Llano resembled the very thing that we both wished could last forever.

The Pedernales River

Light on the Water

by Deborah K. Wilson

It is early spring in Central Texas. I am alone, and it feels good to be driving the "old way" to Pedernales Falls State Park. A busier road would not do on a day like this. I do not want to rush.

Traveling more slowly than usual, I roll down the windows and let the soft air rush around me. I glance down at bare arms, my fully freckled skin, and think that I am looking more and more like my father's mother. A farmer's wife, a rock of love and commitment, she wore all the hours she had spent at the gardens, the barns, the yard, the creeks, and under the sun, right there on her skin.

The road dips across a low water crossing, then rises and curves as it runs up and along the ridge, offering sweeping Hill Country vistas against a backdrop of true blue Texas sky. I am surrounded by thick stands of green cedar with some live oaks mixed in. The oaks have just put on their new leaves, a lighter and brighter green, contrasting beautifully with the darker cedar. It all feels so much like home. Suddenly I get a whiff of exquisite mountain laurel, and my childhood senses come alive.

Where there is room to pull over, I stop to collect a few early wildflowers. Purple verbena, bluebonnets, and Indian paintbrush make a pretty bouquet. I admire their simple beauty. Farther down the way, I stop to look for fossils in a road cut and spot an ancient oyster shell. I can see only a portion of its rippled edge but manage to dislodge it, a nice specimen shaped like a human ear.

Deborah K. Wilson's account of her father's and uncle's deaths during a flash flood was written for the Story Circle Network, a nonprofit organization in Texas dedicated to helping women share the stories of their lives. "Light on the Water" originally appeared in *What Wildness Is This: Women Write about the Southwest*, edited by Susan Wittig Albert et al. University of Texas Press, 2007. Published by permission of Deborah K. Wilson's family.

Continuing on, I soon reach the park road. I feel an aching longing. This was the last road my father traveled, on the last day of his life.

How appropriate it is that he spent his last day here. When we spoke about living and dying, of someone passing on or just going to a nursing home, he would say with his wry smile, "Me? I want to live as long as I can go fishing." I never imagined it would happen so literally.

My father was all things Texas, as was his brother, just as much Texas as any rock, river, or tree. Formed out of the same raw materials, both men followed similar paths, shared similar natures. They were kindred spirits. It seemed somehow fitting that they died together that spring day on the Pedernales River.

I park in an area near the Pedernales Falls and walk to the overlook. From here I can see the grandness of this awesome rock formation, over which falls one of the fastest-flowing rivers in Texas. The rocks are exposed here in huge tilted beds, three hundred million years old, the dark gray-blue limestone masses standing high and proud as the river rushes over and through them. The carving and scouring action of the water has created marvelous textures and structures. There are strange angles, tilted beds lying beneath horizontal beds: angular unconformities that offer clues to dynamic earth movements, to missing intervals of earth history. Somehow, this geological description of missing time created by cataclysmic shifts expresses my feeling of a missing interval in my family's history. At the time of my father's and uncle's deaths, and for weeks after, there was a palpable sense of time standing still. Surreal yet too real. Unbelievable yet undeniable. They were gone, just like that. Time was suspended, although the clocks ticked on.

I gather myself now and walk below the falls, to the place where the water surges downward into a plunge pool, creating swirling eddies that gouge pot-holes in the rocks, some small, some as large as six feet wide and eight feet deep. Some are elliptical, like teardrops, here to catch the tears of those who come to the river to mourn. I am struck by the colors and textures, the angles and shapes meeting, contacting. Within these park boundaries, there are numerous visible examples of geologic contact, points where two different rock formations, two vastly different geologic ages meet, even overlap.

At one location near these falls, I can put one hand on the youngest sand and the other on the oldest limestone, and my hands touch one another at the contact point. This idea of contact intrigues me, and I want to comprehend how, within me, disparate events and ideas can meet and overlap to create my inner landscape. Surely my life is varied and enriched by the inner contact of unrelated things, spiritual and physical. If only I could place one hand on the spiritual plane at the same time as I place one on the physical, as I can with the limestone and sand.

I walk downstream, passing Spanish oak, pecan, mesquite, and sycamore trees. Prickly pear cacti and prairie grasses cover the ground. I reach the old wagon road that leads to Trammel Crossing, where settlers forded the river, and a stand of noble old cypress trees, battered and beaten, scarred by boulders and stones that remain lodged in their roots and trunks from the floods they have endured.

I am near the point where my uncle's body was recovered two days after he disappeared, two miles from the point he went in. He had been fishing with the others at the north end of the park, well above the falls, walking several hundred yards up the channel on exposed rocks in the riverbed. There had been no warning of severe weather and no alert issued to incoming park guests—standard practice if heavy rain was expected. My brother, who barely made it out, said they knew something was coming when the minnow bucket began to bounce. They had no idea how much of a rise to expect, but they knew this river can get fierce, so they gathered their gear and headed back. But in no time, the rocks in the channel disappeared, and a torrent was upon them, a torrent of churning, rushing water filled with boulders, limbs, and debris. They were good swimmers, but even good swimmers can't overcome such a furious force of nature.

I remove from my tote bag the fossil I found earlier, its grayish surface mottled with a crust of rusty brown chert. I place the ancient oyster shell to my ear, and then, remembering my uncle, I hold it to my heart before casting it into the waters that took him back to his source. And the rippling water is all that is left.

I return to my car, retrieve the wildflower bouquet, and head down the less traveled trail that leads to the far north end of the park. The sun hangs motionless in the late cloudless afternoon, and I look up and across the broad expanse of the river to the steep cliffs on the other side. I am here to visit the rocky outcrop where my brother brought my father's body out of the raging water. I shed my shoes and dangle my feet in the Pedernales. The sun's light reflects on the water. It shimmers and dances before me.

At the time of the tragedy, I lived in California. I came back to Texas to bury my father and uncle, comfort my grandparents, and try to understand that the two men I respected and adored were gone. As long as I was near my family, I held up pretty well, but back in California, I was in shock. Nothing seemed right to me. I dreamed of my father constantly, but they were distant dreams, dreams I could barely remember. I felt as if he were somewhere close by, but just out of reach. I would lie in bed, half asleep, thinking the phone was ringing and he was calling, but I could not hear what he was saying. My life was not moving. Time was standing still.

Then three months after my return, something happened. In California, I lived on a beautiful river. My father came to me in a dream, standing by my bed, telling me to wake up. He said he knew I had a heavy heart, and this would bring light into it. I got up, and he led me out to my backyard, to the edge of the river, and told me to look at the scene before me and tell him what I saw.

"I see the river and the mountain behind it," I said.

He said, "Now look at the sky and tell me what you see."

I looked up at the sky. "I see the stars in the night sky."

And he said, "Now look at the water and tell me what you see now."

I looked at the water. "I see the reflections of the stars shimmering on the water."

"That is where I am," he said. "I am the light on the water. Whenever you see the reflection of light on water, know that I am here with you. I am always here with you, in the light on the water."

I rise, holding the flowers for a moment to my face to breathe in their wild sweetness. I untie the ribbon and scatter them across the light on the water.

Angularities of a Creek
Observations from the Pedernales River Basin

by Daniel Oppenheimer

I live along South Grape Creek, a tributary of the Pedernales River, in the Central Texas Hill Country. The creek emerges from limestone in Kendall County and winds past hay fields and scrubland across the Gillespie County line, by the matchless music of Luckenbach, behind a few wineries, to its terminus at a new ranch that has recently reintroduced bison to the Pedernales River Basin.

Most of the year, the spring-fed South Grape Creek flows—and does so clearly. Unless there's a flood, you can see to the bottom—and the fish plainly see you.

By midsummer, the creek recedes, forming pools of captive fish that provide sustenance to a few opportunists, including a lone blue heron and four brown-and-black water snakes that live in the crevices of the creek crossing below my house. Raccoon and fox tracks affirm much more happens after I go to sleep.

In *The Immense Journey*, Loren Eiseley suggests that the secret of life should be sought when one is not confused by the green bustle of spring, but rather when one can "examine in sharp and beautiful angularity the shape of life without its disturbing muddle of juices and leaves." With South Grape Creek, one can see its bare bones in late summer, before the autumn rains—*probable* but not guaranteed—bring reprieve to the fish and the ranchers.

My dog and I love to walk between the pools of water, studying the creek bed. It has topography. There are the valleys, fresh-cut rivulets that hold the last bits of moisture in the channel; there are mesas, the stair-step terraces of exposed Hensel sand and cobble, ascending up one section of the bank; and rolling hills of deposition—each composed of its own unique blend of sand, grit, and rock—that undulate across the channel bottom.

Daniel Oppenheimer is a fifth-generation Texan based in Gillespie County. He is the Land Program Manager for the Hill Country Alliance, a nonprofit organization dedicated to preserving the natural resources and heritage of the Texas Hill Country. © Daniel Oppenheimer, 2019. Published by permission of Daniel Oppenheimer.

While I understand the basic physical processes of erosion and deposition, walking the creek bed suggests levels of nuance that I may need several lifetimes to understand.

Some sections of the creek banks are solid, held together by an intricate web. Fine strands of Eastern gamagrass, switchgrass, and inland sea oats roots weave together with thicker roots of hackberry trees, and the robust, buttress roots of bald cypress trees. These riparian plants are remarkable. Together, they are stronger than rebar, maintaining the integrity of long sections of bank and, in one place, holding an old Super 70 A70-13 tire in its resting place.

When I moved to this little house in the Hill Country, somewhere between Luckenbach and that roaming herd of bison at the confluence of South Grape Creek and the Pedernales River, I was surprised to meet some of the locals. They were beautiful; they were obstinate; they were axis deer.

Indigenous to India and Sri Lanka, axis deer were first introduced to high-fenced ranches in the Hill Country during the 1930s for hunting. Some escaped. With adaptable digestive systems, they are now causing consternation for many, including white-tailed deer, ranchers, and perhaps the creek itself.

Free-ranging herds of axis deer have stripped the creek banks of seedlings and saplings, leaving mature cypress, pecan, and sycamore trees without progeny. In some patches of the creek bottom, there is simply no groundcover or understory left beneath the old trees, but perhaps for an isolated frost weed or the occasional lantana bush.

In the evening, starry nights calmly choreographed by crickets and cicadas are interrupted by a series of bellowing cries. It's an axis buck broadcasting his libido with a jet-powered wheeze that he repeats several times. The noise bears repeating as this buck is seeking a receptive doe amidst a herd that can exceed in size of seventy-five animals.

Occasionally a deer does not make it safely across Luckenbach Road. But we have some hardworking Hill Country buzzards out here that waste little time.

The buzzards stay busy, with the increasing number of visitors traveling down Highway 290 and Luckenbach Road colliding with axis and native white-tailed deer. People come from all corners of the world: for peaches in the summer, locally brewed Oktoberfest beer in the fall, and wine tours year-round.

Some visitors stay for a quick trip, while many people decide to move here. As ranches are sliced into ranchettes, ranchlands converted to homes and manicured lawns, more and more water wells are drilled into the limestone, the same substrate that shapes and is shaped by the creek.

Of course, people need places to live, work, and recreate. However, with the population of the Texas Hill Country projected to double in the next thirty-five to forty years, I wonder when South Grape Creek and other tributaries like it will start to reveal their bones earlier in the summer and later into the fall.

For now, the creek still cleanly flows most of the year below my house. Just this year, I found the bodark tree that gifts to the creek its bright green, softball-sized fruits. Sometimes I'll intercept these bobbing gifts and place them amidst a pile of branches, from whence I hope they will germinate, protected from the axis deer.

If they make it past my place, those floating bodark apples may reach the bison, who, like me, are adapting to their changing surroundings. The new ranch owners are using the bison—along with pasture-raised chickens, pigs, and ducks—to enhance the soil, land, and ultimately the Pedernales River. It's a hopeful story of regeneration that local ranchers and urban foodies alike are following.

We need more stories like these that engage our rural communities and our urban counterparts. Few seem to know that the Pedernales River, which merges with the Colorado River at Lake Travis, provides nearly 25 percent of the drinking water to more than one million people in the greater Austin area. This, to me, is that sharp and beautiful angularity of our Hill Country creeks and rivers: we're all connected, and our decisions matter.

Barton Springs

At the Source

by Stephen Harrigan

I first noticed the springs that feed Barton Springs pool early one summer morning, when I was sitting on the grassy slope gathering my resolve for an initial plunge into the icy water. The pool was calm and vacant, except for a few ducks puttering about at the north end and a half dozen lap swimmers stroking back and forth through the early morning mist, their arms striking the surface with a gentle percussive slap. The previous afternoon's stirred-up silt had settled to the bottom, its slick of suntan oil had dissipated, and the water was so brilliantly clear it almost hurt my eyes to look at it.

Near the diving board, in the deepest, bluest part of the pool, something caught my attention. It was a faint tremor on the placid surface of the water. Since that time, in years when the spring flow has been greater and the artesian pressure more intense, I've often watched the springs discharge themselves in a percolating eruption of bubbles. But that day it was a subtle phenomenon. The slight agitation of the water in that section of the pool reminded me of the quivering surface tension of a soap bubble.

The turbulence, slight as it was, intrigued me greatly. It hinted at some secret commotion below. For the rest of that summer, whenever I came back to Barton Springs, I brought my mask and fins with me and dove down again and again to the main spring opening, which I'd located about fifteen feet below the surface. Taking three deep, quick breaths to saturate my lungs with air, I would plunge down head first, following the vertical fissures in the submerged rock,

Stephen Harrigan is a leading Texas novelist, journalist, and nonfiction writer. He's also written several screenplays for television and film. The author of a dozen books, his many literary honors include the Lifetime Achievement Award from the Texas Institute of Letters. "At the Source" originally appeared in *Barton Springs Eternal: The Soul of a City*, edited by Turk Pipkin and Marshall Frech. Softshoe Publishing, 1990. Published by permission of Stephen Harrigan.

listening to the muffled *ka-thumps* of kids doing cannonballs off the diving board overhead. Jittery shafts of sunlight danced all around me, vectoring toward the distant pebbly bottom where I was headed. By the time I had stopped to squeeze my nostrils and ease the pressure in my ears, I was already running low on breath, and so my inspection of the spring opening, when I finally reached it, was always tantalizingly brief.

From deep in the earth, the water of the aquifer surged into Barton Springs pool through a narrow channel of rock. The opening was about a foot in diameter, and when I sank down in front of it, I could feel a gust of cold water rippling against my face. The velocity of the water caused the heavy pebbles on the bottom of the pool to twitch like Mexican jumping beans, and if I listened closely, I could hear them clack against each other.

That spring opening made me think of an Old Testament miracle—water gushing forth from solid rock, presented as evidence of a power deeper than human understanding. And since that summer I've never thought of Barton Springs as simply a pool, an inert basin of water. To me it has always been a living thing, fed by a system of watery veins and arteries that if they could be traced back to their source, would lead to nothing less than a great beating heart deep beneath the earth.

This summer I went back to Barton Springs, which had recently reopened after months of repairs due to flood damage, I took my hyperventilating breaths as usual and dove down to visit the spring opening. The water was slightly murky, as it tends to be in these days of greedy overdevelopment of the watershed, but it was still thrillingly cold as it poured forth from the sunless hollows of the aquifer.

I was preparing to pinch my nose to clear my ear when I noticed, with a shock, that I was already on the bottom. I thought for a moment that my diving skills had mysteriously improved, but then I understood that the floor of the pool had risen in this spot by a good five or six feet. The spring opening was nowhere to be seen. No doubt flood debris or the heavy machinery brought into the drained pool to clear it away had inadvertently plugged up the opening. For a moment I was alarmed and angered, worried that the pool's supply of pure water had been thoughtlessly choked off. But then, as I turned in slow circles on the bottom, I could feel the slightest underwater breeze on my skin, and I knew that the great heart was still pumping and that the lifeblood of Barton Springs was still coming through.

I felt nostalgic about the old spring opening, but I let it go at that. One door had closed, another was opening, and all I had to do was find it.

The Guadalupe River

Down by the banks of the Guadalupe
On a summer's evening and a haloed moon
Wide-eyed as night owls, naked as a dream
We washed our love in the rippling waters of a rambling stream.

We slept like time itself under diamond skies
Far from the bright lights and the city's lies
Our love arose like a morning dream
And it was washed in the rippling waters of a rambling stream.

Well the mountain dreams of a blanket of snow
And the wild wind dreams of directions it might blow
But the river's dream is a dream of love
And a dream of sweet reflections from above.

—Butch Hancock, from "Banks of the Guadalupe"

Butch Hancock, born in Lubbock, is a world-traveling troubadour, a member of the Flat-landers, and regarded as one of Texas's premiere singer-songwriters. "Banks of the Guada-lupe," © Butch Hancock. Published by permission of Butch Hancock.

Guad Is Great
In Praise of the Guadalupe

by Joe Nick Patoski

*O*ne late afternoon in mid-February, the day after the first significant snowfall in nineteen years, I launched a sit-on-top kayak from the low-water crossing near where I live onto my river, a tributary of the Guadalupe River. It was due for an inspection. It was early in the season for this kind of excursion, but I'd been feeling the tug for weeks.

The calendar said winter, but spring was subtly stirring wherever I looked. A loud scree overhead identified the first pair of zone-tail hawks nesting in the top of a nearby cypress, none too happy with my presence. The first kingfisher flashed right in front of me, then skimmed above the water in full glide. A mockingbird hopped among the bare cypress branches, scouting for nest sites. A small turtle, its shell caked gray with mud, scooted atop a boulder to sun itself. A bass peeked out from under the base of the same boulder, submerged at the bottom of a deep hole.

With each dip of the paddle, I stirred up liquid diamonds that dazzled in the sunlight. The boat moved swiftly as I paddled through placid, deep pools and scraped rock and fought currents. Where I could find them, I rode riffles and rapids, and whenever necessary, I sloshed through shallows, dragging the boat behind me.

While surfing the little rapids, I'd occasionally get in a groove where I didn't have to paddle at all. Rather, I was suspended in the rapid, nose upstream, waves rushing downstream, motionless in the midst of perpetual motion, losing sense of time and even existence. In one of these trances, my meditative state was interrupted by a white-tailed doe stealthily sidling up to the water's edge about one hundred yards upstream to take a drink. She spied me about the same time I spied her. She took another quick drink, stepped gingerly on several flat rocks in the water before bounding into a pool and scampering up

Joe Nick Patoski is a journalist, author, radio host, and renowned expert on many aspects of Texas culture. He's written books on Austin, Willie Nelson, the Dallas Cowboys, Selena, Texas nature, Stevie Ray Vaughan, and more. Originally published in *Texas Parks & Wildlife* magazine, July 2004. Published by permission of Joe Nick Patoski.

to cross over to the other side. Two larger whitetails followed, going through the same routine. Look, drink, scan again, step, step, plunge, step, step across. Negotiating around a particularly large limestone hazard, I glanced back to spot a great blue heron, the giant bird queen of the river, moving upstream, flapping her pterodactyl-like wings just enough to keep her sizeable trunk above the surface of river.

None of the rapids were so much as class II worthy. But on a midwinter's day in Central Texas, I was more than satisfied. I couldn't imagine a better place to be on this earth. That thought stuck with me all the way back to the house even though my butt was numb and I couldn't feel my toes.

Of the fifteen major rivers in Texas, the Guadalupe is the Texas-most river, springing to life in the Hill Country, that sweet spot where east and west, north and south, coast and desert, tropics and prairie all converge and diversity thrives and flourishes. The Guadalupe runs exceptionally cool, swift, and clear until it reaches the fertile rolling plains, where it widens and muddies and roils through hardwood bottomlands and past the historic towns of Seguin, Gonzales, Cuero, and Victoria before reaching the coastal prairie and its delta in San Antonio Bay.

The Guadalupe is the home of the state fish of Texas, the Guadalupe bass. It is the only river in the state that sustains a year-round trout population. Marked with dramatic stretches of limestone cliffs and tall bald cypresses on the upper half and distinguished with water that begins gin clear, evolves into an ethereal green turquoise, and ends an earth brown, it's the prettiest river in Texas. Fed by the state's two biggest springs—the Comal and San Marcos—and supporting abundant wildlife and several endangered species, the Guadalupe has attracted visitors for more than 12,000 years and today is probably enjoyed by more people than any other river in the Southwest.

But the water of this beautiful river is under pressure from growing urban demand. Whether the river will endure for another fifty years, much less three hundred, is not certain. For all its attributes and benefits—and in part because of them—the Guadalupe may be Texas's most troubled river. Coveted by thirsty cities, tenaciously held on to by farmers and ranchers, exploited for new, competing uses as the population of Central Texas booms, the Guadalupe has a forbidding future, and that is a shame when you consider how many Texans take pleasure in it.

Back at the house, I estimated how many other people might have been on the Guadalupe and its main tributaries, the Blanco, San Marcos, and Comal Rivers, that same February day. I figured at least several thousand. Fewer than ten miles south of my little play spot, a flock of sailboats breezed across Canyon Lake, the sole significant lake on the Guadalupe, while several hundred people walked the dam over the course of the afternoon.

Downstream, several hundred more men, women, and children were spread out along the banks, tying flies to their lines, scanning the surface, and casting into the fast-moving, chilly waters for elusive trout. A little farther down, a handful of hard-headed kayakers played in the waves around Hueco Springs and Slumber Falls, the most reliable white water in Texas. Up and down its length, even in winter, the river is a boon to recreationists. Canoeists and kayakers were paddling it, scuba divers were plying its transparent depths at Canyon Lake, duck hunters were sitting expectantly in blinds on its delta, and bird-watchers were searching its forests and marshes.

Once the waters warm in the spring, the thousands enjoying the Guadalupe and its tributaries swell into millions. Each day, thousands of people head to Schlitterbahn on the banks of the Comal in New Braunfels and pay more than $25 to play in America's top-rated water park. On any hot day, some of the best river swimming on earth is in the Guadalupe basin. The curious idyll of "toobing," as it is referred to around New Braunfels, Gruene, and San Marcos, where the pastime is most popular, attracts tens of thousands of aficionados on Easter, Memorial Day, and Fourth of July weekends. The Tube Chute in Prince Solms Park in New Braunfels is a water flume that's been a tourist attraction for many decades. All told, no other river in Texas is so heavily used for recreation. Plain and simple, the Guadalupe is fun.

I have driven the length of the Guadalupe River in stages, exploring its multiple delights, tracing its geography. The river insinuates itself into the rocky oak-and-cedar scrub landscape of western Kerr Country very subtly. There are no specific headwaters, no gushing artesian spring. Dry washes and gullies gradually collect enough moisture from small springs to hold water in pools that stretch longer and longer until a steady, shallow stream trickles over a hard limestone bed and then tumbles out of the craggy hills toward the sea more than two hundred miles away.

At Boneyard Draw, on Farm-to-Market 1340, a sheer sixty-foot limestone bluff in the distance marks a bend in the drainage, the first hint of canyons to come. Just below the crossing is the turnoff to the Kerr Wildlife Management Area, where the Texas Parks and Wildlife Department has been testing cedar (Ashe juniper) eradication, brush clearing, and other water-saving land management strategies. In addition to being a center of white-tailed deer research, this WMA holds one of the great concentrations of wild turkeys in the state.

Less than a mile down the road, I detour down a county road, toward Cherry Springs Ranch, Guadalupe Bluffs Ranch, and the Price's Joy Spring Ranch Bed & Breakfast. At a low-water crossing, I find the river, sparkling in the sun, the palest of greens with a slight tinge of blue, scooting over the hard rock bed.

A mile farther, the river is moving full tilt and roaring to life, with a deeper blue tint, a ribbon of sustenance snaking along a narrow alley guarded by soaring cypress trees and flanked by high bluffs, some rising up one hundred feet above the water surface. Turkey buzzards politely wait on a fence post while I pass before resuming cleanup duty on a mangled piece of roadkill.

A slide leading directly into the water on the banks of Mo Ranch Camp marks the beginning of the "camp run," consisting of Camp Waldemar and Camp Stewart on the North Fork and Camp Mystic, Heart O' the Hills Camp, and Camp Arrowhead on the South Fork. Crider's Rodeo and Dancehall is also on the south fork. There are not too many places in this world where a couple can two-step under the summer stars to the sounds of western swing fiddles and the steady rush of the river.

The Guadalupe widens, narrows, and spills from limestone shelf to limestone shelf as it moves past patios, swings, and ornate rockwork of dream ranches owned by CEOs, corporations, and churches. In one field by the river, scale replicas of Stonehenge and two thirteen-foot-high Easter Island statues have been erected.

The North Fork and South Fork join just below the Hunt Store, a community gathering spot for vacationers, hunters, fishermen, swimmers, and visitors for more than eighty years. Several generations of the wealthiest, most influential Texans have spent the summers of their youth on this part of the river, learning the basics of life and being exposed to a wilder, more untamed version of the natural world than exists near the cities they come from. Small wonder riverfront property here has been the most coveted real estate in the Hill Country for decades.

Anyone can glean a semblance of that experience by passing a night at an old-fashioned resort such as the Waltonia Lodges on the Guadalupe River, or jumping in and cooling off at Schumacher's Crossing, the first significant swimming hole with easy public access on the river.

The bluffs fade farther into the background from the river as it flows between Hunt and Ingram. Ingram Dam creates large enough pools to support a bass boat or a one-man sailboat and offers younger river rats the pleasure of dam sliding.

Parks become more plentiful farther downstream: Louise Hays Park on the south bank through most of Kerrville and Kerrville-Schreiner Park east of town. In both parks, people are disc throwing, fishing, and hanging out. The river gains stature but loses a little bit of its curb appeal as it flows past Kerrville, Center

Point, and Comfort, the bluffs considerably diminished, most of the cypress logged out long ago.

The magic returns just below Comfort and Interstate 10, as the Guadalupe narrows, snakes, and curves through a verdant valley, parts of which have been cultivated by German farmers from the same families for more than 150 years. To stumble upon the hamlets of Welfare and Waring practically hiding under giant oak motts is like discovering a lost fairyland.

Though the entire eighty-nine-mile length of the upper Guadalupe qualifies as a wilderness river experience—save for the dam in Ingram and all the low-water crossings—the thirty-nine-mile middle section between Seidensticker Crossing below Waring to the privately owned Bergheim Campgrounds at FM 3351 conveys the sensation of being somewhere Out There, with more heifers on the banks than humans, more fish in the water than folks.

Below Bergheim and Edge Falls, the 1,939-acre Guadalupe River State Park and the adjacent Honey Creek State Natural Area offer public access to four miles of unspoiled riverfront, more than any park on the Guadalupe and situated a mere thirty miles north of downtown San Antonio. The park attracts hikers and mountain bikers as well as toobers, swimmers, and paddlers. Every Saturday at 9 a.m., Honey Creek opens its gates for a walking tour of the ecologically fragile environment, which encompasses several native species of plants and animals, including the endangered golden-cheeked warbler.

I keep looking for the right superlative to describe the upper Guadalupe's blend of wilderness and playground, and one remark sticks in my mind. At Kerr WMA I stumbled upon Anthony Glorioso, a fresh-faced, curly-headed college student from Poughkeepsie, New York, who was working as a field assistant on a study of wild turkeys by radiotelemetry. Glorioso had never been to this part of the world before, he said.

Asked about his first impressions, he lit up.

"It's like Africa!" he exclaimed.

The New Yorker got it. The Guadalupe is that special.

Paddling the Guadalupe
Canyon Lake to New Braunfels

by Wayne H. McAlister

The conduit from the bottom of Canyon Lake spews out the lifeblood of the Guadalupe River according to the setting of gates beneath the control tower. At this moment, however, we cannot worry if the Guadalupe is tamed, subdued, debased, regulated, or electronically spied upon; we are ready to have our river back on any terms. A cool mist billows from the outlet flume booming into a concrete stilling basin fifty yards above us. Across the frothing channel, the turbines are humming in the six-megawatt Guadalupe-Blanco River Authority hydroelectric facility, tastefully sheathed in Hill Country limestone.

Stashing the gear, I wade alongside the canoe and discover that the water, only about a minute away from the hypolimnic bottom of Canyon Lake, is so cold that it stings my feet, and it feels like a hot wire as the front creeps up my legs. A quick-reading thermometer verifies what my cold corpuscles are already screaming: 54.5°F; too cold for bare legs! There are compensations. On this ninety-degree July day, the refrigerated air in this alcove is 77°F. Over the next five miles, the river will get back to its normal temperature. In the meantime, aquatic life is selectively culled.

We push off into a world of movement, sounds, and shadows, a welcome contrast to the monotony of the reservoir. The water is absolutely clear; I can make out every detail on the bottom eight feet below. We are drifting without ripples, entranced as the silent riverbed of bright Glen Rose limestone and white sand and gravel slides past beneath us. Here and there submerged patches of vegetation stream into the current: brook pimpernel, water primrose, parrot's

Wayne H. McAlister (1935–2018) taught biology at Victoria College and was the author of four books. Excerpted from *Paddling the Guadalupe* by Wayne H. McAlister. Texas A&M University Press, 2008. Published by permission of Texas A&M University Press.

feather, pondweed, stonewort, and long yellow-green tresses of spirogyra. We see no fish or evidence of invertebrates; no caddisfly nets, no ripple bugs. The stream, gripped in unaccustomed cold, lacking its usual load of in-washed nutrients, and acidified by hydrogen sulfide from the bottom of the reservoir, is barren.

The banks, however, are alive and well. The bald cypresses have reclaimed their domain along with a mix of American elm, sycamore, red mulberry, green ash, roughleaf dogwood, soapberry, pecan, a few box elders, and abundant mustang grape. There is movement and melody on all sides: green kingfishers, Carolina wrens, redbirds, yellow-billed cuckoos, wood ducks, green herons, giant swallowtails, and fox squirrels. Nothing like the dismal passage of the reservoir to sweeten our appreciation of the running river.

Across the river, houses sit side-by-side on the high dirt bank, their yards extending down to the water's edge, reflecting affluent America. Most are small but well-built vacation cottages and second homes, each with its own suspect septic system. They are a direct spin-off of the dam, which guarantees security from the river. In addition to its ecological influences and the droves of heedless water enthusiasts that it attracts, the principal adverse impact of Canyon Dam on the downstream Guadalupe River is that it fosters cheek-by-jowl bankside development with its attendant environmental woes.

We glide along, peeping into leisure-living backyards. They have brought it all with them: tables and chairs, hammocks, statuary, croquet hoops, badminton nets, wind chimes, colorful banners, barbecue smokers, gas lights, mercury vapor lights, bug lights—all set on trimmed and fertilized St. Augustine grass traversed by brick walkways bordered with flower beds. Almost every yard has one or more pumps drawing river water for lawn sprinklers. The river bank is decked or curbed and adorned with diving boards, water slides, benches; concrete stairs go down into the clear water. Motor boats, paddle boats, water scooters, and inflated inner tubes are tethered at the ready. Yet despite all this, we see no one. They are all inside their air-conditioned houses or away at their permanent urban homes.

Even if the septic systems are adequate, the cumulative runoff of pesticides, herbicides, fertilizers, detergents, paint thinners, lubricants, and gasoline from so many jammed-up residences must be significant. The result leaves no room for native herbs or communities of wild creatures. Despite the hummingbird feeders and brazen wood ducks, this is a relatively sterile, urbanized environment, perpetually patrolled by overweight but innately deadly house cats.

A mile and a half below the dam, a low concrete parapet marks the Gauging station. As we work the canoe across, the water, at 59°F, still feels uncomfortably cold. My legs are stinging by the time I climb back aboard. Before the dam, the average monthly temperature of the river here was 53° to 84°F, a range of thirty-one degrees; afterward, the range was reduced to thirteen degrees, from 53° to 66°F. No official attention was paid to what that shift did to the lives and life cycles of aquatic creatures, but it is a sure thing the biota noticed.

Just below the Gauging station, the Guadalupe spills through a crescent-shaped notch in a limestone ledge into a boil six feet below. This is Horseshoe Falls, a cataract that even rubber rafts cannot negotiate safely because of the drop and the strong undertow, which draws watercraft down and back beneath the falls. The thunder of the waterfall is a warning, but for daredevils there are explicit signs as well. A billboard strung on a cable above the river proclaims, "Danger Waterfall Ahead. Dangerous Undertow. Many Have Drowned."

As we absorb this message, a fox squirrel gambols jauntily across the swaying cable. On the bank is a second sobering sign designed to be updated as tragedy demands: "Danger Hydraulic Falls. Portage to the Left and Enjoy the Rest of Your Ride. Latest Fatality July 1, 1985: Total to Date 19. Horseshoe Falls Homeowners Assoc." At least the proclamation did not end with the overworked "Have a Nice Day."

Houses, houses, houses on both sides now. Though it is late afternoon, not a soul is outside in the breezy shade, not even kids. The people are not simply inside; they are sealed up inside, behind drawn blinds and insulated walls, doubtless watching a make-believe world on television. Why not stay in the city and watch a video of a river bank? We push on amid the hum and drip of air conditioners, taking the best of the river with us.

The wood ducks we see occasionally are tamer than the ones on remote sections of the river. Some yards have a bomb-shaped plastic duck nest box mounted on a tree. It looks foolproof against raccoons and even fire ants. If the ducklings can avoid house cats and kids, maybe the species will hold its own along here.

We have come to a low concrete dam set on a natural ledge that spans the river. The water, 64°F here, is only knee deep, but where it pours through a sluice near the right bank, the current is so strong, I can hardly keep my balance on the slick bottom while I guide the canoe.

Three miles below Canyon, we come to the high concrete bridge on FM 306, the old Hancock-Fischer Road out of New Braunfels. Hancock is now beneath the lake; Fischer still sits where it has since Herman Fischer opened his store there in 1853, on the high ground north of the reservoir. The Corps of Engineers replaced the old bridge with this modern span in 1964. A colony of chattering English sparrows has converted abandoned cliff swallow nests high among the pilings into a ragged slum.

In the middle of the current, twenty yards ahead, a thumb-sized head with a slender snout pokes up and then disappears. I know, even in this clear water, there is no point in looking for the creature. Although we spot alert and secretive softshell turtles basking on a ledge now and then, they hustle into the water before we can get the binoculars up. Strong swimmers, the thin edge of the turtles' pancake body lets them cleave the swiftest current with a few strokes of their webbed feet.

We have come to the first trout sign stapled to a cypress, encouraging fishermen to participate in a creel survey by the Texas Parks and Wildlife Department. Since the beginning of the program in 1966, when the word goes out in late fall and early spring, expectant fishermen line the banks for miles, eager to cast for the ten-inch, hatchery-raised rainbow and brown trout. These fish are hatched in a federal facility in Arkansas, reared in the Heart o' the Hills state hatchery near Ingram, and dumped into the river from a tank truck to be caught, sometimes within minutes after their release. This is an expensive put-and-take operation; the combination of warm water (warm for trout, that is) and native predators prevents them from developing a thriving population, though a few survive the summers to become six-pound lunkers.

Releasing aliens into the wild is not a good idea, but this instance may be relatively benign. The tailrace below Canyon is already chilled, enough for the trout to survive but not enough to breed or spread farther. Lots of people get enjoyment out of casting kernels of canned corn to pampered fish, then releasing their catch for another try. The program is funded not from general taxes but by sales of fishing licenses, sundry state organizations, and private donations. Why not?

A private camping and river outfitting establishment on the left bank is the first of many between here and New Braunfels. Up the bank at the office, battered and patched canoes are stacked like cordwood, and beyond them a forest of paddles and a leaning mountain of inflated inner tubes. Signs proclaim this to be the place to rent canoes, kayaks, rafts, "toobs," paddles, and life jackets and to arrange for shuttle service and experienced guides. The bare banks and polished cypress roots attest to a booming summertime business.

The next nineteen miles of the Guadalupe hold the dubious distinction of being the most touted, traveled, trashed, and trivialized section of river in Texas. By midmorning on a typical summer weekday, several hundred boisterous recreationists will have launched on excursions of varying lengths; by midafternoon the number will swell to several thousand. A good summer weekend will lure 30,000 revelers and on a prime holiday weekend, a staggering 200,000 suntanned and sunburned bodies of all ages may be bobbing in the water or draped along the banks "having fun" together.

Most of these people are simply out for a good time, to shoot the rapids, picnic, and socialize, but all too frequently, alcohol, drugs, short tempers, and a lack of common courtesy and common sense lead to conflicts. Many have no experience on the river, and a few cannot even swim. Underestimating the strength of the current, they wrap their canoes around rocks, get caught between their craft and a boulder, spill into the path of canoes following close behind, and they egg one another into foolhardy stunts.

Youthful bodies and/or Red Cross volunteers save most but not all. Every year many water-related injuries and half a dozen drownings occur along here due to the lack of effort to control or moderate the traffic. As long as the dollars roll in, those who profit from the congestion encourage such antics.

This influx of recreationists considerably raises the commercial value of the river banks along this stretch, just as it reduces their residential value. Clusters of more or less shabby private campsites, parking lots, liveries, eateries, beer parlors, and dance halls—with garish signs, strings of colored lights, and snapping banners announcing their wares and services—are separated by intervals of undeveloped shoreline. The River Road, running from New Braunfels to Sattler, provides access to these establishments, but every square foot of real estate is protected by a fence and multiple nasty No Trespass signs. The varied signs are consistently vehement: "Private Property, No Camping," "Prosecution for Trespass," "Absolutely No Hunting, Fishing," "Danger, High Voltage," "Beware of Dog," "You Get Out, You Pay," "Property Under Constant Surveillance," "Mantengase Afuera," and "In Case of Emergency, Keep Moving." The signs are a necessary defense against the onslaught of holiday humanity, but they hardly enhance the ambiance of the river.

Despite the escalation in people-use, the problem of trash, happily, has been met and more or less mastered. The banning of glass and Styrofoam containers on this part of the river is generally accepted. If not too inconvenient, most people make some effort to dispose of their wastes properly. Aside from overfilled trash barrels, the biggest problem is aluminum cans casually flipped from watercraft. Since 1976, the River Recreation Association of Texas has sponsored an annual Guadalupe River Cleanup, which attempts to haul out the year's accumulation of solid waste between Canyon Dam and New Braunfels. Refreshments are provided by community groups, canoes and rafts are donated by the outfitters, and dump trucks provided by a local contractor are filled to overflowing with tons of trash dredged up from the bottom and hauled off the banks of the river. The effort attracts the local media and a variety of volunteer outdoor organizations, members of the local community, and a large turnout of bored or concerned young people. Everyone has a ball, and the river benefits from its annual primping.

Through the efforts of many, the unsightly effects of a heedless few are kept to a minimum; and somehow, the Guadalupe rolls on.

Although the flow of humanity makes a sacrifice zone of one of the prettiest runs of river, it also sways public opinion toward protecting the natural ruggedness of the stream and its valley. In the end, then, we prepare to ignore the people and enjoy a demanding piece of the Guadalupe that is relatively secure from worse. In this age, that is about as good as it gets.

In the Rapids
Guadalupe River

by James Hoggard

Drowning my body below my brain, I sat
defying the sworl between moss-slick rock,
my heels fighting too-smooth stone,
my fingerpads and palmbutts rubbed raw,
and, heady, I howled, waterdrunk.

Over my thighs and around my wrists, like hairs,
short filaments of moss, small leeches clung,
squiggled by delirious wash,
and my heavy flesh jostled, a wet
wave-undulant rug.

Sensuous bellowing through water and throat,
easing toward the cool calm pool, resistance
of fight, insurance of fight,
skin scraped, struggle for blood, but no mud,
only the feel of depthless flush.

Then downstream, where it's shallow and still, canoes
streamed up toward my violence as if they,
graceful silver bananas,
were sent with their young tee-shirted priests
to civilize my pleasure-rage.

James Hoggard (1941–2021) was a Distinguished Professor of English at Midwestern State University, a Fellow of the Texas Institute of Letters, and the author of twenty-six books, including poetry, novels, essays, short stories, and plays. © James Hoggard, 1982. Published by permission of James and Lynn Hoggard.

Rigid, I dared them to come, held breath,
felt fish nipping under my thighs, I itched,
baby leeches on my neck.
The canoes were too late to save me.
I slipped and washed hard against rock,
learning in the rapids' run the grand tumult of heathen's grace.

The Blanco River

The Blanco River

by Wes Ferguson

One morning I went for a walk in the middle of the Blanco River. It was the dead of summer in Texas, and the Blanco had run dry, other than a few low pools trapped in depressions of the riverbed. From bank to bank, drifts of gravel rose and fell like the undulating dunes of a white desert. In less than nine months, a terrible flood would sweep down this river. The raging Blanco would destroy hundreds of homes, fell an estimated 15,000 trees, and kill twelve people. As I hiked across the desiccated riverbed, however, the perils of flood were far from mind.

The Blanco, at a length of eighty-seven miles, is not considered one of the state's major rivers. Rather, it is a tributary of a tributary, a small, delicate stream in a network of streams that rise from the rough slopes of the Edwards Plateau. Locals call it the "Blank-oh," emphasis on the first syllable. It begins about sixty miles southwest of Austin, as the crow flies, and is more or less equidistant from San Antonio to the south. Fed by springs, the Blanco drifts eastward by southeastward, as most rivers in Central Texas do.

The Blanco can be breathtakingly pretty, as long as you know where to look. The stream courses through sheer canyons, rolling hills, and flat, green valleys. On lazy afternoons, visitors enjoy cool flows and clear green swimming holes where bald cypress trees and craggy limestone bluffs offer much-needed shade from the summer sun. Before achieving national infamy for the flood that struck on the Memorial Day weekend of 2015, the Blanco was most widely known as an idyllic summer retreat and low-key tourism destination.

Wes Ferguson grew up in the Piney Woods outside Kilgore. An award-winning journalist and the author of two books on Texas rivers, he is a Senior Editor at *Texas Monthly*. Excerpted from *The Blanco River* by Wes Ferguson. Texas A&M University Press, 2017. Published by permission of Wes Ferguson and Texas A&M University Press.

But stories of confrontation are not uncommon. Fisherman Harry Hause tells one. He lives with his wife, Nancy, and their dogs beyond a tall river bluff near the Hill Country town of Wimberley. As he paddles downstream, Hause occasionally runs into fences erected across the riverbed. Twice, he and his fishing buddies were in the process of working their boats through a wire fence when they came face-to-face with the property owner. The elderly rancher was not happy to see them.

"I don't know if he thought he was God or what," recalls Hause. "If he was around, he would approach you. He made it perfectly clear he owned all this land. You're talking to a guy armed with a shotgun, and you have to go through his fence. You don't get too smart-assy. I heard from other people, he did that to them, too. People are very aggressive about their land rights. They don't want you there; they think they own everything. They don't care if you're just boating through."

Gun-toting or otherwise, ranchers are a dwindling breed on the Blanco. The old-timers increasingly share the river with multimillionaires and billionaires who have turned riverfront ownership into an exclusive club that includes some of Texas's most influential political donors; a part-owner of an NBA team; the founder of Mexico's most powerful newspaper conglomerate; and George P. Mitchell, the late business magnate and real estate developer who pioneered hydraulic fracturing for natural gas, earning him the nickname the "Father of Fracking." Throw in two of the Big Five trial lawyers who negotiated Texas's legendary $17 billion legal settlement with the tobacco industry in the late 1990s, and you get the picture.

With so many riverfront ranches converted into vacation homes for well-to-do Texans, it might seem strange that an attorney, oil tycoon, or investment banker would harass a person for paddling or swimming the Blanco. But property rights are sacrosanct in Texas, ranking somewhere between love for God and Mama, and Hause's story gave me pause. and I contemplated the red-and-white "No Trespassing" signs on the gravel bar.

I scrambled up and down the dunes, through a world of white. Two years earlier, I had swum in water so deep here, my toes could not touch bottom. Texas rivers are always changing, but the Blanco offers extreme evidence as it runs from bend to bend and day to day. On this morning, my toes were dry. Chalky river pebbles crunched underfoot, and outcrops of craggy limestone rose beyond the opposite bank. Sun-bleached rocks of many sizes were scattered like dusty bones across the riverbed.

There could be no doubt about it: this was el Río Blanco, the White River.

Little Blanco River

by Naomi Shihab Nye

You're only a foot deep
Under green water
Your smooth shale skull
Is slick & cool
Blue dragonfly
Skims you
Like a stone
    Skipping
        Skipping
It never goes under
You square-dance with boulders
Make clean swishing sound
Centuries of skirts
Lifting & falling in delicate rounds
No one makes a state park out of you
You're not deep enough
Little blanco river
Don't ever get too big

Naomi Shihab Nye is a San Antonio–based "wandering poet," songwriter, and novelist born to a Palestinian father and an American mother. Among her many honors are lifetime achievement awards from the Texas Institute of Letters and the National Critics Book Circle. "Little Blanco River" originally appeared in *A Maze Me: Poems for Girls* by Naomi Shihab Nye. Greenwillow Books, 2014. Published by permission of Naomi Shihab Nye.

The Comal River

The waters . . . are clear, crystal, and so abundant that it seemed almost incredible to us that its source arose so near. Composing this river are three principal springs of water which, together with other smaller ones, unite as soon as they begin to flow. There the growth of the walnut trees competes with the poplars. All are crowned by the wild grapevines, which climb up their trunks. They gave promise already in their blossom for the good prospect of their fruit. The white and the black mulberry trees, whose leaves were more than eight inches in length, showed in their sprouts how sharp were the frosts. Willow trees beautified the region of this river with their luxuriant foliage and there was a great variety of plants. It makes a delightful grove for recreation and the enjoyment of the melodious songs of different birds.

—Isidro Félix de Espinosa, 1716

The location and general aspect of New Braunfels is very pleasing, and in all of Western Texas, no more beautiful and suitable spot could have been chosen for a settlement . . . The Guadalupe, flowing east of the city, is a stream about thirty paces wide, abounding in water that runs rapidly and tempestuously in its rocky bed due to its considerable fall. Unlike other streams and creeks of the low coastal country, its water is pure and clear, almost excelling that of an Alpine stream. A narrow strip of forest, scarcely classed as bottom, confines the river to its bed. The Comal, which has an equal volume of water but which excels the former in the clearness of its water and the luxuriant growth of trees on its

Isidro Félix de Espinosa (1679–1755) was a Franciscan missionary who accompanied several expeditions into Texas during the early 1700s.

Ferdinand von Roemer (1818–1891) was a prominent German geologist and paleontologist who visited Texas in the 1840s.

banks, forms a junction with the Guadalupe above the city. The Comal owes its existence to the confluence of the Comal Springs and the Comal Creek, which takes place near New Braunfels. The unexcelled beautiful Comal Spring has its source at the base of a mountain range, hardly a half mile distant from the city.

—Ferdinand von Roemer, from *Texas*, 1849

The Comal River

by Patnarain

*I*t's a Saturday in December, and a small crowd is gathered on the concrete banks, drinking beer and vaping e-tobacco. The crystal green river sings out to me, and I dive in. Emerging from the rushing cold water, I hear "You're going to drown in that thing!"

"One day, perhaps," I respond and murmur "god willing" under my breath. I've started a new phase in life. An empty nest now gathering twigs askew. Alone and unwashed I choose to be, salvation comes looking for me . . . at least that is my hope.

As I climb out of the water, a graybeard regular, Randy, tells me that he is glad when the visitors come and even happier when they go. He's an old hand at snorkeling this river, always looking to laugh and share tales of the small treasures he's recovered from capsized tourists. He brags about his refrigerator of river beers and his shade tree of lost sunglasses. He says a good day is when he finds a twenty-dollar bill in the water. He adds with a hint of skilled casualness the money often turns up where the current hits a retaining wall, just below Stinky Falls. Twenty dollars means he's buying the beer. It was Randy's ex-wife who told me I was going to drown. They amicably split, and each got a wiener dog in the divorce. Now they only see each other on these nice days in the winter. She avoids the crowds and the heat, but he's at the river every day searching for fresh spoils.

The springs that birth the Comal went dry in the 1950s, and the next time that happens, it might be for good. For now, the river always embraces me when I dive in. It is truly a mother that welcomes all her children: the summer crowds of beer-guzzling toobers, casual swimmers looking for relief from the heat, fussy wetsuit divers, the families with still-fearless children. But like any other water, the river doesn't always give back.

I first encountered this river as a kid forty years ago, and like a thousand other perfect childhood moments, I forgot about it. But years later, after rediscovery, I took my little fingerling and plopped her in an inner tube. As we floated,

Patnarain is the pen name for Jeffrey S. Davis, who lives in New Braunfels and is a Senior Research Librarian at a major law firm. In his spare time he coaches youth soccer and enjoys the rivers of Texas. © Jeffrey S. Davis, 2020. Published by permission of Jeffrey S. Davis.

she heard another parent say that if the current pulls you down, then just relax; it will shoot you back up. She wanted me to hang on, but when we reached the falls the river set her loose. She got caught underwater in the current—and fortunately remembered the advice she'd heard. The lifeguard threw down a ring, and she, gasping, caught it and clung tight. Never again, she swore. The river has marked her soul and taught her that parents are not as powerful as they make themselves believe.

As the months pass in my new home, I find myself visiting the river at these same falls nearly every day. The rush of the water pulls me into its depths, and the current slams my quads and knees into rocks. The bruises help me feel that I somehow belong here. I genuflect to the river. There is no liturgy amongst the sunfish and the turtles, but I am one with brother heron and sister caracara.

Above the falls, I swim completely submerged with mask and snorkel. I marvel at this miracle I've become a part of, watching the light-dappled fish swim beside me. When summer arrives, the snakes, turtles, and fish do their best to avoid the massed hordes of floating party-goers. I quickly learned to do the same and get to the river early in the morning, before the first armada of toobers. At this hour, the rod and reelers silently cast from above while I swim below, drifting in the current, pushed downstream to moments of joy and being.

The river grows sluggish in summer, seemingly drowsy from overuse. I've visited the vaunted springs, watching them sputter to keep breathing life into this water. My morning swims are peaceful, but I become distracted by the underwater spoils left behind by tourists: the Yetis, phones, driver's licenses, GoPros, and, of course, sunshades. I recover missing car keys that must have ruined peoples' vacations, a lost wedding band that maybe broke someone's heart. I haven't seen any twenty-dollar bills yet, but I am discovering thousands of beer bottles, beer cans, and the flotsam of feel-good excess. I began to gather this detritus and heap it ashore. Above, I see a kindly couple picking up litter along the banks, and we nod at each other.

One bright morning, I'm snorkeling past a washed-out maxi pad that clings to a boulder when I spy the crawdad. The crustacean is sticking its pincer into a Corona bottle and stretching for all it's worth, yet it's oh so far from the lime at the bottom of the bottle. I swim around debating what would Jesus do, and I end up leaving it for another day. Enough days and the bottle will be buried in the soft bed of the river.

Yes, this river has become my salvation, or at least my salve. I know this will end one day too soon. I have only one prayer: Let it be me that departs.

The San Marcos River

The Perfect River

by Stephen Harrigan

It is only a little river. From where the San Marcos rises abruptly out of the earth to the point at which—as a nineteenth-century poet phrased it—she gives "her royal hand in marriage to the waiting Guadalupe" is a distance of only fifty-nine miles. Well before that union, at an earlier confluence with the Blanco and an encounter with effluvia from the San Marcos wastewater treatment plant, the river begins to lose its character. Its clear, spring-fed waters are suddenly a soapy, opaque green; the stream seems bloated, sullied, prodded toward the Gulf.

But within its first few miles, as it meanders through the city limits of San Marcos, the river possesses a simple, radiant beauty. Its waters rise pure and temperate through the porous limestone strata of the vast underground filtration system known as the Edwards Aquifer. Here, at its headwaters, the river has been impounded to form a small body of water known as Spring Lake, but a quarter of a mile downstream, it flows again more or less according to its natural inclinations. It runs through the heart of San Marcos—it is the heart of San Marcos—and along its way, it passes through three public parks, beneath numerous footbridges and trestles, and over a series of broken stone dams, the remains of nineteenth-century mills. Beyond the Interstate 35 bridge, the

Stephen Harrigan is a leading Texas novelist, journalist, and nonfiction writer. He's also written several screenplays for television and film. The author of a dozen books, his many literary honors include the Lifetime Achievement Award from the Texas Institute of Letters. "The Perfect River" originally appeared in *Texas Monthly*, July 1981. Published by permission of Stephen Harrigan and *Texas Monthly*.

In the 1990s, Texas State University purchased Aquarena Springs and began the process of dismantling the theme park and restoring the natural habitat. Today the swimming pigs are gone but glass-bottom boats remain. The site is home to the Meadows Center for Water and the Environment.

river is deeper, murkier, and perhaps a little wilder, and there are occasional minor rapids.

In its upper stretch, the San Marcos is essentially an urban river, relentlessly prettified, its banks shored up by concrete or bordered with philodendrons, its waters stocked with gold-colored carp and Mozambique tilapia, and jammed on summer weekends with rowdy college students slung into inner tubes. But the San Marcos is also a delicate and highly specialized environment for a number of indigenous creatures. Most of them are inconspicuous: a few species of the moth-like caddis flies, which in their larval stage are aquatic; tiny fish like the fountain darter and the San Marcos gambusia; and a salamander, *Eurycea nana*, that occurs in the headwaters of the river and nowhere else in the wide world.

I have seen *Eurycea nana*. A water-quality scientist named Glenn Longley scooped one up for me from the lake in front of the Aquarena Springs Inn. It was perhaps an inch long, a pale, wriggly form with exotic feather-boa gills. We looked down into the net, where the salamander wriggled in and out of a clump of algae. There did not seem to be much to say about it. "Well," Longley said, shrugging, "that's what they look like."

The creature was returned to the water to browse among the algae for copepods and other nearly invisible things that it consumes. I had a vague interest in the salamander, but I was stirred by a broader appreciation of the river itself, responding to it not just because it harbored a number of phylo-genetic curiosities but because it was simply so pretty. The river is certifiably extraordinary. It has been designated by the government as a "critical habitat" and described in the *Federal Register* as "one of the planet's most precious resources." But I found myself drawn to the river for only the most ordinary reasons: for the way the water sounded and the way it held light. The sala-mander favored the stream because the water temperature is a more or less constant 72 degrees. The human longing is not so specific, and certainly not so benign in its consequences, but over the millennia, it has proved to be no less real. Recent archeological evidence suggests that the river is the oldest continually inhabited site in North America. Despite all the damage we have done to it, our claim to the river is secure.

"A fairyland" was the way one correspondent of the last century described the headwaters of the San Marcos, where a series of first-magnitude springs rises from the Edwards Aquifer. Another imagined it "peopled with laughing water nymphs." The outflow from the springs was more spectacular in those days; the water surged forth from its ancient limestone channels with such force that there was an incessant frothing and fountaining at the surface. Because the lake into which the springs discharge is now deeper, the impounded headwaters of the river are barely riled by the artesian force below.

At its origin the river runs even with the Balcones Fault, the great geological event that created the distinction between the Hill Country and the plains that slough away to the coast. It was the fault that created the river as well, causing cracks in the limestone through which the rising groundwater worried its way to the open air, enlarging the passages in the process.

The springs have never failed, at least in all the time that humans have kept track of them, and the water has retained its astonishing clarity. If you take one of the glass-bottomed boat rides at Aquarena Springs, the big tourist sprawl that dominates the headwaters of the river, you can make out—twenty-five feet below the surface—the miniature grottoes among the riverbed through which the high-volume springs discharge.

There are other springs, with less force, that are visible only as ceaseless percolations through the aerated sand covering the limestone. Most of the time, the boats skim across a thick bed of aquatic vegetation that is dominated by vertical growths of fanwort and the matted, interwoven strands of *Hydrilla* and riverweed. It's like soaring above the canopy of some surreal rain forest, now and then coming across a clearing. "The white stuff down there is limestone," the guide says, "and the dark stuff is humus—a fancy name for mud." At such points you can see the huge undulating caverns in the vegetation, floored with ossified tree limbs and teeming with Río Grande perch, aquatic turtles, and assorted sunfish, to which the guide, assuming her place in the ecology, tosses a dose of food pellets.

The San Marcos is not a "natural" river, unless one is generous enough to consider the meddling attentions that humans have paid it over the years to be a natural process. Although much of the river is choked with plant life, there is no telling how many of the species that inhabit it are indigenous. For years the river was a major source of commercial aquatic vegetation for use in the home aquarium. It was a thriving industry that required a kind of periodic clear-cutting, a harvesting of the cabomba and elodea crops. If, in his travels, a gentleman horticulturist came across a species he thought might look pretty in the river, he'd toss it in and see what happened. Often enough, in the clear, mild water, it would thrive to nightmare proportions.

The river's most prolific introduced species is water hyacinth, a species of floating plant originally from South America. Individually the plants are very picturesque, seemingly just the thing for a burbling, tranquil stream like the San Marcos. They have broad, thick leaves that seem to have been designed to function as airfoils, bulbous stalks filled with pockets of air to keep the plant afloat, and a submerged system of trailing, purplish roots that are reminiscent of soft coral. Each plant produces a prominent flower, but the hyacinths reproduce in a grass-like manner as well, sending out rhizomes and creating new plants, eventually knitting together a floating colony that then becomes part of one of the massive hyacinth blankets that clot the flow of the river whenever it encounters an abutment or a piling.

It was partly to control the water hyacinths that nutrias, the infamous South American water rats, were introduced into the river in the early fifties. Unfortunately, the nutrias left the water hyacinths alone. Otherwise they were like some unstoppable microbe from outer space, ravaging the native vegetation, supplanting indigenous mammals like the woodchuck, and scaring untold numbers of swimmers out of their wits. Over the years the nutrias have proven to be indefatigable pests whose life energies seem to be exclusively devoted to gnawing through the landscape with their big rodent teeth and replicating themselves with astonishing alacrity.

The river begins its public course beneath an old dam through which the water spills out in an ice-blue, translucent flume. This is an ancestral swimming hole, deep enough in its center to make practicable a rope swing attached to a cypress tree on the bank. There is a restaurant going up here, on the other bank there are student apartments, and a few yards downstream, just above the University Drive bridge, is one of two storm drains that are channeled directly into the river.

I stood there one afternoon at dusk and tried to imagine what the river had been like two hundred years ago, before the dam had created the falls behind me, before the philodendrons and the water hyacinths and the hordes of bikini-clad coeds lying indolent and oily in the afternoon sun. The river would have been shallower then (though it is rarely more than eight or ten feet deep now) and lined with the great cypress trees that were eventually cut down and sunk into the riverbed to provide the foundations for the dams that powered the mills along the river a century ago.

But there was no point in trying to imagine it. That particular manifestation of the river is gone, and those of us who have come to love the San Marcos must make do with its present form. And anyway, I was far from being a pure admirer of the river. I wanted it for my own use, just like everyone else, and I was willing to ignore whatever habitat damage I might do to it as I snorkeled along its length, displacing who knew what tiny creatures as my big power fins churned up the silt along its bottom.

I put on my wet-suit top and entered the river near the falls, feeling the first rush of cold and the cyclical thrumming of the agitated water. My notion that day was to swim off in search of the giant freshwater prawn, the elusive crustacean that inhabits the river and was supposedly the basis of a thriving shrimping industry here in the last century. I had seen only one pickled in a jar in Glenn Langley's office—and had been startled by its size. It was as big as a lobster, with huge meaty claws, and in the preserving fluid, its color was a brilliant calcareous white. Since then I had looked for the prawn every time I entered the river, but I had come to the conclusion that it was as mythical as the yeti. I let my face mask rest half under the surface and saw a stinkpot turtle traveling upstream near the bottom of the river. The stinkpot, aware of my presence, picked up its pace, striding along upon the riverbed in a manner that was at once heavy and buoyant, reminding me of the way astronauts bound, not quite airborne, on the surface of the moon.

The turtle hid among the wide green blades of some water potato plants, and I let the current take me through the shallow, pebbly stretch of the river that led under the bridge and into the concrete sluiceway of Sewell Park, a natural swimming pool where it is customary for local college students to take their ease. Toward the end of this stretch, the vegetation was so thick that I had to get out and portage myself to a reentry point a hundred yards downstream near City Park. Here the water was deeper and filled with bass and bluegills and Río Grande perch. Above the surface there were turtles—cooters—sunning themselves on half-submerged limbs. At one point I counted eighteen of them; as I drew closer they all dropped off the log with as little grace as a falling stack of dishes.

A green heron took off from the same log, using its deep, loping wingbeats to propel it to a similar station downstream. There was a yellow-crowned night heron in a tree limb above me, and a rotting snake carcass was looped around the piling of a footbridge. The current was stronger here, and like the fish, I faced it and watched what it washed downstream. Now and then they would lunge at something I couldn't see—a tiny crustacean or water bug—but the only things visible to me were the endless parade of water hyacinths and unidentifiable vegetative debris.

I was washed down to the train trestle at Rio Vista Park, where I wended my way in and out of the pilings, looking under the canopy of water hyacinths for one of the monster prawns. Instead there were crawfish, as lividly red as boiled lobsters, and minute damselfly larvae, structurally indeterminate little beings that looked as if they could as easily evolve into fish as into the flying insects they were destined to become.

I settled to the bottom and as long as my breath lasted watched the lazy, respirating mantle of a half-buried clam and the bluegills that hovered above their prey and then suddenly dived into the mud like kingfishers. In the mat of water hyacinths above, there were sometimes gaps through which the sun penetrated, illuminating the underwater landscape so that it resembled a gloomy storybook illustration of a deep forest glade.

The tourist economy of San Marcos is keyed to the stability of the springs that feed the river, and the city's chief attraction is Aquarena Springs, which, together with a negligible fault-line cavern known as Wonder Cave, siphons off a consistent stream of travelers from the interstate. Aquarena Springs began in the twenties, when A.B. Rogers—"a rancher, a sportsman, a leading furniture dealer and undertaker, and a progressive citizen," according to the local newspaper—bought the land surrounding Spring Lake and began to develop the site. He built a hotel and a golf course and over the years outfitted the lake with glass-bottomed boats and an underwater show like the one he had seen at Florida's Weeki Wachee Spring. Rogers's basic philosophy for this enterprise, according to Gene Phillips, the park's present manager, was to "take natural beauty and manicure it."

A variety of exotic things have taken place at Aquarena Springs. Performing seals were brought in, but they did not flourish. Once a four-hundred-pound sea turtle was released in the river, but it promptly sank into the alien biomass and died. On the positive side, Aquarena is proud of the underwater wedding that took place in the submerged theater in 1954, a formal affair in which the groom wore twelve-pound shoes, the bride's skirt was lined with lead hoops, and all "bridal attire" was sprayed with lacquer to "keep its appearance fresh." An event of equal magnitude was the filming of the movie *Piranha*, which featured a now-classic line of dialogue—"Sir, the piranhas are eating the guests!"—spoken on the shores of Spring Lake.

Aquarena now features a sky ride, which angles up from the east bank of the river to the top of the scarp on the other side. There is also a machine called a sky spiral, a rotating observation deck that travels up and down a glaring white metallic shaft that looks like some immense public utility project. Other amenities include the standard "authentic" Western town and a disturbing arcade in which ducks and chickens and rabbits sit in cages and, at the insertion of a coin, proceed in the most dim and perfunctory manner to ring a fire bell or walk a tightrope for their daily niblets. "Welcome to my show," says a sign on these cages. "I am happy and eager to perform for you. My classmates and I were taught at Animal Behavior Enterprises, Hot Springs, Arkansas, using the reward system."

One of the mainstay attractions at Aquarena Springs is Ralph the Swimming Pig, who performs as part of the underwater show. There has been, in fact, a succession of Ralphs; when each one, after about a year, grows too big and persnickety to perform, he is—to put it quite bluntly—eaten.

When I attended the underwater show, a little Ralph piglet was being trained off to the side of the Polynesian "volcano" that is the theater's centerpiece.

A college girl in a green sequined bathing suit—an Aquamaid—was trying to entice the creature into the water with a bottle of milk. "Come on," she said, tapping him on the nose with the nipple and then withdrawing it. "Come on, or I'm gonna pop you one."

The performing area for the underwater show is a calm, lucent pool about fifteen feet deep, created by the diversion of a natural spring that rises in the lake behind it. The theater itself is a kind of submarine that, by means of a ballast system that was once the subject of a cover story in *Popular Mechanics*, submerges so that its viewing windows are just below the surface of the water.

On the day I entered the submarine, there were few patrons—mostly young parents with bewildered, frenetic toddlers who seemed determined to focus their attention everywhere except on what was happening on the other side of the windows. A young man in a Hawaiian shirt stood at a microphone in the center of the theater and asked us to think of him as our skipper. We observed a feeding frenzy by a group of ducks as we began our descent, and soon we were looking from below at a teeming surface of disembodied paddling feet. Now and then one of the ducks would dive deep for a sinking pellet, fighting hard with those feet to submerge and then finally rocketing to the surface with the buoyancy of a football.

Two "Polynesian witch doctors" named Glurpo and Bubblio jumped into the water from the volcano, pulled two long rubber hoses from its base, and began to breathe from them as they clowned about in the weightless atmosphere of the pool. The South Seas verisimilitude was a little slack. It was apparent when Ralph came onto the scene that the Swimming Pig was not fond of his role. Glurpo coaxed him into the water with a milk bottle and led him around the viewing window. The pig, his wild eyes fixed on the bottle, churned the water with his cloven feet, struggling to keep his snout in the air.

"Glurpo," said the skipper when the pig had completed his rounds, "is going to use his magic on that clamshell and on the mouth of the volcano and bring forth two beautiful, shapely native girls. Hopefully with any luck at all, we'll have some beautiful native girls." A giant clamshell opened and, as in some Botticellian nightmare, an Aquamaid sprang forth. Another soared boldly from the archway in the submerged half of the volcano. Their bathing suits were iridescent; the sequins glittered like fish scales. As they performed acrobatics, their blonde hair flowed above their heads like some barely rooted algal mass. The Aquamaids cocked their right legs, arched their backs, and began to rotate, flailing gently with their hands at the water in a manner that suggested the strumming of a harp. Next they demonstrated their prodigious buoyancy control. By inhaling through the hoses, then exhaling, they were able to rise and fall in the pool like counterbalances. Then, retaining just the proper amount of

air, they hung motionless, in perfect harmony with the complex hydrodynam-
ics all about them. There was something magnificent about the Aquamaids; it
was their poise in such an unsettled element, the touching nonchalance with
which, later, they sat on giant concrete lily pads and had an underwater picnic,
munching on celery and then somehow managing to gurgle an entire twelve-
ounce soft drink into their systems.

For several years an archeological excavation has been taking place in the
bottom of Spring Lake, and it is not unusual for patrons of the glass-bottomed
boats to look down and see a group of divers picking through a section of
river bottom marked off into a grid by red plastic tape.

I spent a few hours here and there working with the archeologists, fanning
away the overburden of mud and then picking up flint chips and anything else
that seemed to my indiscriminate eye to have significance. The boats came
overhead with ceaseless regularity, and whenever I heard the electric whirr of
their motors, I would look up through fifteen feet of water and marvel at the
detail of the faces peering at us through the glass.

At so shallow a depth, there is no concern about the bends, and so it's possible for a diver to stay underwater all day, which was the normal operating
procedure of the archeologists. It was not unusual for them to put in forty hours
a week of total submersion.

Most of them were SMU students, supervised by an anthropology professor
named Joel Shiner. Shiner is in his sixties, but he looks younger, and he has a
glowering, cynical edge that is not unappealing. He first began digging in the lake
two years ago, after a San Marcos acquaintance told him about an abundance
of projectile points he had found just below the falls. When Shiner went to look
for himself, he found that the reports were correct and that besides the points
there were large numbers of exotic rocks—quartz crystals from Arkansas and
red metamorphic rocks from West Texas. Since all the artifacts appeared to be
in no order whatsoever, it was unclear to Shiner whether they belonged to this
site or had merely washed over the falls from their original matrices in the lake.

Shiner got a digging permit from the Texas Antiquities Committee and
obtained permission from Aquarena to work in the lake. He chose a spot along
the ancient river terrace, above the channel where the river must have flowed
long before the dam was built and the rising waters diffused its original identity.
Shiner wanted to do what he termed a "humanistic" report, to do more than simply catalog the artifacts and their associated strata. He wanted to reconstruct
the lives of the Indian cultures that dwelt here, to discover if he could what
sort of intangible resources—spiritual resources—they derived from the river.

In the process of sorting through the evidence in the river bottom, Shiner and his students turned up a treasure trove of artifacts—hundreds of thousands of points and tools dating back through the Paleo-Indian and Archaic periods and suggesting that a sedentary population had lived along the river for 12,000 years.

"One way or another," he told me in his Dallas office, which was filled with boxes of projectile points and bison bones and primitive hacking tools, "we're going to make some activity sense out of this site. As people—full-fledged, card-carrying people—they had to appreciate the beauty of the place. No way you can avoid it. There's absolutely no reason to believe that these people were inferior in any way. Maybe they didn't make votive offerings to the springs. Maybe the only damn thing the river inspired them to do was sing and dance, but I bet you they sang and danced well.

"From an economic viewpoint, this place was a blessing for the Indians. I'm sure they saw beauty in it. I'd sum it up this way: anybody who left the San Marcos to go someplace else was a damn fool."

Earth Day, April 22, was a dismal, overcast day, and the people who showed up on the banks of City Park to participate in the annual River Cleanup were not legion. There were perhaps twenty or thirty of them. One of the leaders was Tom Goynes, who owns a canoe livery down the river and is the usual winner of the Texas Water Safari canoe race, which begins at the San Marcos and ends 265 miles later in San Antonio Bay. "I can remember," he said, "about ten years ago, it wasn't unusual for schools to let out a half day for Earth Day. But noooooo, not anymore."

The volunteers took garbage bags and worked up and down the river by canoe or on foot. I put on my snorkeling gear and combed the bottom of the river at City Park. There were hundreds of pop-tops within an area no larger than an average swimming pool, and the bottom was also littered with beer bottle shards, Easter egg shells, Fritos bags, marbles, even a tire tool. It was peaceful, solitary work, and every now and, then I would stop and admire the underwater topography, the way a turtle stood motionless underwater on a submerged limb, the constant stream of air bubbles that rose from the center of the white flowers that extended sunward on long, fragile stalks.

When I came out of the water, I noticed perhaps a thousand young people singing and parading toward City Park, and I was seized for a moment with the inspiring thought that this throng had come to help with the cleanup. But they were only the Derby Day contestants from the college, who had come to the banks of the river for an afternoon of sack races and crab walks.

"Ooooooh," said a girl, a member of an organization named Friends of the River that had helped organize the cleanup. "If I see any of them throwing down their beer cups . . . ooooooh!"

There was a river festival the next Saturday, consisting of an art fair and one or two country bands and demonstrations of synchronized swimming and children's gymnastics. The highlight of the day was an aquatic parade through Sewell Park, which comprised only four or five floats. There was a river queen who waved to the sparse crowd from a canoe decorated with crepe paper and pom-poms, an inner tube with a papier-mâché zebra's head that did not clear the footbridge and had to be retired, and the Friends of the River float, which consisted of two canoes tied together and heaped high with full garbage bags.

One night I went along with a group of divers who, under some official pretext or other, were making a tour of Spring Lake. There was a good moon, and in the deep holes where the vegetation was kept cleared, there was already illumination enough for us to see without lights. I dropped down to the opening of a high-volume spring and lay basking in the silence and the half-light and in the steady pressure of the water that sluiced upward—magically, I thought—from the depths of the aquifer. How long that water will continue to flow is an open question. The San Marcos springs have never failed, but our demands on the groundwater that supports them grow every day. In another few decades, when the populations of San Antonio and all the other communities that depend on the aquifer have dramatically increased, the water table may very well be too low to feed the San Marcos springs, and then the river itself will be gone.

We saw a big eel and a spotted gar and several bullhead catfish that were swimming around beneath the submarine theater. I descended to the bottom of that performance pool and remembered the Aquamaids as they had performed their buoyancy skills, hovering there in the water in perfect, ravishing balance. The moonlight played upon the fluted edges of the giant clamshell. Aquarena seemed a mysterious place that night. It seemed almost like a place of worship, the most recent evidence of the ageless, imperfect human infatuation with the river. Our love for such gleaming places has always been ungovernable and devastating.

I stayed in the pool awhile longer, staring through the glass of the submarine into the dark, empty auditorium and then wandering aimlessly around the base of the volcano. Then I swam out of the theater and back into the wellspring of the river. I was looking for the giant freshwater prawn.

The Sabinal River

The Clear Sabinal

by Gardner Smith with Robert Reitz

*D*ry Can Canyon isn't so dry at this time of year. It's full of water, and its rocky walls are dripping from places too numerous to mention. The mountain laurel is full of blue flowers, and the pink of the buckeye is pretty too. About halfway up the canyon is one of the creek's many springs, this one rising up in the middle of a pool next to an old Indian rock shelter. That spring doesn't just flow; it comes out of that hole the way the Baptists pray, belling up the middle of the pool. If you've ever sat on top of Langford's hot spring on the Río Grande, you'll have an idea how strong Dry Can Spring comes out of that limestone.

We paused on our journey at the rock shelter by Dry Can Spring for a while just to get the feel of the place. It has a taste and a smell to it that awakens tribal memories before television, freeways, and shopping malls; before airplanes flew and radio crackled, before railroads, even. Yes, it was right here our Indian brothers and sisters rejoiced in their successes or mourned a death in the Family.

> At dawn they rose
> splashing water on their faces
> and in the middle of the night
> someone got up to toss
> another log on the fire.

Gardner Smith and **Robert Reitz**, fellow Vietnam veterans, made dozens of trips throughout Texas and the Southwest from the 1990s to the 2000s. Influenced by early Texas landscape painter Frank Reaugh and Japanese haiku poet Bashō, they published their observations in a series of handmade books. Excerpted from *The Clear Sabinal* by Gardner Smith with Robert Reitz. Los Madrugadores, 2017. Published by permission of Gardner Smith and Robert Reitz.

How can we ever undo
the harm we inflicted
on our brothers and our sisters?

Oh brothers, sisters of the Sabinal
we are the pipe carriers
keeping alive your memories.

Come, spirits of the dead,
we'll dance this rocky dance
just once and pass along.

The Fountain of Youth

The whispers of the Indians are loud in Can Canyon at this time of year. This is one of the many side canyons of the Sabinal, nice and secluded, out of the main stream and out of the way of the Comanche. Water comes pouring out of the rock in Can Canyon like a fire hydrant in some places, and with a drip drip and splatter and splash in most other places. You're never out of hearing of water that sounds the same way now as it did thousands of years ago to those who came here to give thanks for the blessings of life, and like us, drank deep of these cold, clear waters and rejoiced in the renewal of the year.

Learn the Large, Know the Small

A certain time of day—
the sun streams straight down
the limestone canyon walls
where moss spikes are pushing up
mightily at the sky.

The Limestone Symphony

The ring of rock on rock
as we walk along Can Canyon
is a melody of the limestone sea.

The top of the divide between the Dry and Wet Can Canyons is littered with Edwards chert, or flint, as Texans call it. This stuff weathers out of the limestone formations of the plateau. The Indians just loved this stuff for their projectile points, for it is really sharp. I sat down on some of it and jumped up faster than a man my age is thought capable of. Indian artifacts made of this chert are found all over Texas, New Mexico, Oklahoma, and Kansas. It was as highly prized as Alibates flint, though not so handsome in color. And it was not just the Kiowa and Comanche who came here to supply their arrow and spear points. Edwards chert was known to the Paleo-Indians. The Cooper Site, for instance, up on the Beaver River of Oklahoma revealed lots of Edwards chert. We are talking about Folsom Man here, who lived in Texas about 12,000 years ago. They lived among plenty of now extinct species, including several species of bison no longer found on the plains, but they did not have horses. Folsom Man was a walking son of a gun. He got his projectile points from the Edwards Plateau in the Texas Hill Country, from Alibates on the Canadian River in the Panhandle, and as the Cooper site has shown, he also got his points from the Niobrara River jasper deposits in northern Nebraska, almost into the Dakotas.

In the rocky canyons of the Sabinal and its aunts and its uncles, there's a curious kind of limestone that is as shot full of holes as a "Drive Friendly" sign west of the Pecos. "This is your brain on drugs," I joked the first time we saw a piece of the stuff. This vermicular limestone looks wormy as old pinewood. Most of it is high and dry in the hills now, but occasionally you can see that same process is still underway farther down where the water table now flows, the rock all honeycombed, water pouring out of hundreds of holes. Lyell really was correct when he said you can see the same processes that formed the ancient world still underway today.

> As with rock, people too—
> the ancient ones feel
> as we do.

We sit in the grass and the scattered chunks of limestone and flint at the top of the divide and have a little lunch.

> There's nothing quite so compact
> as a chunk of flint
> particularly if you're sitting on it.

An attractive chunk of blue flint weathered out of a vanished limestone ledge—

I try it out,
the feel in the hand is pleasing
but I put it back.

In the upper reaches of Can Canyon, coming down the divide from Dry Can, we encountered the head springs of the creek, and from that point we had the music of a thousand and one watersounds. In the brush along the path at the foot of some cliffs, we saw a porcupine. With impish impudence the fellow stopped and took a Nixon right in front of us then slowly, leisurely climbed the cliffs with all his bristliness.

The prickly pear
of the animal world—
right at home in Texas.

They've dammed Can Creek a mile above the place where it joins the Sabinal to make a pond a good twelve feet deep.

So clear it's almost air
the surface ripples
echoed on the cobbled bottom.

Everyone we've talked to about the lost maple has agreed that the tree certainly is green. Green is a color you don't see much of in Texas west of the Balcones, and a lot of it is cedar green or live oak green, colors only distantly related to lost maple green. In the sunshine the leaves are just a little too bright to look directly at.

In the shade of rock cliffs
or on cloudy days the maples
seem to glow with a light
that comes from within,
like the human species.

Lost Maples has more of the feel of West Texas than the rest of the Hill Country. We got our photographs back the other day, and Bob and I are convinced that the light is different too. The photos from Enchanted Rock are normal, from Luckenbach and Hye and the Pedernales Valley, all normal. The photos of Lost Maples, though on the same roll as the others, all have weird colors. Greens have shifted noticeably toward the yellow. The color of the sky is off too.

Lost Maples is in a space warp.
It comes as no surprise
that it bends the light a little too.

The Sycamores on the Sabinal do not attain adulthood. They're too skinny and a little awkward, like gangly teenagers. The Sabinal bottoms are largely an illusion—it's a harsh life just beyond these canyons. Fingers of the great Chihuahuan Desert are probing into the fringes of the Hill Country. Down along the river, though, there's plenty of water flowing out of the rock, which at Lost Maples is Edwards limestone, shot full of holes, and there are springs that gush like fire hydrants. The side canyons are cool and shady, but it's a little overhot out in the river, and we seek what shade can be obtained in a grove of sycamores, not much, but enough.

"Just for a while,"
I said, leaning back
to take a nap.

The Frio River

Things Water Whispers to Limestone

by Andrew Geyer

I was the only one who wanted to be the river.

There were six of us, a motley crew of brothers and sisters and first cousins, three boys and three girls. One of us wanted to grow up to be an astronaut, one a composer, one a fashion model. Two weren't sure.

Me? The Frio River.

Seriously. I didn't just want to float on the river, or swim in the river, or smash feet-first into the river from a boulder or a rope swing. I didn't just want to haul bass and sunfish and catfish out of its clear and chilly depths. I wanted to *be* the river.

Why?

Reason number one was growing up on a working cattle ranch in Frio County—a ranch that the Frio River did not flow through. The only surface liquid for miles filled the thirty-five-foot circular trough in the water lot (courtesy of the electric irrigation motor) or the smaller water troughs located at the bases of various windmills scattered across the brush and cactus-covered acreage of the Geyer spread. Those of you who have ever tried to swim in a thirty-five-foot circular cattle trough might appreciate why this Southwest Texas ranch boy wanted to become one with the Frio River; those of you who haven't might want to take a look inside the mouth of a cow.

Need a second reason? Alright. Let's think Southwest Texas. Mesquite. Scrub brush. Prickly pear. The low rolling hills bristled with chaparral as far as the eye could see from the high home hill that my parents' ranch house sat atop

Andrew Geyer grew up on a working cattle ranch in southwest Texas and is an avid canoeist. The author of several books, he currently serves as Professor and Chair of English at the University of South Carolina-Aiken and as fiction editor for *Concho River Review*. © Andrew Geyer, 2020. Published by permission of Andrew Geyer.

there in our arid corner of the Chihuahuan Desert. Here's a challenge for you: try *not* wanting to be the Frio River next time you make the dusty drive from San Antonio south down I-35 to Hwy. 57 and then west-southwest over to the Kickapoo Lucky Casino in Eagle Pass.

Number three? During a typical year in Frio County, of the ninety-two days spanning the months of June, July, and August, around seventy have high temperatures of 100 degrees Fahrenheit or above—and about 99.9 percent of the ranch work I grew up doing was done outside. If you have ever burned prickly pear in the middle of a summer drought, with hungry cattle crowding around you to gobble up the newly dethorned cacti the minute you finish torching off the spines, then you have absolutely wanted to be the Frio River—whether or not you realized it at the time.

Now that the why of it has been established, let's focus on becoming one with that magical ribbon of sixty-eight-degree water, which stretches twelve miles through the Frio River Valley from the FM 1050 bridge just above Garner State Park down to Neal's Crossing at Concan. Visualize floating at the base of the towering cliffs of Old Baldy in the clear river water, with its sudden jets of cold from subterranean springs. Daydream about the majestic Bald Cypress trees lining both banks, festooned with dangling rope swings ready to fling wannabe Tarzans into the wide warmer pools and swimming holes that get colder and darker the deeper you dive. Be mindful, though, of the limestone bed that can change without warning from slippery-smooth to jagged, of the sudden rapids, of the hydraulics that lurk below the low-head dams and crossings.

The first week of June, after school let out, my Nana would always spring the six of us Geyer kids—all born within four years of each other, the progeny of a pair of brothers (her only sons)—from the dry and dusty heat of our daily lives and haul us up to Concan, where her lifelong best friend had a house on the Frio. While we kids were becoming one with the river (well, while one of us was doing his best to, anyway), our grandmother and her bestie and their cronies stayed at the house—sometimes at the domino table on the screened porch overlooking the river and sometimes on the riverbank with cane poles—and played forty-two or hauled fish from the clear water while they drank and smoked and told tales.

When we were little, even though we each had our own inner tube, the grown-ups made the smallest of us wear life jackets. Nana's best friend's husband had an old Ford truck, a faded pea green stepside with a wooden bed, and he would stuff all of us into the back with our tubes and haul us up to the FM 1050 bridge, strap neon-orange life vests onto his squealing victims, and then release us into the river. He would always wait until the last of us disappeared around the bend at the foot of Old Baldy. Then he'd head back to the doings at the river house, and we'd shuck our life vests and float through Garner State Park together and on down.

This was long before every suburbanite in Austin and Houston and DFW had discovered that magical twelve-mile ribbon of the Frio and converged. So once we got through Garner, particularly if it was a weekday, we'd have long stretches of river pretty much to ourselves.

I remember floating that first three miles through Garner, dodging the paddle-boats and the swimmers, then clearing the low-head dam at the foot of the park and trying not to be the first to flip. I remember scooting over the Old Leakey Road at Mager's Crossing (still trying not to flip), then scooting over the River Road at Seven Bluff Crossing (and feeling pretty good if I still hadn't flipped), and then clearing another low-head dam and shooting through the little rapid below it. I remember floating on down into The Chute, where the limestone banks closed in tight and a series of standing waves always made at least some of us flip. I remember recovering my tube (it seems like I was almost always the first one who flipped) and heading on down to the gleeful madness of Comanche Crossing and, after a lazy half-mile, shooting under the bridge at Kenneth Arthur Crossing, then winding on down through the boulder garden rapid and into the three-and-a-half-foot drop at The Falls (where we nearly always flipped, all of us, especially if we didn't stay to the right). I remember finally taking out on the beach at Neal's, even though we had our own tubes, and then enjoying the best swimming hole in the state of Texas until that old pea green Ford came and hauled us back to the river house.

We had the time of our lives.

As the years passed, the smallest of us finally got to leave our life vests behind. At long last, when we were teenagers, some of us even left behind our inner tubes. In their place, we brought along snorkeling gear and floated and swam through the clear river water down to Concan. Of course, we still enjoyed the boulder diving and the rope swings and the swimming hole at Neal's. But those last couple of goggles-and-fins trips down the river were the closest I ever came to becoming one with the Frio. The whisper of water over rocks is almost comprehensible to the submerged ear. I always thought that maybe, if I could just translate a couple of syllables, I could learn the river's language—that I could come to know the things water whispers to limestone.

As the years passed, though, the river got more and more crowded. The boulders didn't tower quite as high, the rope swings didn't fling us quite as fast or far, and the swimming holes didn't seem quite as deep. Divorce came for my uncle's family, and our rambunctious band of brothers and sisters and first cousins was divided across the Lone Star State.

And of course, as we grew through adolescence and into adulthood, our wannabes changed into realities. The six of us scattered across the country. One is now a partner at a tech firm in DFW, by way of the Air Force. One is a homemaker in San Antonio. One is in the penitentiary in Wisconsin. Two are in trailer parks. One is a university professor in South Carolina, by way of the Army.

We don't see each other anymore, and we don't talk much even on Facebook. But I think of them often, particularly when I'm in my beat-up old green canoe paddling my way down yet another ribbon of river. I still listen just as intensely to the whisper of water over limestone rocks, and I'm still hoping to figure out those first two key syllables. But sometimes, especially when I'm camped below a little rapid, I take a break from listening—and wonder whether any of those other five still remember the magic of our time together during the first week of every June.

When I die, I will be cremated. My wife has promised to scatter my ashes in the three or four places that have the greatest significance to me. One of those places is that twelve-mile stretch of heaven that so occupied the thoughts and dreams of a Southwest Texas ranch boy. So the day will come when I finally do achieve my original wannabe and become one, at least in some sense, with the Frio.

In the meantime, I will remember for all of us. I will remember the river.

North Texas

The Red River

The river rises on the Llano Estacado, the Staked Plains of Coronado, who sought Seven Cities of Gold and found instead the plains, the canyon, the river, treachery, despair, and death. Water falling on the plains begins its downward course to the sea, seeking an outlet off the level mesa, plunging into the canyon, the Palo Duro, cutting deep through clay and sandstone, cutting through the ages, leaving perpendicular blue, red, yellow walls, eroded bluffs, high, lonesome sentinels and towers that brood over their own desolation. Rushing downward through narrow defiles, the river spreads free, mile-wide-and foot-deep thin over a broad, sandy bed through a semi-arid plain. Free now of its headlong plunge, the river sinks into the sand, separating into several channels, slow, sullen, through chalk bluffs, sand hills, among the cattails, salt cedars, past tangles of mustang grapes, thickets of wild plums, past forgotten Indian campfires and cowboys' graves, over deep holes where catfish big as hogs lie deep in shadows and bump lazily against the red prison walls, treacherous with shifting sands where cattle and horses mire and die.

But when it rained on the high plains, the river had another face. Heavy, thick, ponderous with its own power. Tearing out new channels, washing away old bluffs, rising up out of its bed to sweep away cottonwood and hackberry, mesquite and willow, here and there carrying away a field of cotton or a stand of corn, or a farmhouse built solidly upon a crumbling bluff. High, turgid, out of its banks, the river lay athwart the trail. Death and destruction were on its face.

—Robert Flynn, from *North to Yesterday*

Robert Lopez Flynn was born in Chillicothe, Texas, about ten miles south of the Red River. He grew up picking cotton and became a playwright, the author of thirteen books, and Professor Emeritus at Trinity University. His literary honors include the Lifetime Achievement Award from the Texas Institute of Letters.

The Meanest River

by Jan Reid

I've never heard of a swimming hole on Red River. No canoeists navigate its rapids, and no college revelers float by in cutoffs and inner tubes, towing coolers of beer. Through seasons wet and dry, with rare exceptions, it runs the color of chocolate milk, and it smells bad. Unlike our sightlier streams, it never washes clean over beds of limestone, granite, or gravel. To love this body of water, you have to forgive its ugliness and work your way back from there.

Nevertheless, a richly layered mythology has grown up around this muddy and moody waterway that separates Texans from Oklahomans east of the Panhandle. Part of the romance of the great American West, the Red River has inspired cowboy ballads, scores of historical novels, and some choice westerns. In Howard Hawks's 1948 classic, *Red River*, John Wayne drives nine thousand head of Texas cattle north toward the nearest railhead. He spurs his horse out into the shallows of this river of promise, of starting over. The big trail boss points at clear pools and warns the drovers of quicksand here, quicksand there. Earlier, Wayne had nodded in the general direction of the Río Grande—a glance of six hundred miles—and declared that all the land between the two streams now belonged to him. "Someday that'll all be covered with good beef," he vowed. "Good beef for hungry people." At his signal, cattle crowd down the grassy slope and wade into the Red with scarcely a splash. They don't get their noses wet.

But the scene, which was filmed in Arizona, completely misses the power of its title stream. The Red was the bitch river—the moment of truth and the psychological point of departure. South of it, trail drivers endured the resentment of farmers who did not want a million hoofprints in their fields. North of it, they encountered bands of Comanches and Kiowas, who were openly hostile in the early years. Later, when theoretically pacified on the reservations, the Indians extorted beefs of tribute, which they called "wohaw." Trail bosses tried to give them cripples. And the river showed the cowboys what

Jan Reid (1945–2020) was a journalist at *Texas Monthly* and the author of more than a dozen books of fiction and nonfiction. Two of his novels, *Comanche Sundown* (2009) and *Sins of the Younger Sons* (2017), won the Texas Institute of Letters Award for Best Fiction. "The Meanest River" originally appeared in *Texas Monthly*, July 1988. Published by permission of *Texas Monthly*.

they were in for. If they caught the Red "on a rise," all the rivers north were apt to be "up and swimming," too. The Washita and the North Canadian ran just as fast, deadly, and cold.

The Red begins with intermittent creeks and flash-flood draws south of Tucumcari, New Mexico, but it becomes a flowing river in the Panhandle's geological showcase of soil erosion, Palo Duro Canyon. Between the 99th and 100th meridians, its forks and tributaries continue to cut through the buttes and mesas of a crumbling, calcareous clay formation called the Permian Redbeds. Farther east, Oklahoma creeks deepen the water's rusty shade with iron and other minerals washed down from the Wichita Mountains. From streams, gullies, and bar ditches above Lake Texoma, about twenty million tons of dirt erode toward Red River every year. Below the dam, loam banks slough off and hit the water with a startling sound effect: *Galoomp!* The loose banks stir more mud in the mixture all the way to Arkansas, where the river makes its big south bend, and on through Louisiana, where it broadens and eventually joins the Mississippi delta. The Red can't help its color.

In the North Texas counties where I grew up, soil conservationists and highway engineers have used junk cars to keep good dirt and bridges out of Red River. Against the caving banks, the Hudsons, Studebakers, and Olds 88s are planted side by side with the heavy engines down, windows broken out, connected by strands of oilfield cable—a nostalgic kind of boondock pop art, I always thought.

The river's charm and value lie in the bottomland. Teenagers make sunning beaches of sandbars that can be as white and soft as any dunes on Padre Island. When I was in college, we sang, boozed, and kissed around blazing campfires on the Red. River bottom parties were high points of the year.

Other nights, we crossed the bridges and descended on latter-day juke joints that served up fried catfish, hush puppies, beer, mountain oysters, and yowling country-western, all under the same roof. A vestige of days when the majority of North Texans voted to keep their counties dry and sober, these service establishments are strung all along the southern Oklahoma border. Boundary streams are more than bodies of water; depending on the direction of travel, they stir feelings of safety and homecoming, peril and adventure. And in Oklahoma, that strangely foreign land, anything could happen. You might fall in love. You might get killed.

Between 1867 and 1895, nearly ten million cattle and a million horses moved up the trails that crossed the Red. Unlike the movie cowboys, the men who drove the longhorns north feared stampedes far less than they feared rivers.

Stampedes frayed their nerves and kept them up all night; river crossings killed them.

The cowboys' tales are as hair-raising today as they were when told around the campfire. Drovers used drowned horses for pontoons to float wagons across. One cowboy risked his life to rescue a mule that desperately treaded water because a cracked willow limb had snagged hobbles tied around its neck. Another time, in a flooding Red, two drovers somehow unsaddled a panicked horse that refused to swim. Their motives were less humane. Tied to the saddle was a cowboy's watch and his three-hundred-dollar stash.

The Chisholm Trail, named after a half-breed Choctaw, Jesse Chisholm, crossed the Red near the mouth of Salt Creek, a tributary in Montague County. The crossing at Red River Station was marked by a store-saloon and a raft ferry. Due to the exigencies of grazing and market, the longhorns usually came up the trail during the spring storm season. One cowboy described an 1871 flood that had thirty outfits and sixty thousand head backed up forty miles south of the Red. Another vividly remembered the Red's power: "We had some exciting times getting our herd across Red River, which was on a big rise, and nearly a mile wide, with all kinds of large trees floating down on big foam-capped waves that looked larger than a wagon sheet, but we had to put our herd over to the other side . . . Three herds crossed the river that day, and one man was drowned, besides several cattle."

Even today the Chisholm Trail is at the heart of Red River folklore. To find the crossing, you take FM 103 north out of Nocona, wind off westward on Montague County roads (some unpaved), and finally ask a farmer, busy dosing his dirt with ammonia, if this is the right plowed field. Next one over, he replies. Landscaped with yucca and wildflowers and protected by a chain-link fence, the state's monument to Red River Station explains that an abrupt bend in the river checked its flow and created the fording spot; at the peak of traffic on the Chisholm Trail, some days the cattle were so crowded that cowboys walked on their backs. A few yards away, almost hidden by brush, a bullet-dented metal sign denotes the Scenic Chisholm Trail Walking Tour. It slopes down about a hundred yards, but you wouldn't want to picnic on the bank. The shallows look creamy and stagnant. The air sings with mosquitoes and gnats.

Local people know a prettier spot not far downstream. As you come into its stretch of river bottom, the flatness negates any sense of decreased elevation. But all at once the pecans, sycamores, black walnuts, and cottonwood shoot fifteen feet higher in the air. Sandbars on the Texas side offer a fine view of a sheer and pocketed sandstone cliff. A fallen concrete abutment lies in pieces in an adjoining pasture, and rusted steel cables hang in the water from the Oklahoma bluff: fishermen know the place as Burnt Out Bridge.

Spanish Fort, the nearest town, is about five miles downstream from Red River Station. On a punitive expedition against all Indians in 1789, Spanish soldiers attacked a large settlement of Comanches and Wichitas there and got themselves thrashed. The Spaniards said the Indians had constructed moats and swore the stockade flew a French flag. Today, fewer than a hundred people live in the historic town. At the onetime grocery store and post office, an old-timer named Virgil Hutson lives with his wife, Mary. He sells hunting clothes and dog collars and posts neighbors' bulletins on his wall. "Wanted," says one. "Broke mule—15 hands or taller." The Hutsons do some truck farming. The fertility of the valley's alluvial soil enables Mary to brag on a seven-acre plot that yields twenty bushels of tomatoes a day. But the river also takes the bounty away. She tells me she's seen it twelve feet deep behind that white house at the end of the road. The actual bed, she goes on, is a mile and a half away.

The paved road runs out at Spanish Fort. On Texas highway maps, the Red River's farm-to-market roads are often dead-end streets. The Mississippi's southernmost major tributary, Red River flows twelve hundred miles from its headwaters on the dry plains of New Mexico to its mouth through reasonably populous country. But above Shreveport, Louisiana, no town or city is properly built upon it. Not one. The Red's uncontrollability has created one of the longest corridors of rural lifestyle to be found in this country. If rivers can be invested with human traits, this one chortles at our expense.

The land grabs associated with Red River were shameless from the start. When Thomas Jefferson purchased 800 million acres of wilderness from France for $15 million in 1803, Louisiana was very loosely defined. Because the French explorer Sieur de LaSalle had oversailed the mouth of the Mississippi 219 years earlier and camped for a few months on Galveston Island, Jefferson proposed a southern boundary of the Río Grande. "Absurd reasoning!" replied a Spanish diplomat. Red River became the Americans' fallback position.

The wrangling over the Louisiana Purchase continued until 1819, when John Quincy Adams, as Secretary of State in the administration of James Monroe, negotiated the treaty with Spain. When a river becomes an international boundary, ordinarily the territorial claims meet at the midpoint of the stream. Ensuring the Americans' navigation and water rights, this treaty defined the boundary as the Red's *south bank*. In turn, the treaty had to be honored, if renegotiated, by revolutionary Mexico, and then by the Republic of Texas.

The first Anglo-Americans were fugitives from justice; in 1811 about a dozen outlaws pitched camp in the woods near an ancient buffalo crossing of the Red. The name "Pecan Point" referred to both sides of the river, but along with Jonesborough, a ferry crossing and village just upstream, it was the first permanent Anglo settlement in Texas—and the busy crossings of the Red River foretold the end of Hispanic dominion. The migratory trail channeled Sam Houston and Davy Crockett, with other pioneer Texans, to that narrow stretch of river valley. On the Oklahoma side, the United States government settled Indians whom it had forced off their homelands. Land north of the Red River was ceded to the Choctaws. A village called Shawneetown existed for a time. The Trail of Tears led to the Red's north bank.

When Davy Crockett crossed the river two months before his death at the Alamo, he saw a virgin valley. Spotted with meadow prairies and cut with tributary brooks, the forest of red cedar and bald cypress teemed with buffalo, black bear, whooping cranes, ivory-billed woodpeckers, green and yellow Carolina parakeets. Crockett wrote home: "I expect to settle on Bodarka Choctaw Bayou of Red River that I have no doubt is the richest country in the world, good land and plenty of timber and the best springs and good mill streams, good range, clear water . . . game a plenty . . . I am rejoiced at my fate."

Anglo-Americans soon overran the river's eastern portions, but the upper Red posed an entirely different set of problems. The government could only theorize about its source, for the river cut through plains controlled by hostile Indians. In 1852 an Army captain named Randolph Marcy set out to find the Red's headwaters. In the granite Wichita Mountains, fifty miles north of Red River, Wichitas told Marcy that all tribes feared the ride that he proposed. Westward, the Red was a stream of foul-tasting water that could not be healthily swallowed. Marcy calculated that the surface gypsum belt that dosed area rivers with purgative salts was 50 to 100 miles wide and 350 miles long. Along with the water, the soldiers and animals suffered 104-degree heat and horseflies that Marcy claimed were as big as hummingbirds. During that summer, the column was reported massacred by Comanches. The War Department passed on this report to Marcy's family, who donned clothes of mourning. A minister preached his funeral sermon.

Not yet informed of their demise, the explorers ventured up the Red's North Fork. Marcy wrote that Comanches and Kiowas favored that stream, which crosses southwest Oklahoma and heads in the eastern Texas Panhandle, because of its rich prairies and abundant cottonwoods. When snow buried the grass, the Indians fed the trees' sweet bark to their horses. But Marcy correctly read the North Fork as a tributary. Returning to the parent stream, the column resumed its westward march along the Prairie Dog Town Fork. Four months after receiving his orders, Marcy found headwater springs, if not the true source. For the first time, the water was clear and sweet. Above the cottonwoods were magnificent multi-colored cliffs.

Unknown to Americans of Marcy's time, Palo Duro Canyon drove the captain to the far reaches of his prose style: "Occasionally might be seen a good representation of the towering walls of a castle of the feudal ages . . . Then again, our fancy pictured a colossal specimen of sculpture, representing the human figure, with all the features of the face distinctly defined. This, standing upon its lofty pedestal, overlooks the valley, as if it had been designed and executed by the Almighty Artist as the presiding genius of these dismal solitudes."

Claude Zachry's picture window and patio overlook the bluffs of Red River in Clay County. From his backyard Bermuda grass, the red clay drops off two hundred feet. Though the Burkburnett oil field is just twenty miles upstream, I saw none of the nodding horsehead pump jacks that enable other cattlemen to hedge against the price of beef. Zachry's land value is bolstered by orchards of pecan trees that are evenly spaced in fields of maroon dirt, which he keeps planted in wheat and rye. Because of the frequency of floods, Zachry doesn't try to grow that grain to harvest; fat Herefords eat the greenshoots. About a mile away, the sand flats and cocoa-colored river make a hairpin curve back toward the house and then disappear in the trees, seeking the mouth of the Little Wichita. Morning sun was burning through the night's rain clouds.

Tall and long-legged, Claude Zachry has lived on this ranch since 1929. I kept thinking of the old-timers in Larry McMurtry's early novels.

"When the river floods, how fast does it rise?" I asked him.

"Depends on how much water there is down below," he said. "If they've had rain downstream, that holds the head rise up. But it's not always gradual. Flood of '35, I saw horses and cattle and logs all come down together. Parts of houses with chickens still sitting on the roof." He rose from his easy chair and stared at the bottom. "I drowned a horse in that flood. I was trying to get to some stranded cows and didn't know how bad it was. I swam him back toward the bluff, and he climbed up in tree branches and hung on. But it was too much for him. He just gave out and died."

Ranching the bottomland is not the same as running a place up on the plains. On grassland wooded with mesquite, cattlemen thank their stars for knee-high clumps of little bluestem. Down among the pecans, big bluestem and Indian grass rustle chest-high in the breeze. But while plains ranchers can leave tractors in a partially plowed hayfield, every night Zachry moves his machinery to high ground for fear of losing it. Because the last big flood in 1983 deposited so much sand, he needs a four-wheel-drive pickup in the bottom pastures.

Riding away from the house in his pickup, Zachry descended a steep graded road and cut through the plowed fields of his pecan orchard. When he stopped the truck, he glanced at my feet to see if I was properly shod. The grass was wet, and snakes were out. "This place can really grow the cottonwoods," I enthused.

Zachry followed my upward gaze with less rapture. "Yeah. If there was any market for 'em, we'd sure be set."

The red ground underfoot was broken up in triangles and trapezoids of half-inch crust. Short grass grew beyond the point where it looked solid. Along the bank, the cracks in the soil were wider, predicting the next collapse. Served by crude gullies and festooned with dead or dying shrubs and grass, the wet sandbars and silent river offered a sullen contrast to all this luxuriant green.

"You are standing," said Zachry, "on Red River's south cut bank."

"It just breaks off in the river, doesn't it?"

"Farmers lost half-acres of cotton in the old days."

Quicksand, which pervades the Red's legends, is created by upward-flowing ground water that holds soil particles in suspension. But if you look for the cinematic gloop that has the consistency of Malt-O-Meal and slowly sucks you under, you won't find it. In dry seasons, the bed is laced with wind-arranged sand and alkaline grit. Near the dividing and intertwining streams, which may run no more than shin-deep, the ground looks damp but easily supports the weight of a horse. The mud makes squelching sounds under its hooves. The horse takes another step on ground that looks identical—and the bottom falls out. Plunging and pitching, it strikes for anything solid. If it topples and rolls, a rider can be crushed and buried.

"Some horses have a light step and a sense of just where they can go," said Zachry. "We called them river horses and needed them because we were always digging out bogged cows. For some reason, the river's not as *quickie* now as it used to be. Cows wouldn't sink out of sight, but the stuff flowed in and set like concrete. If they got eighteen inches of a leg caught, it would hold them till they died."

He moved the truck and showed me a spot with a higher cut bank. Pointing at willows and salt cedar, he said the changing river had given that acreage to Oklahoma. "It used to be yours?" I asked.

"Oh, yeah. I've ridden those woods a thousand times."

He stared at the sandbars and reminisced. "In fact, when I was a young man, we used to cross it here every Saturday night. The closest dances were over in Ryan. When the moon's up on it, I never have seen it when it didn't look half a mile wide."

⌒

The prettiest stretch of river valley lies due north of Dallas. Here the longest of the Oklahoma tributaries, the Washita, angles down through the eastern Cross

Timbers. Fringing the rich tall-grass prairie, the narrow strip of oak and elm forest attracted settlers because it supplied fuel and lumber. Preston Road in Dallas was once the Butterfield stagecoach line to Oklahoma Territory. But the Red's history is least recognizable along this stretch of river. If downstream towns and thousands of acres of farmland were ever to be spared its floods, a dam had to stop the Washita, too. Planning of the dam at Denison, ten miles below the Washita's mouth, officially began in Congress in 1929.

Since Lake Texoma would back far up the tributary and remove 200,000 acres from cultivation and property tax rolls, an Oklahoma governor named "Alfalfa Bill" Murray called it "the biggest folly ever proposed." During the dam's construction, Oklahoma twice sought work-stop injunctions from the United States Supreme Court. But no Oklahoma politician wielded as much power in Washington as Sam Rayburn, the Texas congressman from downstream Bonham. Because it was a domestic priority of the Speaker of the House, the Red River dam was completed in 1944—one of the only public works projects allowed to continue during World War II.

With 585 miles of shoreline, Lake Texoma is now the country's tenth-largest reservoir. The four-state apportionment of water rights irrigates some farms, and two generators in the dam provide backup electricity for towns and rural cooperatives in Texas and Oklahoma. But the lake's primary purpose is flood control. When a flood crests near Wichita Falls, it takes about three days to reach the Denison dam. Gauges up and down the river beam signals to satellites, which relay them to computers of the United States Army Corps of Engineers in Tulsa. That data governs the release of water through the dam. A June flood in 1957 cleared the dam by three feet and made a beautiful and frightening waterfall of the spillway—the only time the system failed. Ordinarily, the deepness of the lake turns the river's homely brown water a pretty jade green.

More than eight million tourists visit Lake Texoma every year. Convenient to Dallas-Fort Worth and Oklahoma City, docks of yachts and sailboats and hillsides of condominiums have begun to appear. Urbanity encroaches, but the submerged cut bank and foibles won't go away. Anglers can fish with special Texoma permits or take their chances with different game wardens and laws on either side of an imaginary Texas-Oklahoma boundary in the middle of the lake. Authorities briefly tried to mark the state line with a thirty-mile string of bobbing floats, but they proved impractical and were soon removed.

Below the even grass lawn of the earthwork dam, the Red reemerges from twenty-foot tubes. Frothing and slowing the water is a grid of concrete bulwarks patterned like a waffle iron. A reinforced building at the foot of the dam contains the generators.

⌒

Twenty miles downstream, near Bonham, a bored kid passed the time peeling out on the Highway 78 bridge. Driving a mud-splattered pickup, he raced to the end of the rusting steel bridge, turned around, and peeled out again. The truck had Oklahoma tags. On a gray Friday in early spring, I had set out for a long drive in the country—a nature trek. An old friend named Roy rode along. We crossed into Oklahoma wherever we could, but pavement over there was scarce along the river, all the land was plowed, and the farmhouses looked like John Steinbeck's hard travelers had just gone down the road, feeling bad.

Back on the Texas side, we passed through lush meadows and hardwood forest. Though we seldom saw the river, we sensed its nearness in long spaces that opened up in the horizon of blue-green foliage. This country has long had a reputation for hideouts of criminals on the lam. But the Texas villages—Ivanhoe, Tulip, Telephone, Monkstown, Direct, Chocota—have an appearance of rustic contentment and prosperity. "Since 1883," boasted the sign of a small Baptist church. "Until Christ comes again."

On the shoulder of Highway 271, which connects Paris with Hugo, Oklahoma, we hammed and photographed each other beside the upright granite map of Texas that marks the state line. The boundary markers are strapping and friendly things; you want to stand up against the Sabine and throw an arm around the Panhandle. Across the bridge and back in Oklahoma, we circled past a drive-in with a tersely worded sign—Bob's Beer—and left the car on the lot of a large dance hall. Red River Junction was painted across its front. The river here was a quarter mile wide. It rose against the bridge abutments and swelled around them with a sound of rapids you wouldn't want to swim. Brush and brown foam gyrated in whirlpools. Roy looked back at the empty dance hall and laughed, imagining its conversations. "Let's get drunk and go fall in the river," he said.

The Red is no River Jordan, and it's not half as pretty as the Seine. It's just a muddy border stream. But coming southward, I always breathe easier when I hear the clicks under my tires of the narrow two-lane bridge. I know I'm back where I belong.

The Washita River

Washita River

by Karla K. Morton

I never asked why they stopped
to bathe her—
my mother, two years old,

bare buttocks in the Washita,
plump baby legs reaching
for those holy red waters.

Driving there now
in late Indian Summer;
I see them down there, watching:

my grandparents,
two sets of Oklahoman great-grandparents—
all younger than I am now.

What magic breaks a river
through earth and flint and time;
what makes our lives eternal
but each legend of bloodline.

Karla K. Morton, born in Fort Worth, is the author of several books of poetry and was the 2010 Texas Poet Laureate. In 2016, she and poet Alan Birkelbach launched a three-year project to visit all sixty-one US national parks, documenting their journeys through poetry and photography. © Karla K. Morton, 2019. Published by permission of Karla K. Morton.

What power is there in a snippet of story
told every crossing of that bridge.

Look, see the ridged prints of your mother
held deep in the mouth of the clay.

The Washita remembers.
See how she played—
lifted wet fingers to her mouth,
the same mouth of your daughter.

This is why we return again and again
to the story;
to the River.

feel how it floods and bends your soul
years after you depart;
the way it still hums the hymn of your name;
how it carries your wistful heart.

The Wichita River

The Falls Return to Wichita Falls

by William Hauptman

ichita Falls had an image problem of almost metaphysical proportions: it was a city of just under 100,000 people, but nobody knew exactly where it was. The other cities of the plains—Amarillo, Lubbock, Midland, and Odessa—were all relatively familiar names, but people outside of Texas invariably thought Wichita Falls was somewhere in Kansas. And where were the falls themselves? They had been destroyed by a flood sometime in the 1890s.

So Wichita Falls built an artificial waterfall to "put the falls back in Wichita Falls" and give the city what then mayor Charles Harper called "a symbol of hope." The new falls were inaugurated on June 5, 1987, during a three-day FallsFest, which organizers called "the biggest turn-on in North Texas." The entertainment included the country-rock singer Joe Ely and the United States Army's Golden Knights parachute team. Willard Scott of NBC's *Today* show even broadcast the weather from there.

All this took me by surprise. In the two years since I had last visited my mother and my brother, who still live there, the bottom had fallen out of the price of oil, and Texas was going through some hard times. But Wichita Falls was getting better—or at least some people there seemed to think so.

This year, I went home during FallsFest '88, hoping to better understand my hometown—why it is the town it is, how it got that way, and how it's changed in the more than twenty years since I left.

William Hauptman, born in Wichita Falls, is a Tony Award–winning playwright who lives in Brooklyn. His short fiction has appeared in *Best American Short Stories*, and his acclaimed 1992 novel about tornado chasers, *The Storm Season*, was later republished in the Wittliff Collections Literary Series. © William Hauptman, 1987. Published by permission of William Hauptman.

I left New York and flew to Dallas, where I changed to a small commuter plane, which took me to Wichita Falls, 150 miles to the northwest. For thirty minutes we flew over wooded farmland. Then the country below suddenly changed. The pastures were covered with thorny mesquite. The soil turned to a clay that my father, a geologist, used to call "Permian red." In the spring, when it rains, this clay saturates the local water, giving the Red River its name. We were over the high plains. Ahead, I could see the broadcast towers of Wichita Falls.

My mother drove me into town from the north, on the Central Expressway, from which Wichita Falls shows its best aspect. From there, the four or five large downtown buildings form an impressive group. On the hill above downtown is the Memorial Auditorium, as large as many Broadway theatres, and the Acropolis-like First Baptist Church, which covers a whole city block. Pouring down from the bluff below Riverside Cemetery is the falls. The unpredictability of the Wichita River—most of the year it's dry, but in the spring it often floods—made it impossible to build the falls in the riverbed itself. So water is pumped up from the river, then sent streaming over an eighty-foot cascade.

The notion of rebuilding the falls had been around for a long time. By 1985, a local group called Streams and Valleys decided the time had come to do something and offered to raise $250,000 by public subscription. Not everyone was for it. Many people, especially older residents, were stubbornly opposed, for various reasons—it was a waste of money, it was in the wrong place. I spoke to one of these older residents, whom I'll call Mr. Bud Stone, to protect the anonymity he requested.

Someone had sent me to Mr. Stone because he had taken part in an early attempt, twenty years ago, to clean up the Wichita River, and allegedly knew the true location of the original falls. Mr. Stone, who is in the oil business, was born in Burkburnett in the year of the boom. His father was a driller. Our conversation took place in his office, where he sat in a battered leather chair, chain-smoking Winstons, his dog at his feet. On the wall was a photograph of an old jackknife rig, spouting oil.

Mr. Stone first told me he wanted no publicity. When I asked him to show me the letter of thanks the Chamber of Commerce had given him for his efforts, he refused. Then he gave me a lecture, in wonderfully blunt language, on how writers regularly distort the facts of what goes on in Washington, that made me glad I had never worked for him as a roughneck. At one point, his dog even joined in, giving me a few barks.

Once Mr. Stone got started on the history of Wichita Falls, however, he was hard to stop. His favorite subject was mesquite. He asked me if I knew how it had gotten here. I did—it was brought up from Mexico in the excrement of cattle—but I didn't know why there was so much of it around Wichita Falls, until Mr. Stone told me cowboys used to pasture trail herds here for five days, to fatten them up before they crossed the Red River. It took five days, he explained, for a steer to relieve himself of all the excrement in his system. Could I quote him on that? No, I could not—and I had wasted enough of his time. The whole thing was a lot of damned nonsense, anyway.

The last thing he told me was, "You see, the real falls was in coloredtown, and that's why people pretend they don't know where it was."

Actually, there was no attempt at deception—the new location was chosen for maximum visibility from the interstate and its proximity to the Sheraton Hotel. The falls were designed by Groves & Associates, a San Antonio engineering and landscape architecture firm that has previously designed river-beautification projects for San Antonio and Waco, and is working on one for Lima, Peru. The finished product is satisfyingly impressive, especially at close range. "We wanted noise, volume," Mr. Groves told me. "That's the secret."

After the falls were unveiled at FallsFest in 1987, everyone who had opposed the project came around overnight. The falls are an unqualified success. Several people told me it was "the best thing that ever happened to this town."

The events of that FallsFest have already passed into legend. The Wichita River was in flood, and the Sheraton was surrounded by water. The visiting dignitaries (which included the mayor of Niagara Falls) had to be taken to the ceremonies in the "Wichita Falls Navy," a fleet of canoes. I watched all this from a hospital in New York City, where my son was being born. The *Today* show coverage began before daybreak with Willard Scott, wearing a red "gimme" cap, his arm around the mayor, saying, "I want you to meet America's number-one fall guy, Charles Harper."

As the show went on, coming back to Willard every half hour for his weather summary, I thought I began to detect a note of condescension in his voice. (I learned later that off camera, when told that putting the falls back in Wichita Falls had cost $400,000, Willard Scott asked Mayor Harper, "Why didn't you just change the name?") On his last spot, Willard appeared wearing a fez to introduce Carl Wilson, the aged potentate of Maskat Temple, the Order of the Shrine. "What am I, if you're the potentate?" he said, shoving his microphone under Mr. Wilson's chin.

"You're the impotentate," Mr. Wilson said, and at that moment, I experienced the strongest feeling of pride I had had for my hometown in several years.

On the Saturday night after I arrived in Wichita Falls the following year, I went to FallsFest '88 with my brother and his wife. We parked in the municipal lot and took a motorized trolley to the city park. Tents, concessions, and rides were set up in a large meadow.

For a while, we watched the Twin Spins—a children's gymnastic team—perform. One little girl, no more than five years old, did a spectacular series of cartwheels that brought us to our feet. Then we went to the longhorn pork skins concession, where pork skins were made before your very eyes—something I had never seen before. A woman took a handful of "rendered bacon rind pellets" and dropped them in a pot of hot oil, where they ballooned up like cumulus clouds on a summer day. I had always thought pork skins should be well-aged, bought at a 7-Eleven, and eaten after midnight. These were so transcendently fresh, they seemed almost nourishing.

We walked along, crunching great mouthfuls of pork and air, washing them down with beer. At the arts and crafts tent, I saw some good local folk art, including some wagons fashioned from old Dr. Pepper crates that looked just like the one my grandfather had made for me when I was a child. There were farmers and their families, city people wearing shorts and tennis shoes, and lots of long-haired teenagers. It was much the same crowd I had seen at any number of county fairs in my youth, with one exception: there were no fistfights. There was not even any shoving at the beer tent. The five policemen I saw seemed to be on good terms with the crowd, and no one even gave them a hostile look.

Later, I walked a mile or so through the park to the falls. A handful of people were there—mostly older, taking pictures. I stood at the foot of the lowest cascade and looked up. Four thousand gallons a minute were pouring over the lip, filling the air with humidity. The artificiality of the falls was evident—it looked something like the Roaring Rapids at Six Flags Over Texas—but somehow this didn't bother me. I was reminded of the earth art of the late Robert Smithson, works like *Amarillo Ramp* and *Spiral Jetty*. Authenticity had nothing to do with it; this was a site, a location on which people could pin their associations and, in this case, their hopes.

In this, the falls may be a better symbol than people know. Wichita Falls may have run out of oil, but it does have water. Since the 1920s, the city has built four artificial lakes—Kemp, Kickapoo, Diversion, and Arrowhead—and wants to build another. It's not the best drinking water in the world, but it's perfectly suitable for industrial use, and its availability was one of the reasons the industries came here.

When I was a child, water was rationed, and my father struggled to keep the lawn alive. Now—in the spring, at least—Wichita Falls is green and pleasant, a much more attractive town, for my money, than Lubbock, Abilene, or Amarillo.

In fact, water may be the element that determines the future of Wichita Falls. If those lakes don't turn to salt, they could be the reason why, in one hundred years, Wichita Falls is still here.

As for tourism as the future of Wichita Falls, I'm not qualified to judge. It may be that if they build the riverwalk and the convention center, Wichita Falls will become a tourist center. But it may be that this is a case of "Rain Following the Plough."

At the end of my time in Wichita Falls, I began to feel a little uncomfortable. One night, at a 7-Eleven, I heard myself tell the counterman, "Appreciate it," and thought I sounded like an actor trying to pass for a Texan.

The truth is, I don't belong here anymore. But I love Wichita Falls—I love it with a writer's love for his hometown—and I wish the people well. Over the years, a strange thing has happened: the town has gotten more interesting. I might even say that to me, it has become the most interesting—and therefore the most beautiful—place on earth.

On my last evening there, I drove downtown, which is now my favorite part of town. Unfortunately, many of the old buildings have been torn down and replaced by parking lots. But many are still standing, and they are best seen in the low, clear light of sunset, which seems to last for hours.

There was not a car, nor a person, nor another living thing—until I saw a box turtle, big as a plate, inching his way across Scott Street. There was no telling how he had gotten here or where he was going; the river was a mile away. I wondered how long he had traveled and how, even on these deserted streets, he had escaped being crushed.

It pleases me to think these turtles can be one hundred years old. I picked him up—his head and feet disappeared—and put him on the floor of the car. Then I drove to the park, where I placed him on the grassy bank of the river and stood off to one side to watch. After five minutes, his head poked out. Then he shuffled rapidly into the muddy red water and disappeared.

The Canadian River

*A*merican folklore abounds in songs and stories about lazy rivers and mighty rivers and quiet rivers and rivers that call you back to the pleasant memories of childhood. The Canadian has inspired nothing like this. It is a wicked, perverse, stingy river. Stephen Foster couldn't have written a sweet ditty about the Canadian; he would have been too busy swatting at deer flies. If Mark Twain had sent Huck and Jim down the Canadian, American literature would have been deprived of its best example of River-as-Universal-Being; Huck and Jim would not have found enough water to float a feather, much less a raft.

—John Erickson, from *Through Time and the Valley*

John Erickson is the creator and author of the beloved Hank the Cowdog series. His first book, *Through Time and the Valley*, chronicled his horseback journey through the Canadian River valley and was published by Shoal Creek Publishers, 1978.

The Canadian River

by Joe Holley

*I*n a thinly populated area northeast of Amarillo, where rumpled hills and flat-topped mesas belie the stereotype of the billiard table-flat Panhandle, where the nearest town of any size is not Amarillo but Liberal, Kansas, I've found a region chock full of fascinating history and populated by accommodating people with stories to tell about their Texas home. A river runs through it.

It's called the Canadian. Starting out as snowmelt in the Sangre de Cristo range of southern Colorado and meandering across five Texas counties before mingling in eastern Oklahoma with the Arkansas River, the Canadian is the Panhandle's only river.

Where the river got its misleading name is open to conjecture to this day. Perhaps seventeenth-century French explorers christened it, assuming it flowed northward into Canada. The writer John Graves leaned toward the notion that the word is a corruption of *la canada*, Spanish for ravine or gully; the river does, in fact, flow through rugged canyon country in the Panhandle. Another possibility: French-Canadian fur traders may have made their way down the Mississippi, up the Arkansas, and into at least the lower part of the river.

Spanish explorers couldn't agree on what to call it. Flowing southward past today's Raton, New Mexico, their Rio Buenaventura, Rio Colorado, or Rio Santa Magdalena hollows out a dramatic gorge almost 1,500 feet deep near Las Vegas, New Mexico. At its juncture with the Conchas River near Tucumcari, it makes a ninety-degree turn and begins a meandering flow across the arid plains of northeastern New Mexico and into the Panhandle, where it forms the northern border of the Llano Estacado, decisively separating the fabled staked plains from the rest of the Great Plains. Along most of its 906-mile course from mountain to plain, the Canadian is a braided stream with interlacing channels that drains an area of 46,900 square miles.

Joe Holley, born and raised in Waco, is an acclaimed journalist and the author of several books, including *Sutherland Springs*, which won the 2021 Texas Institute of Letters Award for Best Nonfiction. For many years, he's written the popular "Native Texan" Sunday column for the *Houston Chronicle*. © Joe Holley, 2020. Published by permission of Joe Holley.

John Erickson, Hank the Cowdog's creator, knows the Canadian well. A rancher as well as a prolific writer, he has lived most of his life in and around the Canadian River Valley. In a memoir called *Through Time and the Valley*, he describes the Canadian as "a wicked, perverse, stingy river."

His Canadian is the river I know too, although I'm not sure I'd be as severe about it as he is, particularly since the river no longer breaches its banks periodically, wreaking havoc on Panhandle people, property, and livestock. Still, I understand what he means. The Canadian is no warbling, spring-fed stream like the Comal or the San Marcos. Sluggish and slow for much of its quicksand-pocked course, occasionally disappearing altogether, it bears no resemblance to the mighty Colorado or the wide Missouri. I call it a workaday river, a resource to be used and enjoyed, if not necessarily appreciated.

My acquaintance with the Canadian is primarily the result of visits to the pleasant, little northeastern Panhandle town that took the river's name when it was founded in 1887. With its hilly, red brick–paved Main Street and a leafy residential neighborhood of well-preserved Victorian homes, Canadian, like the area itself, refutes the fading small-town stereotype. Salem Abraham, whose Lebanese great-grandparents immigrated in the 1920s to Canadian, where they established a mercantile store, says that his hometown has prospered over the years because of ranching and oil and because families like his have maintained ties and have given back. Abraham himself runs a futures-trading concern from offices in a venerable downtown hotel, one of several downtown buildings he and his wife, Sally, have restored; the business successfully competes with firms in Chicago and New York.

The Abrahams own a 3,000-acre ranch that abuts the river, but the town itself grew up about a mile south of the Canadian, a necessity in years past when the river went on its rampages. Occasionally I jog across Canadian's historic wagon bridge over the Canadian, a bridge nearly a mile long that the town has transformed into a handsome pedestrian span. (The bridge is so long because of the river's sandy banks and because of the floodwaters that used to spread like a roiling inland sea across the countryside.) These days the river where the bridge crosses, tamed to practical use decades ago, is relatively shallow and maybe fifty yards wide. It flows through a marshy, jungle-like flood plain that's home and hideout to white-tailed deer, raccoons, jackrabbits, waterfowl, bobwhite quail, and wild turkeys. A few miles beyond the bridge, the flood plain narrows, and the Canadian becomes a pleasant stream drifting eastward through field and pasture toward the nearby Oklahoma state line and its eventual melding with the Arkansas.

"Huck and Jim," in Erickson's disparaging words about the Canadian, "would not have found enough water to float a feather, much less a raft." Maybe so,

and yet there's more to the domesticated Canadian than is immediately obvious. The river may not have inspired writers and poets, but it does boast an
engaging history.

One afternoon I stood along a narrow trail winding through scrub vegetation ninety miles upstream from Canadian's pedestrian bridge. On the ground
at my feet was a large, rectangular-shaped limestone rock lying flat on the
ground, a hundred yards or so from the narrow, red-tinged river. Early-morning
dew congealed into ice had partially filled a perfectly rounded cylinder worn
into the scarred, gray stone. I was looking at a metate, a tool the so-called
Antelope Creek People relied on more than a thousand years ago for grinding corn and seed. They were not the first to live along the Canadian. "The
Breaks," as the river's double valley is called, has been inhabited for eons.

I learned about those inhabitants in Borger, a town a few miles south of the
river that's been in existence not for eons but for less than a century. In downtown Borger, I met Ricky Say, a retired public school teacher and volunteer at
the Hutchinson County Historical Museum whose forebears arrived from Titus-
ville, Pennsylvania (birthplace of the oil industry), during "Booger's" raucous
oil boom in 1926. Say knows his river history.

"The Canadian River was the first superhighway of the Great Plains," he told
me as we perused exhibits of the cavalcade of cultures that have relied on the
river. More than 10,000 years before the Antelope Creek villagers lived among
the bluffs and tributaries of the Canadian, and hundreds of years since, the river
has been, in Say's words, "a natural highway between plains and mountains."
The prehistoric inhabitants found water in the Canadian River Valley; they
relied on springs bubbling up from the ancient waters of the Ogallala Aquifer.
The river's tributaries provided wood, shelter, an abundance of wild game, and
easy access to trade routes spanning the continent.

The metate I encountered near the river lies within a mile or so of the visitors' center of the Alibates Quarries National Monument. Just south of Fritch,
an unassuming, little town on the shores of Lake Meredith, Alibates is one of
the *least* visited national monuments in the United States, park ranger Joe
Mihm told me.

On the weekday morning I showed up, Mihm was free to lock the front door
and escort his two visitors—me and a Chicago retiree checking off his national-
park bucket list—on a two-hour hike into the bluffs and mesas cosseting the
center. The retired power-company lineman from Borger led us up a steep,
winding trail—cut by modern-day Navajo trail builders from Arizona—past
rust-red sandstone freckled with white limestone rocks. With a brilliant blue
sky as backdrop, the rugged red-white-and-blue terrain was a pleasant surprise
to my Chicago companion, who favorably compared the isolated area to other

national parks he had visited. (He had never heard of the Canadian, glinting in the sun in the distance.)

Our hilltop destination was a group of small quarries where skilled men and women six or seven hundred years ago worked flint into tools and weapons revered for their sharpness and efficiency. The quarries are shallow pits littered with rock shards—red, gray, purple, maroon, white, and multicolored—that were the detritus of carefully chiseled spear points, scrapers, drills, awls, knives, and hammers. The finished products were so prized that the Antelope Creek People were able to trade them for shells from the Pacific coast, dried fish from the Gulf of Mexico, and animal furs from the Rocky Mountains. As a crisp hilltop breeze blew, the three of us stared down at a quarry the native people had used for at least 12,000 years, from the close of the most recent Ice Age until about 1870.

Mihm explained that before the Antelope Creek People arrived, the Canadian River Valley was inhabited by the Clovis culture, perhaps as long ago as roughly 12,000 BCE. Following the Clovis people were the Folsom people, who, like the Clovis, were big-game hunters who stalked the giant bison. The Antelope Creek People arrived in the 600s or 700s CE and were the last to live permanently in the valley until shepherds (*pastores*) from New Mexico ventured onto the Great Plains in the mid-1800s.

The Antelope Creek People left the area in about 1500; archaeologists aren't sure why. Then came the Comanches and the Apaches. Both groups hunted the bison of the Great Plains and the deer, elk, bear, and other game that sheltered in the Breaks.

Coronado crossed the Canadian in 1541 in his search for cities of gold. New Mexico's Spanish governor Juan de Oñate followed the river onto Oklahoma's western plains in 1601; Spanish traders and buffalo hunters followed. In 1719, French explorer Bernard de la Harpe followed the river's course to its mouth. In 1740, Pierre and Paul Mallet also explored the river's entire length and inaugurated a decades-long period of French trade with the Osage and Wichita tribes in Oklahoma.

Buffalo hunters filtered into the area in the 1840s, slaughtering the shaggy creatures in numbers almost impossible to imagine. After the discovery of gold in California in 1849, Capt. Randolph B. Marcy commanded troops that laid out the California Road along the Canadian, a route that westward-yearning pioneers and forty-niners relied on until 1861.

In 1864, Kit Carson led a force of 350 volunteers and Indian scouts out of New Mexico to pursue a group of Comanches and Kiowas whose raids had disrupted trade along the Santa Fe Trail. Following the Canadian, Carson and his men attacked a Kiowa village in a grassy meadow about two miles north of the river in what's now Hutchinson County. The battle, near an old buffalo hunter's camp called Adobe Walls, was inconclusive, and the soldiers made their way back up the river to Fort Union, New Mexico.

On an upstairs wall of Borger's history museum is an oil portrait of a sober-looking young man with straight, shoulder-length black hair and a droopy black mustache. His name was Billy Dixon, a buffalo hunter who made a name for himself at the second Battle of Adobe Walls in 1874. Dixon is credited with using his Sharps .50 hunting rifle to fell a Comanche warrior sitting on his horse on a low butte at least three-quarters of a mile away. He was so far away, he tumbled to the ground before anyone near him heard the crack of the rifle that killed him.

After his buffalo-hunting days, Dixon settled near the Canadian. As he recalled in his autobiography, he found along the river "pure air, good water, fruitful soil and room enough for a man to turn around without stepping on some fellow's toes." (The area's not all that different today.)

By the time Dixon died of pneumonia in 1913, the Comanches had, of course, been subdued, but the Canadian was still running wild nearly every spring. The river could be a raging torrent two-and-a-half miles wide and ten feet deep. Say, the museum volunteer in Borger, tells the story of a farmer living near a settlement on the north bank of the Canadian called Plemons (now a ghost town) who relied on his winsome daughters to lure travelers to presumably safe crossings. Somehow the Panhandle Sirens invariably got the trusting travelers stuck in the mud (or quicksand), and their enterprising ol' dad would just happen to arrive, hitch up his mule team, and pull them out of their predicament. For a price.

The treacherous Canadian was finally subdued in 1965, when Sanford Dam was completed forty miles northeast of Amarillo. Behind the dam, Lake Meredith became the Panhandle's playground, a lure for fishermen, campers, hikers, and water skiers. Today the lake supplies water to a half million people in eleven Panhandle cities and towns.

"We've pulled a trillion gallons of water out of Lake Meredith in the last fifty years," said Kent Satterwhite, general manager of the Canadian River Municipal Water Authority. "The reason that's important is because that's water that otherwise would have come out of the Ogallala Aquifer. Ogallala water is not renewable."

Satterwhite was sitting behind his desk in the CRMWA office, the dam and the blue waters of the lake visible on a blustery day through a picture window behind him. Despite the growth of Amarillo and other cities and towns of the plain, the valley of the Canadian still seems isolated, lightly inhabited. I think that's why I'm drawn to the area and to the river that shaped it. Standing beside the Canadian one cold, sunny afternoon, the banks lined with yellowed marsh grass, the red bluffs casting shadows across the gently flowing water, I saw no one, heard no one. A hawk soared above me.

The river and rugged environs felt haunted, though not in a threatening way. I was alone, but I knew, or felt, that spirits inhabited the place. Not far from where I stood was a metate and flint spear points, pictographs, and slab-house dugouts that people who lived along the river built and used long, long ago. The artifacts are mute evidence of cultures that lived and died and disappeared, just as we will one day. The river remains.

Interlude

Half-Forgotten Rivers
The James and the Pease

by Michael Barnes and Joe Starr

*H*ow does a Texas river become half-forgotten? Remote and rugged terrain can play a part. Distance from population centers adds obstacles.

The flood-ravaged James River, for instance, is short, at 45 miles long, confined entirely to a fairly isolated part of the Hill Country and only intermittently accessible before it pours into Llano River. Meanwhile, the 100-mile-long Pease River, which flows from near the Caprock in West Texas northeasterly to the Red River across wooded grasslands, passes through some public land but is unloved for a reason that we did not learn until our second round of Texas river tracings.

Some necessary background: Our urge to trace Texas rivers started out with a hankering for the Great Empty. A stretch of road with no cars in sight, ahead or behind. Since sharing a dorm room at the University of Houston in the late 1970s, the two of us had taken any number of epic road trips. By the early twenty-first century, we had traveled by car, van, or truck across almost the entire Lower 48, visiting parks, monuments, museums, and whatever else the road happened to throw in our way. In 2003, we decided to track the route of the Lewis and Clark expedition, from Camp Dubois in Hartford, Illinois, all the way to Fort Clatsop, Oregon. Like the early explorers, we followed the rivers.

One particular impression stayed with us: the contrast between the vast mouth of the Missouri River as seen across the Mississippi River from Camp Dubois, and the tiny presumed source of the river at Lemhi Pass on the Continental Divide in Idaho, a burble of water that could have been—and in fact was—straddled by a child.

For years, **Michael Barnes** and **Joe Starr** have been tracing Texas rivers, writing about their observations for the *Austin American-Statesman*, where Barnes is a longtime columnist. **Barnes** is a native Texan who earned his PhD at the University of Texas and is the author of three books. **Starr** is a native Californian who fully embraced Texas after moving here in the 1970s. He currently teaches English as a Second Language to international students at Houston Community College. "Half-Forgotten Rivers" originally appeared in *Texas Highways*, July 2020. Published by permission of Michael Barnes and Joe Starr.

A few years after that, standing on Bryan Beach at the mouth of the Brazos River, it hit us: What if we followed every significant river in Texas from its source to its mouth, or vice versa, by car and on foot, with occasional dips into the water?

That was exactly what we did.

We had read a couple of dozen books about those streams, then crisscrossed the Texas countryside along back roads, documented our hikes to the rivers, visited scores of parks, sampled hundreds of local eateries, photographed a great many courthouses, and stopped at just about every historical marker along the way.

We tried very hard not to trespass on private property and stuck to wet-unto-navigable riverbeds, which are fair game, according to a legal expert at the Texas Parks and Wildlife Department. We started out with good old-fashioned maps, including some very detailed—and at the time expensive—ones published by the US Geological Survey.

The main thing: we saw Texas in a completely fresh way.

The James

Called "The Unknown River of Central Texas" by the Environmental Defense Fund, the James is the only major tributary of the Llano if you don't count the North Llano and the South Llano, which join neatly in the aptly named town of Junction. This pristine river is fed from springs that flow out of the Edwards-Trinity Aquifer. It begins along the line between Kimble and Kerr Counties and continues northeast, joining the Llano as part of the Colorado River basin just south of Mason.

Its crystal-clear waters wind through a lush, verdant canyon teeming with fish, something that has not gone unnoticed by fishermen, including authors Fred Gipson (*Old Yeller*) and John Graves (*Goodbye to a River*), who both wrote poignantly about the river.

It suffered major floods in June 1935, November 1980, and October 2018. Perhaps that was why there were so few structures or mature trees along the river or the James River Road, which follows the canyon for much of its length.

On our second visit, we started at the true headwaters of the James, located on private land. There, Russell Rogas looked out over the low, smooth, tilted canyon. "After the big floods, just about everything you see had changed," said the Brenham resident whose family owns the land in Kimble County. "That boulder was over here. This pond was over there."

His father-in-law, Larry Tegeler, also of Brenham, purchased the terraced valley on Ranch Road 479 between Harper and Junction "for the view and the water," which are ardently enjoyed by Russell; his wife, Amey Rogas; and their four outdoorsy sons. They have survived epic floods, wildfires, and three years ago, a tornado that did not damage what remains of the Creed Taylor Ranch Home, once dubbed "the finest home west of San Antonio," according to a historical marker at the pull-off to their land. It burned down in 1926 and again in 1956. A single-story house now sits on the nineteenth-century foundation.

"We just come and relax," Russell said. "In this world where everything goes on, this is a nice respite for the boys." Britt, seventeen; twins Ben and Grant, fifteen; and Jack, eleven, are all over these highlands in ATVs. Just this morning, Jack killed a "gun hog," and the boys estimate they shoot thirty feral hogs a month on the land during the summer. They invited us to sift through the remains of a Native American midden littered with chert that rises slightly above clear, cold first waters of the James.

"There are springs all through here," Amey said. "In the summer, you can hear it. It sounds like a bathtub with the faucet on full."

Below this spot, the casual visitor comes in direct contact with the James and its shorter tributary, the Little Devils River, at only a few spots along RR 479 and RR 385, as well as the granite-gravel James River Road, which shadows the lower James until it converges with the Llano River near RR 2389 in Mason County. Yet there are plenty of sights along the way, including an especially helpful historical marker that explains how a Spanish expedition in 1808 forged through these canyons on the way to Santa Fe.

We stopped in the dry bed as the road crossed recharge zones. There we marveled at the stratified rock canyon walls and the pools of water teeming with tiny perch and, we later learned, Guadalupe bass.

The day's ride ended just past an exotic game ranch, where we encountered an expanse of the river stretching hundreds of yards to the farther bank. Dare we cross it in our Volvo SUV? Had we known what we discovered later, that the water was less than a foot deep with a hard limestone bed, we might have forged ahead, but instead we listened to the inner public-service announcement in our heads that urged, "Turn around, don't drown."

We do not trifle with Texas rivers.

John Karges, an affable and well-informed biologist with the Nature Conservancy of Texas, met us the next morning at a tiny roadside park at the intersection of US 87 and RR 1723, just south of Mason. After exchanging enthusiasms about the James River, we followed Karges to RR 2389. Our destination was the Eckert James River Bat Cave, owned and operated by the nonprofit conservancy. But first we had a surprise for the San Antonio–based Karges: his first view of the confluence of the James and Llano.

One of the few public amenities on this stretch of river is the Dos Rios RV Park, which perches on a bluff above this confluence, serving as a base for fishing, wading, and kayaking. Our journey took us up the James River Road, where Karges stopped to show us an ideal natural grotto and a smooth-edged box canyon above the James.

"This really reminds me more of the geology of West Texas," he said.

Under Karges's direction, we crossed the wide ford that had held us up the previous day. A few yards away is the well-marked and well-gated entrance to the eight-acre bat cave preserve, named after Phillip Eckert, a rancher who discovered the cave in 1907. His grandson, Clinton Schulze, and his wife, Anne Schulze, are credited with saving the land and shaping the well-tended interpretative trail that leads to the cave's mouth. During the summer months, the conservancy takes as many as one hundred people at a time on weekends to two viewing spots outside the cave. The water-carved cavern is home to four million bats of two varieties, Mexican free-tailed and cave myotis, which live in separate colonies inside the cave and emerge in pulses containing an estimated 100,000 flying mammals at a time. Predators lie in wait at the entrance, but since the bats number in the millions, numbers are on their side.

"They make vortex spirals as they emerge," Karges said. "And now we know that there are exchanges among the Central Texas bat colonies. They are hard to monitor, but we are learning more all the time."

The Pease

The Pease is utterly gorgeous from its source, northwest of Paducah, to the point where it disgorges into the Red River after flowing through untidy ranchland near the town of Vernon. It also passes by Quanah, which we wanted to explore for its associations with the last Comanche chief, Quanah Parker, and his mother, the twice-kidnapped Cynthia Ann Parker. After Quanah, the Pease curves northward toward Vernon and its terminus at the Red.

Early on, it looks like a West Texas river, cutting through grass-tufted mesa and gurgling across pebbled limestone beds. Near its mouth, a hundred miles from the confluence of its forks, it more closely resembles a North Texas prairie river, bending around muddy pastures covered with tall grasses and big trees. It was in this lower region that we encountered signs of agricultural and industrial stress along with significant erosion.

Two handsome plots of public land, the Matador Wildlife Management Area and Copper Breaks State Park, await visitors along its banks. So why is the Pease unloved and perhaps best known for a late battle in the state's Indian Wars that wasn't really a battle at all?

We found out the answers to those questions at the end of our second visit, but first we encountered the North, Middle, and South Pease Rivers up and down county roads off US 62 between Childress and Paducah. At the Matador Wildlife Management Area, 28,000 acres of rolling high-grass prairie dotted with mesquite, juniper, and shinnery oaks, two of the three forks were set out as if on display for tourists.

"Quail season is our busiest time of year," said the park's manager, Chip Ruthven. "If it's a good quail season."

Northwest of Paducah, the full Pease is crossed at one of our favorite river sites in Texas by a relatively new bridge on Cottle County Road 104. Here one can easily park on the north side of the bridge and walk down to wide sand-bars, braided streamlets, and high white bluffs pocked with overhangs and caves. (We stuck to the wet riverbed.) So half-forgotten is the Pease that if you browse online for images of it, among the top returns are photographs of this spot taken on our two trips.

At Copper Breaks State Park, a few miles below Quanah on Texas 6, park interpreter Will Speer answered our lingering questions while we toured the excellent museum at the headquarters.

Why copper?

"The surface of the land here is covered with it," said Speer, who grew up on the Bosque River. "But none of it was worth anything. Little chunks of copper buried in clay. Basically, it could not be smelted."

Why breaks?

"You can look at the broken topography," Speer said. "The sandstone and mudstone from the San Angelo formation and the Permian bedrock are quite rugged above the creek."

Why did the Comanche gather here?

"The Big Pond spring," he said. "And the four conical Medicine Mounds are just to the northeast; you can see them from the highway. This area was one of their strongholds, revered as sacred or ceremonial grounds."

Then why, after all this, is the Pease so unloved?

"Gypsum," Speer said. "There's too much in the water. It's not good to drink."

This piece of vital news dovetailed with what we had learned earlier in the day from Shane Lance, who showed us around the Quanah, Acme & Pacific Railway Depot Museum. The town of Quanah, backed financially by the Comanche chief Quanah Parker, was built on the fortunes of that railroad and a giant nearby gypsum mine and plant. Acme, the plant's company town, was founded by the grandfather of the billionaire Koch brothers.

So where was the Battle of Pease River?

"It wasn't a battle, actually," Speer said. "It was a massacre of fifteen or so women and one brave down in Foard County. They were camped on the south side of the river and were surprised by Sul Ross and his rangers, who killed everybody except Cynthia Ann Parker, because her hair was light and her eyes blue."

Surely the state's most famous kidnapping victim, Quanah Parker's mother was taken by the Comanches in what is now Limestone County in 1836 and then retaken by Texans in 1860. She had become the beloved only wife of Chief Peta Nacona and mother of their three children, including Quanah. Her later life among the Texans was miserable, but that is another story.

"There's a marker along County Road 3103 to Margaret where Cynthia Ann was recaptured," Speer said. "It is said by local legend that when Quanah visited the location, he picked up some barbed wire, balled it up, and threw it fifty feet and said, 'That's exactly where it happened.'"

Try as we might, we could not find the marker or the battlefield.

Part of the satisfaction of tracing Texas rivers has always been the surprising pleasure of being thrown off balance: learning from what we sought but could not find, and getting lost in parts of Texas we did not recognize. And who knows? We might return to this half-forgotten, alluring—even if partly unpotable—waterway.

West Texas

Río Grande / Río Bravo

The sierras here round grandly in, to form the famous Pass of the North, and approach each other parallel within a mile, for a distance of about five miles. The sloping deserts of gravel on both sides of the river are compressed into an elevated plain, through which is trenched the Río Grande. There is no sublimity of mountain grandeur at all, but the panorama is highly impressive and even imposing, by reason of its mighty vistas, its vast deserts, its blue-stretching sierras, and the cheerful greenery of the river region, like a flat-iron for shape, with its point shoved into the pass.

From the haggard, and scarred, and ghastly heights of the plain you look down on the river, and feel that there is fertility yet left in the world some-where. Over on the Mexican side, you see pale straw-colored, or milky, or rich creamy cliffs of limestone, some of them wavy-streaked with yellowish amber, like gigantic agates. The exquisitely tender green of the mountain mesquite, dotting with little clumps these mellow and milky cliffs, gives indescribably beautiful effects of color.

Thus, in more senses than one, the view I had of Texas in leaving it, as Dr. Johnson said of Scotland, was the finest I saw.

—Stephen Powers, 1871

Old río, you and I live in two countries.
What crooked memories.
What crooked journeys.

—Pat Mora, from *Encantado: Desert Monologues*

Stephen Powers (1840–1904) was born in Ohio and reported on the Civil War as a Union Army correspondent. After the war, he walked to California. He published an account of his journey in 1871 as *Afoot and Alone: A Walk from Sea to Sea by the Southern Route*.

Pat Mora, born and raised in El Paso, is a poet and author of books for adults, teens, and children. Her many literary honors include the Lifetime Achievement Award from the Texas Institute of Letters. She is the founder of Día / Children's Day / Book Day, a national celebration of children, families, and reading.

And the River Runs Through

by Bobby Byrd and Sasha Pimentel

El Paso is rooted like a thicket of salt cedar and cottonwood on the Río Grande. El río cuts through mountains to make this place a natural passage. That's what *el paso* means, the pass. For centuries many different peoples—like ourselves, right now, standing here—have passed through El Paso, going north, going south, going west, going east. On the other side is La Ciudad Juárez, Chihuahua, México. Los mexicanos call this river "el Río Bravo," and they know down deep in their hearts and minds, like we know down deep in our hearts and minds, that we are all brothers and sisters. We breathe the same air, we drink the same water. We are border people. Somos fronterizos. We are without end.

Begin from water, the great stillness of desert night and cooling air, our river violet and inky. La luz de la luna en las colinas. And a word rustles across the page, between mouths, at the edge of state and country. El Paso, sólo el Río Bravo tiembla entre tú y el rostro brillante de Juárez—and when the plane descends, both cities glisten in the window, a single ocean of light. Begin now, too, in ascent of flight—the altitude of shared breath, and how, below clouds, our land breaks through: like puddles of star.

Bobby Byrd is the author of numerous books of poetry, and much of his work is set in the southwestern borderlands. He and his wife, novelist Lee Merrill Byrd, founded El Paso–based Cinco Puntos Press. **Sasha Pimentel**, born in Manila, Philippines, is the author of two collections of poetry and winner of the American Book Award. She is an Associate Professor in the bilingual Department of Creative Writing at the University of Texas at El Paso. "And the River Runs Through" © Bobby Byrd and Sasha Pimentel, 2016. This poem is part of a public art installation at El Paso International Airport. Published by permission of Bobby Byrd and Sasha Pimentel.

El Río Grande

by Pat Mora

Maybe La Llorona is el Río Grande
    who carries voices wherever she flows,
the voices of women who speak only Spanish,
    who hold their breath, fluttering
like a new bird, cupped in their own hands high
    above their heads.

Maybe La Llorona is el Río Grande
    who rolls over on her back some afternoons
and gazes straight into the sun,
    her hair streaming brown into fields of onion
and chile, gathering voices of women who laugh
    with their own fear.

Maybe La Llorona is el Río Grande
    who penetrates even granite, gathers the stars
and moon and tells her cuentos all night long,
    of women who scoop her to them in the heat,
lick her on their lips, their voices rising
    like the morning star.

Pat Mora, born and raised in El Paso, is a poet and author of books for adults, teens, and children. Her many literary honors include the Lifetime Achievement Award from the Texas Institute of Letters. She is the founder of Día / Children's Day / Book Day, a national celebration of children, families, and reading. From *Agua santa = Holy water* by Pat Mora. Beacon Press, 1995. Published by permission of Pat Mora.

The River That Runs Through Me

by Beatriz Terrazas

I miss the Río Grande. In my mind I see it, and I smell menudo spiced with oregano. I see it and I hear the clop of horses' hooves outside my grandfather's house in Juarez, feel the beat of a corrido lifting my feet. I've been away from El Paso/Juarez for twenty years now, but I still call it home. Early this year, driving along Interstate 10, I caught a glimpse of the Río Grande. The river lay there between the two cities where I grew up, dry and bare in spots, looking more like a snake that had slithered up to the wrong end of a farmer's hoe than the mighty force implied by its name. It lay there, broken, totally passable for anyone wishing to cross it either north or south but for the white Border Patrol vehicles planted like sentinels along it.

The river—and all it stands for to me—has become invisible despite being in the background of our daily political discourse. I read or hear story after story about international border fences in Texas: The town of McAllen agreed to reinforce its flood walls rather than submit to new fencing to deter trespassers. A federal judge ordered Eagle Pass to surrender more than two hundred acres of land for fence construction.

I keep hoping others will see what I see: not borders and fences and illegal immigrants but the Río Grande itself. To those of us who love it, the river is not merely a boundary with Mexico; it's a living thing. And to those of us who carry it in our veins, it is the story of our lives. The river haunts me. Several years ago, I traveled long stretches of the Río Grande, from its headwaters in Colorado to its mouth in South Texas. Meeting others along its trajectory was a lesson in how this bony, nearly 1,900-mile channel has shaped and influenced people. I came to see how the river is irrevocably intertwined with the child I was, the woman I am. It tethers my soul to the arid landscape in West Texas, and to Mexico. But today's Río Grande is oh so different from the river I once knew.

The river of my youth flowed deep and strong near Las Cruces, New Mexico, where my family used to picnic. Once, when I was six or seven, my mother

Beatriz Terrazas, born in El Paso, is a writer, photographer, and video producer. She received a Nieman Fellowship at Harvard and was part of a *Dallas Morning News* team that won a Pulitzer Prize for a series about violence against women around the globe. "The River That Runs Through Me" originally appeared in *Literary El Paso*, edited by Marcia Hatfield Daudistel. TCU Press, 2009. Published by permission of Beatriz Terrazas.

commanded my siblings and me to stay on the bank and wait for our father before jumping in to play. While he unloaded sandwiches and chips from the trunk, she stepped into the water for a quick swim. Then she was shouting, and in just seconds, her voice sounded far away and she looked tiny, her arm a matchstick floating on the water. She was drowning! I shouted to my father: "Mi mamise esta ahogando!" My father, all white skin and plaid trunks, leaped into the water, but by the time he reached her, she was standing on a sandbar. Later, she told us that la corriente, the current, swift and unseen beneath the river's surface, had carried her away from us, but shhhh, it's okay now.

Another memory: I was about ten and in Juarez playing quinceañera with my cousins on a packed-earth patio. We dreamed about that first dance and the white pearly dress like an upside-down tulip that would signal our passage to womanhood. We shuffled our feet to the song we sang aloud, our budding hips bending to the beat of the cumbia: "Ven a bailar quinceañera. Ven a gozar, quinceañera." And though we couldn't see the river, as dusk fell, coloring the neighborhood purple and gray, its ghosts beckoned us. You know La Llorona drowned her children in the river. You know that, right? Now she wanders the river crying, looking for other children, so watch out!

In high school, some Latino boys threatened to throw into the river a white kid one of my friends was dating. Looking back, I wonder: Were they thinking of the deep symbolism of drowning a white boy in the waters that embodied their different ethnic histories? Probably not; they were just angry, disenfranchised in the way that brown-skinned boys were then, looking for a way to vent their feelings.

But what some people fail to understand—about me, about those boys—is that for us, the river wasn't a barrier. An inconvenience, perhaps, when we had to cross the international bridge to visit our abuelas and primos or wait in long lines of chugging, overheated cars on the way back to our American lives. But the river was our connection, a witness to our attempts at straddling two cultures—to the fact that we could learn US history in school during the week and spend Saturday nights celebrating weddings al otro lado. To the struggles of navigating two languages, two collective histories, and finding that with the passage of time, we were completely at home in neither one nor the other.

That's why seeing the disappearing Río Grande fills me with such longing. I see it and taste the cinnamon coffee of mornings in my grandmother's kitchen. I see it and feel the sweat trickle down my back on a hot day, while my grandfather is lowered to his final resting place in a dusty cemetery. I see it and hear it calling my name as only a loved one can. It is the mirror that reflects the middle space between cultures and countries where I spent my formative years. Yet for several months out of the year, even Google Earth would be hard-pressed to find this river between El Paso and, say, Presidio. During the summer it is dammed upstream for irrigation, its flow so greatly compromised that it dries up in some places and disappears.

The river seems to be vanishing just as I've realized I can't live without it. I worry that for all of our border talk, we are so blinded by political and economic issues that we don't really see the Río Grande. I worry that we won't be able to control the invasive salt cedar breaking up its banks. I worry that we will divert its waters to the point of no return.

What happens then? La Llorona, the restless spirit whose existence calls for water, will have a tough time calling forth a child by a dry channel. As for me, would losing the river mean losing a part of myself? Sunday picnics, high school raft races, crossing into Mexico to watch my grandfather die—would all these memories dry up as well? I hope and pray the river outlives my family as the natural world is supposed to do.

And if I'm lucky, the Río Grande will have been the great witness I think it is and will have carried the bones of my memories to be cradled in the sea.

The Ninth Dream
War (In The City In Which I Live)

by Benjamín Alire Sáenz

All my life—let me say this so you understand—*all my life*
I have heard stories of the river and how people were willing
To die to cross it. To die just to get to other side. The other
Side was the side I lived on. "And people die to get here?"
My mother nodded at my question in that way that told me
She was too busy to discuss the matter and went back
To her ritual of rolling out tortillas for her seven children, some
Of whom asked questions she had no answers for. We were
Poor as a summer without rain; we had an outhouse and a pipe
Bringing in cold water from a well that was unreliable
As the white man's treaties with the Indians, unreliable
As my drunk uncles, unreliable as my father's Studebaker
Truck. I was six. It was impossible for me to fathom
Why anyone would risk death for the chance to live like us.

I have heard people laugh when
They see the Río Grande for the first time. *That is the river?*
But that river has claimed a thousand lives, Mexicans caught
In its currents mistaking the river as something tame, and in
One second the river devoured them whole. The survivors
Have handed down this lesson: Nothing in the desert is
Tame. Not the people, not the sand, not the winds, not
The sun, not even the river that resembles a large ditch,
That's laughed at by visitors and locals alike. Nothing
In the desert has ever had anything resembling mercy

Benjamín Alire Sáenz is the author of several books and a longtime Professor of Creative Writing at the University of Texas at El Paso. The recipient of many literary honors, he was the first Latino to win the PEN/Faulkner Award. From *Dreaming the End of War: Poems* by Benjamín Alire Sáenz. Copper Canyon Press, 2006. Published by permission of Benjamín Alire Sáenz.

On Mexicans attempting to leave their land, to become
Something they weren't meant to be.

          People are still crossing. People are still dying. Some have
Died suffocating in boxcars. Some have drowned. Some
Have been killed by vigilantes who protect us in the name
Of all that is white. Some have died in a desert larger than
Their dreams. Some were found, no hint of their names
On their remains. In the city that is my home, Border Control
Vans are as ubiquitous as taxicabs in New York. Green vans
Are a part of my landscape, a part of my imagination, no less
Than the sky or the river or the ocotillos blooming in spring.
The West is made of things that make you bleed. I no longer
Hang images of summer clouds or Indians carrying pots on their
Talented heads or Mexican peasants working the land with magic
Hands. On my walls, I no longer hang paintings of the Holy Poor.

          We have been fighting a war on this border
For hundreds of years. We have been fighting the war so long
That the war has become as invisible as the desert sands we
Trample on.
          I do not know how long all this will continue. Peace
Is like the horizon. We can see it in the distance,
But it is always far, and we can never touch it.

                                        Every day
In what passes for a newspaper in the city in which
I live, someone writes a letter ranting against the use
Of the Spanish language because this is America, and I can
Taste the hate in the letter, can almost feel the spit
In the letter writer's mouth, and I know we could not
Ever speak about this without one of us wanting to hurt
The other in the city in which I live.

I will tell you a sad story: White people are moving away
From this city that has claimed my heart. They are running away

From my people. They are running away from all that keeps
Us poor. I want them to stay and fight. I want them
To stay and live with my people. We have chased them
Away. I want them to love the people who make the food
They love. *We have chased them away—are you happy? Are you*
Happy? And there are people waiting in line, spending
Their fortunes just for a chance to enter, waiting, just blocks
Away from where I sit, waiting to come over, waiting in Juárez
Just to cross the river, from China and India and all the nations
Of Africa and Central America and Asia. No poet, no engineer, no
Politician, no philosopher, no artist, no novelist has ever
Dreamed a solution. I am tired of living in exile. I am tired
Of chasing others off the land.

Let me say this again. Again. Again.
I want, I want this war to end. To end.

Early Morning, Front Porch
—El Paso, Texas

by Bobby Byrd

I boiled water to clean up
the pigeon shit on the front porch.
That's why I'm outside
broom in hand
on such a beautiful morning—
from here I can see
the whole wide horizon,
the sun rising, desert mountains
to the east to the west,
flowering from the emptiness,
the Río Grande running through
two cities, two countries, two
languages, this side, that side,
so much sorrow, so much
love and hatred, good news,
bad news, the old lady
who said it's all the same,
even in the midst of her suffering,
the death of children,
a husband wandered away—
"Pay attention," she said,
"the water is flowing,
and still the pigeons coo,
the cats sleep, the earth
swings round on its cosmic string."

Bobby Byrd is the author of numerous books of poetry, and much of his work is set in the southwestern borderlands. He and his wife, novelist Lee Merrill Byrd, founded El Paso–based Cinco Puntos Press. © Bobby Byrd, 2020. Published by permission of Bobby Byrd.

Jeep in the Water

by Octavio Solis

The Río Grande we call it on the US side. Río Bravo is what they call it in Mexico. The difference is the difference. Somewhere in the murky depths of this beleaguered band of water is a demarcation line invisible to all but the respective governments of both nations.

One morning a long time ago, which in El Paso could mean either fifty years ago or yesterday, two Border Patrol field agents on their rounds spot a dealer-fresh cherry-red Jeep parked in the shallow Rio. It sits unattended right in the center, the brown water coursing halfway up the doors, loaded with kilos of marijuana. Upon inspection, the agents surmise that some audacious drug runners from Juárez somehow got it into their *cabezas* that if they had the right vehicle, they could simply drive through the river at its shallowest point and safely transport their cargo to its destination. It almost worked. They probably felt like geniuses as their Jeep readily churned through the water in the dead of night. But right at midstream, with no horses to jump to, the Jeep had come to a gurgling halt, mired in deep silty sludge. The dried spatters of mud on the shiny red exterior suggest to the agents some recent desperate heaving back and forth of the vehicle. Apparently, the deflated smugglers abandoned their mission and waded back to Juárez, sans Mary Jane.

Pleased with their catch, the Border Patrol field agents notify their superiors and summon a tow truck to drag the Jeep to shore. By now, a small crowd of people has gathered on both sides of the river to gawk, alerted to the spectacle by the traffic choppers of morning radio. The congregations seem harmless enough, more bemused than alarmed at the sight of a stranded Jeep in the middle of the river, so the agents take only standard cursory notice.

The tow truck appears on the scene in due time, and the young attendant begins running a long tow line to the Jeep. That's when things take an ugly turn. Before he can reach the vehicle, he's being pelted by the Juárez assembly with stones, slabs of concrete, bottles, and whatever else is handy, and he is driven

Octavio Solís, born and raised in El Paso, has written over twenty-five plays and has won dozens of awards, including the Distinguished Achievement in the American Theater Award from the William Inge Center for the Arts. Excerpted from *Retablos: Stories from a Life Lived Along the Border* by Octavio Solis. City Lights Books, 2018. Published by permission of Octavio Solis and City Lights Books.

back out of the water. The agents shout admonitions to the suddenly bristling mob, but at that moment, a tow truck on the Mexican side backs up to the bank, and two men charge into the river with their own tow line. This brazen act affords some incentive to the Border Patrol tow man, and he barrels back into the water. An uproar of curses rises from both sides of the river in two languages as the men slosh like lunatics to the Jeep with their tow lines. The Mexicans secure theirs to the rear fender of the Jeep while the American ties his to the front. Then the contest begins.

The tow trucks rev their engines, pull the tow lines taut, and proceed to pull on the Jeep in opposite directions. An international tug-of-war commences with great noise and cheering from the gathered spectators, many of them already picnicking on the promontories with churros and beer. Back and forth lurches the Jeep, first toward Mexico, then toward the US, then back Mexico-way. Wagers are taken on who will prevail. Some brave boys even grab the line and tug hard to stack the odds in Juárez's favor. The Border Patrol fire warning shots in the air to disperse the crowd and demand the tow-truck desperados cease their criminal acts, but it's no use. Nobody can hear the shots above the shouting and the clamor of the news choppers directly overhead. This is now a full-blown international incident.

At long last, a larger heavy-duty tow behemoth designed for hauling eighteen-wheelers pulls up to the US embankment, and its seasoned driver, long in the tooth and short in the saddle, dodging various projectiles, succeeds in attaching his own tow line to the derelict Jeep. Once ashore, he climbs into his cab and sets to towing it out of the water. The crowds fall silent as the steel cable tautens. *Señor* Jeep heaves mournfully for a moment over the loud grind of the overheating engine of the Mexican tow truck. Then a hideous crunch is heard as the rear fender snaps off and flies into the air like a catfish being reeled in. To cheers from the Americans, and jeers from the Mexicans, the Jeep slowly taxis northward to America, but not before some daring half-naked Mexican kids rush to snatch some bags of pot, souvenirs of this mighty Pan-American match.

The Jeep is impounded, the marijuana seized, displayed and destroyed, and the story, widely circulated for a time throughout the Southwest with many a chuckle, is eventually forgotten in the mix of more sensational and bloodier stories of the War on Drugs bedeviling the region.

But somewhere below the surface of this river, covered over by the silt of years like the footprints of an ancient dinosaur, lies the imprint of tire tracks from a solitary Jeep that challenged the legitimacy of this invisible line we call the Border.

A River of Women

by Pat Mora

A river of women
softened this valley,
hummed through the heart
of night lulling
babies and abuelas
into petals of sleep.

El rio de mujeres
gathered the peach light
of dawn for warmth like a shawl,
slid the glow
into the desert's roots,
eased its greyest thirst.

The river of women
penetrates boulders, climbs
crags jagged as hate,
weaves through clawing thorns
to depths parched, shriveled
offers ripples of hope.

Rio de mujeres,
soften our valley,
braid through its silence
carving your freedom
to the song you learn
on your winding way.

Pat Mora, born and raised in El Paso, is a poet and author of books for adults, teens, and children. Her many literary honors include the Lifetime Achievement Award from the Texas Institute of Letters. She is the founder of Día / Children's Day / Book Day, a national celebration of children, families, and reading. From *Agua santa = Holy water* by Pat Mora. Beacon Press, 1995. Published by permission of Pat Mora.

River of women,
stream on in this valley,
gather all spirits,
deepen and rise,
sustaining your daughters
who dream in the sun.

Monsoon Season

by Sasha von Oldershausen

I left early to beat the heat. The screen door crashed behind me, and I walked past my car, my feet crunching the earth underfoot. Where the dirt road met highway FM 170, here known as the "River Road," I began to run. On the two-lane highway, you could hear a car coming a minute before it was there, like a wave that crests, then washes past. No cars this time.

I had run this path many times before. Farther south, opposite the direction I was headed, the road follows the Río Grande's circuitous path and snakes through dramatic canyonlands that open up like a broken geode, finally concluding in Big Bend National Park. But here at the outset, in the small border town of Presidio, the view was less bombastic. Still, I never tired of it.

The highway was flanked by thorny mesquite and yellow creosote, their branches tangled and unpretty. A cardinal posted up on a telephone line, a prick of blood. It was springtime, and the cottontails bounded across the road with manic velocity; I'd hold my breath until they made it safely to the other side. The turkey vultures wheeled overhead, cruising on thermals.

I ran along the shoulder of the highway until I saw the sign demarcating the Presidio wetlands. These were man-made wetlands, a project spearheaded in 2015 by some of the Far West Texas town's residents. Using the effluent water from Presidio's wastewater system, they created a riparian habitat resembling the wetlands that used to exist all along the Río Grande—before irrigation and mining would undo these ecosystems, before the land became peopled.

Here along the river was evidence of its depletion. Invasive plants like the salt cedar, which was introduced by the United States in the early nineteenth century to prevent soil erosion, had narrowed the river's path and slowed its flow. The Río Grande, defying its name, was a motionless band of silty water, supplied mostly by the Rio Conchos, which runs from its headwaters in the Mexican state of Chihuahua, joining the Río Grande at the Presidio–Ojinaga border. *La junta*—the juncture, it's called.

Sasha von Oldershausen is an Iranian-American journalist who grew up in New York and lived in Presidio, Texas, while writing about immigration and the border. Her work has appeared in the *New York Times*, the *Atlantic*, *Harper's*, and the *Paris Review*. © Sasha von Oldershausen, 2019. Published by permission of Sasha von Oldershausen.

At the sign I turned onto the dirt road that descended upon the ten-acre wetlands' outer limit, connected to a path that ran along its length. The wetlands path ended at the levee, built in 2008 after a massive flood drowned most of the town's farmland. On the other side of the levee was the river, unpredictable and unyielding.

On days after rain, this dirt road was littered with prehistoric-looking millipedes dressed in tawny, segmented armor, who emerged from seven years underground for an opportunity to mate. They impassively pedaled hundreds of legs like gears in a machine, covering an impressive amount of ground from one minute to the next.

Normally, the descent was my favorite part. Like a scene out of *Jurassic Park*, the still desert suddenly transformed, teeming with a live replica of what had once existed there. Dozens of species of bird swooped overhead, crying out and skimming the recycled water with their webbed feet. It was amazing to see how far just a little bit of water could go.

But for the past several months, the wetlands had turned dry. City officials told me they were having issues with the salinity of the water. It was killing everything, they said. Most of the birds had already left. I held out hope for their return, and still each morning I ran.

I moved from my home in New York to the Far West Texas town of Presidio to work as a reporter on the US-Mexico border. Two thousand miles away, I was constantly seeking some connection to home and found myself drawn to the Río Grande, a life source that centuries-old civilizations had gravitated to for food, for water, for respite.

On the hottest days, we'd head to the river's pebbly banks to swim in its warm water that cooled us still, our hair and skin covered in a film of silt when we dried. The first time I floated the river in a kayak, I was reminded of its long, arterial history. Ancient-looking turkey vultures settled onto branches on either shore, all part of the same flock. Cliff swallows would build gourd-shaped nests out of the muddy banks. They'd pinch the earth with their beaks and spit it back out in sticky pellets in the bare, cavernous space beneath each bluff.

Through my work, I learned that within the past century and a half, the countries on either side of this river designated the Río Grande a line, and suddenly the water was political, too. But nature made a mockery of these human arbitrations; monsoon storms swept through, flooded the plains, and changed the river's course.

The Spanish word for storm is *tormenta*, an apt term to describe the drama of it all. During the late summer monsoon season, cumulus clouds would build all day, along with the heat, and turn a dark bluish gray by late afternoon. The sudden and impetuous rainfall drowned the land, causing flash floods and filling arroyos with fast-moving water that washed away roads and unearthed what lay beneath. The river flooded. By next morning, the millipedes would emerge from their seven-year slump. The skeletal ocotillo plant, like a bundle of doodled lines during the hot and dry summer months, would plump with leaves, blooming red at the tips like painted fingernails.

In the aftermath of these major storm events, officials from both countries scratched their heads as they were forced to reckon with the complications of using a natural resource that was fluid to designate a rigid border.

Another consequence of these politics, the river had become a place of separation—from family, from past lives, from violence—and sometimes, a grave. Migrants, attempting to cross the border, caught in its flux. Their bodies were found tangling in the river cane, bloated and blue.

Over time, my love of the desert grew. People will describe the desert with words that connote its harshness. Rugged. Caustic. Stark. I've used these words, too. But these words are wrong. It is delicate and discreet. Its subtlety shivers in breezes invisible to the touch. Nothing is slipshod; everything is precise. That plant exists over there because it could and it had to. The pads of the cacti, beneath their pricks, are as tender as an earlobe.

After living in Texas for long enough, my hair quite suddenly turned from wavy to straight. The skin around my eyes bloomed with creases from squinting at the sun. I continued to run, and my destination was always the river, where I stood at its banks watching the muddy surface. It seemed to me that the water gave as much as it took. I thought, the water is not like us. We take and we take until there's nothing left.

Once, after days of rain, I pulled over to the side of the River Road, where a path led to a clearing that offered a view of the rapids. The river was bigger than I'd ever seen it; water cascaded through, muddy and frothing and carrying bits of debris and mesquite branches, and I thought how easy it would be to drown.

On assignment, I illegally crossed over from a Texas border colony into Mexico with an undocumented woman named Clara and her granddaughter, Clarisa. The two towns, divided by the river, functioned as one—though there was no sanctioned way to cross directly—and Clara had houses on both sides. It was late summer, and when we crossed, the riverbed was parched; we walked across with ease.

In the Mexican town, Clara knocked on the door of a small adobe home on a hill. A middle-aged man opened the door smiling, and kissed her. I tried to mask my surprise. I'd only interacted with Clara at her home in Texas, and had assumed there was no man in her life. There, I learned she was married, only her husband lived across the river.

We ate lunch at her house, and after, she showed me outside to her yard, where she kept a bucket filled with stones. She filled a coffee can with water, submerged each stone, and wiped its surface with her thumb. She showed me how the inscribed lines of fossils—relics of the desert's aqueous past—would reveal themselves in the dark, wet shadows.

That afternoon, a violent storm blew through. Since there would be no way for us to cross the river, I stayed the night. With nowhere to go, I lay on a bed in one of the rooms, watching Clara by the light of the doorway as she mopped the wet that crept across the threshold.

The next morning, we walked to the riverbed that just a day earlier ran dry. Now it raged with water, murky with sediment. Clara led me to a couple of steel cables that hung across the width of the river, tethered to either side—my only means of crossing back over. Clara and Clarisa would stay in Mexico until the river subsided, but I couldn't wait. I took a step on the bottom line and clutched the top with my hands, sidling across and trembling and trying not to look down until I'd safely reached the other side.

The Big Bend region's mountains, banded by thick deposits of limestone and shale, serve as perpetual reminders of a history that precedes civilization and resounding evidence to those who reside here that a border wall—no more impassable than the mountains themselves—needn't exist.

At the Texas town-turned-golf resort, Lajitas, I reported on the Voices From Both Sides Festival. On this day, families displayed matching T-shirts as a show of solidarity. The festival drew hundreds from both sides of the US-Mexico border to the Río Grande's muddy banks. There, families and friends met in the middle of the river, an international boundary, to celebrate their cross-border community.

Jeff Haislip and Collie Ryan, residents on the Texas side, along with their friend from across the river, Ramón Garcia, founded the party in 2013 as a protest of the tightened border-security measures enacted after 9/11.

On a stage on the Texas side, musicians serenaded Mexico with songs about la frontera. Their faces gleamed with sweat as they withstood 100-plus-degree heat. Others found respite from the sun in the cool but murky river. A couple danced to cumbia music calf-deep in water, impervious to the hard stones beneath their feet.

A yellow line spanning the width of the river and tethered to either side provided a guide for those crossing. On the Mexican shore, vendors sold tacos, elote, and heaping bowls of fruit doused red with chile. On the Texas side, attendees brought aluminum trays filled with pasta salad, while others cooked burgers and frozen pizza on a flat grill. People crossed back and forth across the river freely and in clear sight.

Though the Border Patrol is aware of the annual celebration, there were no agents in sight. A handful of deputies from the Brewster County Sheriff's Office stood by nonchalantly, chatting amicably with attendees.

Historically, the swath of river between the two towns served as a key transit point. In the nineteenth century, the area became a trading post. Until 2002, the stretch between them was one of several unofficial ports of entry, where a lone boatman would ferry people across the river.

Some hold out hope that the port of entry will once again reopen. Others say they won't hold their breath. Or maybe this river will eventually dry, and only then the two sides will connect as one continuous stretch of parched earth, the sunken riverbed inscribed like a scar.

Running the Cañons of the Río Grande

by Robert T. Hill, 1901

*J*ust above Presidio the Rio Conchos enters the Río Grande from Chihuahua. This is a long stream, and brings the first permanent water to the main river. In fact, the Conchos is the mother stream of the Río Grande. Above the mouth of the Conchos, the Río Grande was a dry sand-bed. Below, it was a good stream one hundred feet wide, with a strong current, which was to carry us along at a rate of three miles an hour. At this season of the year, the Conchos is flooded by the summer rains that come from the Pacific. Our plans were based upon the assistance of one of these rises, and we were not disappointed. Two days after our arrival at Presidio the river rose a foot, giving exactly the desired stage of water.

At noon, October 5, 1899, we pushed out into the river at Presidio and started on our long journey into the unknown. Hardly had we begun to enjoy the pleasant sensation of drifting down the stream when a roaring noise was heard ahead. This came from seething and dangerous torrents of water foaming over huge rounded boulders of volcanic rock which everywhere formed the bottom of the river. Reaching the rapids, we had to get out of the boats and wade beside them, pushing them off or over the stones, or holding them back by their stern lines. This process had to be repeated many times a day for the entire distance, and, as a consequence, all hands were constantly wet. The swift current and uncertain footing of the hidden rocks made these rapids very dangerous. A loss of balance or a fall meant almost certain death. It was our very good fortune not to upset a boat or lose a man.

The second morning we reached the appropriately named village of Polvo ("dust"), the last settlement for 150 miles. It consists of half a dozen dreary adobe houses on a mud-bank, the remains of the old United States military post of Fort Leaton. A few miles below Polvo the huge chocolate-colored cliffs and domes of the Bofecillos Mountains began to overhang the river, and before

Robert T. Hill (1858–1941) was an early Texas geologist who mapped and named many formations, including the Balcones Fault Zone in Central Texas. In October 1899, he led an expedition to explore the little-known canyons of the Big Bend. Excerpted from *The Century Magazine*, January 1901.

night we entered the first of the series of cañons of the Río Grande, in which we were to be entombed for the succeeding weeks.

This and the Fresno Cañon, a few miles below, are vertical cuts about six hundred feet deep through massive walls of red volcanic rock. All the other cañons are of massive limestone. The rocks are serrated into vertical columns of jointed structure, and when touched by the sunlight become a golden yellow. The sky-line is a ragged crest, with many little side cañons nicking the profile. When evening came we were glad to camp on a narrow bank of sandy silt between the river and its walls. Lying upon our backs and relieved of the concentration of our wits upon the cares of navigation, we were able to study and appreciate the beauties of this wild gorge.

The river itself, here as everywhere, is a muddy yellow stream. In places, patches of fine white silt form bordering sand-bars; about twenty-five feet above these, there is a second bench, covered by a growth of dark green mesquite. The whole is enclosed by vertically steep, jointed rock walls. The thread of water and the green ribbon of the mesquite bench are refreshing sights, for immediately above the latter, on both sides, the desert vegetation always sets in.

Toward sunset I scaled a break in the cañon to reach the upland and obtain a lookout. Above the narrow alluvial bench forming the green ribbon of river verdure, I suddenly came upon the stony, soilless hills forming the matrix out of which the valley is cut, glaring in the brilliant sunshine and covered with the mocking desert flora. The sight of this aridity almost within reach of the torrent of life-giving waters below, the blessing of which it was never to receive, was shocking and repulsive. It also recalled a danger which ever after haunted us. Should we lose our boats and escape the cañons, what chance for life should we have in crossing these merciless, waterless wastes of thorn for a hundred miles or more to food and succor?

The Big River is Kept in a Stone Box

by Sandra Lynn

1.

Inside the canyon
mounds   green as the graves of saints
                jewel the river's verge.

(Picture the saints embarking.
Robed in white
                        desert chieftains
their breath like pollen
                                they ride the rapids in balsam boats.
Craning their necks, leaning over the gunwales
they adore the cathedral walls
                the towering sanctuaries of light and
                                wheeling hawk
                the river pale as the thoughts of the dying
                        honey worked out of a box hive.
They go gloriously and intently
                to splinters
                                so as never to leave.)

Sandra Lynn (1944–2013) was a poet from Jacksonville, Texas, who taught at universities in Texas and New Mexico. From *Where Rainbows Wait for Rain: The Big Bend Country*, poems by Sandra Lynn. Tangram Press, 1989. Published by permission of the Center for Southwest Research, University of New Mexico.

2.

the river   however   is no saint
look at this stupendous heave of wall
chewed clear through!
obviously this humble old rio
with its muddy knuckles
knocking on the lowest doors of the stones
possesses   hidden
a devilish   handsome
set of teeth

Rafting the Big Bend

by Edwin "Bud" Shrake

I am having a hard time reading this notebook because it got very wet, but I can remember that it was about a year ago when Don Kennard asked if I would like to paddle a canoe ninety-odd miles down the Río Grande through what he promised would be spectacular canyons. He asked it one sultry midnight at a party in Austin, Texas. At that hour almost anything sounds like a wonderful idea, and I have promised to do a lot of things then that I never got around to. A little twang inside my head told me Kennard wouldn't forget about this in the morning, but I kept listening anyhow.

"We're going to see, feel, taste, and record that section of the river," he said, flushed with what I assume was enthusiasm. "We'll be the first working scientific expedition to go through there since the Hill Expedition in 1899. There are thousands of prehistoric Indian sites no scientist has ever looked at, and Lord knows how many rare plants to be found, and the geology is fantastic. Besides that, there are some pretty good rapids to run, and some good old boys to sit around the fire with, and at night the stars are right in your face."

Kennard is a robust, speckle-bearded fellow in his early forties who played football at North Texas State University and was for twenty years a member of the Texas legislature, where he set a senate filibuster record of twenty-nine hours, twenty-two minutes. To use up the time, he proposed a Texas Hall of Heroes and discussed 460 candidates for membership before two senators finally surrendered the votes he wanted. Now Kennard was with the Lyndon B. Johnson School of Public Affairs, working on a wilderness preservation project.

"We're going to explore the area in more than a cursory way," Kennard said. "It'll be a trip you'll never forget, you can count on that. How much do you know about canoeing?"

"You paddle on one side and then the other."

Edwin "Bud" Shrake (1931–2009) wrote the classic Texas novels *Blessed McGill* and *Strange Peaches*. He was also a Hollywood screenwriter, a literary journalist at *Sports Illustrated*, a Willie Nelson biographer, and coauthor of *Harvey Penick's Little Red Book*, the best-selling sports book in history. Originally appeared as "Rapids Round the Bend" in *Sports Illustrated*, April 15, 1974. Also appears in *Land of the Permanent Wave: An Edwin "Bud" Shrake Reader*, edited by Steven L. Davis. University of Texas Press, 2008. Published by permission of Ben Shrake.

"Sure. It's easy. You'll catch on. When you turn over, what the hell, every-body does."

"Everybody turns over?"

"Sooner or later everybody tumps over. Nothing to worry about if you don't get caught under the canoe against a rock or hurt yourself too bad. What do you say? Got the sporting blood?"

"Sounds like a wonderful idea to me."

Kennard didn't forget. He phoned and brought over a couple of US Marine surplus waterproof packs. "Here's how this thing started," he said while I was wondering what to put into the packs besides my knife and sleeping bag. "The Parks and Wildlife Commission, the General Land Office, and the Texas Historical Commission asked the LBJ School to conduct a survey of areas of Texas that should be preserved. So we're beginning to look at fourteen natural and rare sites and write them up from the standpoints of botany, archaeology, zoology, and geology. Graduate students from all over the state will follow up and do a more thorough job on what we begin.

"In the next five or ten years, we hope to cover 150 sites that should be protected as parks or wilderness areas. But this is the first one."

A few days later, I drove to the home of Anders Saustrup, field director of the Rare Plants Study Center of the University of Texas, and threw my two waterproof packs in the back of a pickup truck hitched to a trailer hauling six aluminum canoes. "See you on the river," Kennard said. He and a geologist got into a truck for the all-night drive down to Black Gap at the edge of the Big Bend. I was to fly down the next day with Texas Land Commissioner Bob Armstrong in his Beechcraft Bonanza. The weather was clear and warm. A lovely Texas spring.

> The trip [from Black Gap through the canyons] could be disastrous if someone broke a leg. There would be no way to get an injured person out other than to float out over a period of several days. It would be extremely difficult to float an injured person out in a canoe without capsizing several times. The discomfort of being thrown into the rapids with a crudely splinted broken leg can hardly be described. For this reason, my strict instructions to members of the expedition before leaving are don't break no legs.
>
> —Bill Kugle, member of the Texas Explorers Club and a Peggy Eaton founder.

> EMERGENCY EXIT FROM THE CANYONS: The Border Patrol flies these canyons every few days, and you could possibly signal them with a mirror.
>
> —Bob Burleson, member of the Parks and Wildlife Commission.

"I hear Anders has refused to let women go on this trip," said the hostess at a dinner party. "You know why? Macho stuff, that's why. He doesn't want to be sitting at the Scholz Garten drinking beer and bragging and suddenly hear some girlish voice pipe up, 'Oh, I did that trip last Easter. Isn't it fun?'"

"Well, I saw some of the canoes today," I said.

"How'd they look?"

"They had a lot of dents."

The lovely Texas spring suddenly turned nasty. It began raining before dawn. At noon Bob Armstrong called. "How's your courage quotient?" he said.

"I'll just let it ride along with yours."

"I don't mind this rain," Armstrong said. "Flying on instruments is fine. But there's a few thunderstorms between here and Pecos. It probably won't be too bad. It just won't be good, is all."

The General Land Office in Texas controls 22 million acres of land and mineral resources, an area larger than Maine and only slightly smaller than Indiana. Armstrong, who is about forty, was elected land commissioner in 1970. He rides a motorcycle to the office, skis, backpacks into the mountains, plays the guitar, raises cattle, is a good photographer and a good canoeist. His wife, Shannon, used to teach canoeing someplace. The words that would have told me where she taught are a blue muddle now in my notebook.

A young woman from the Land Office picked me up in her car. "Last year they took twenty canoes down that part of the river you're going on," she said cheerfully. "Only three or four didn't turn over. I think Kennard turned over twice."

We stopped at a big white wooden house on a street with many trees. Stephen Spurr, the president of the University of Texas, came to the door and looked out at the rain. "Some of these guys may not be very well organized, but we'll bungle through and have a good time," Spurr said. "I've canoed about all the canoeable rivers in Michigan and Minnesota. Been on a lot of float trips around the country. But I can't say I'm an expert white water canoeist. It's by guess and by God with me. How about you?"

"I can't remember whether I've ever actually been in a canoe before."

"Oh. Well. You're in for an interesting time, aren't you?"

Spurr is a forester with a PhD from Yale. He taught and did field research for nineteen years at the University of Michigan. Later he became a compromise dean at Michigan following a campus political struggle. He was hired by Texas in the midst of another political fight, which at the time of our trip was nowhere near over. Spurr picked up a small bag, put on a straw farmer's hat, and kissed his wife. "If they fire me here," he said, "we can go back to the woods and be just as happy."

The two-and-a-half-hour flight to a landing strip on a ranch outside the town of Marathon wasn't bad, considering it rained most of the way and the plane iced up. Clifton Caldwell met us at the airstrip with his truck. He is the chairman of the Texas Historical Commission and a West Point graduate who owns a ranch outside of Albany, Texas, on the Clear Fork of the Brazos River. "My nearest neighbor is eleven miles," Caldwell said, "and it's thirty-five miles from my house to a bottle of beer."

The truck sped along a highway cut through greasewood and cactus. The mountains turned gold and purple in the dusk, and beyond, higher mountains rose across the river in Mexico. Caldwell told about driving into this area looking for a place called Stillwell Crossing. "At the river we ran into a snaggletoothed old man and asked if we were at Stillwell Crossing. The old man said if we had an airplane, we could just fly right over that mountain and be there in no time. If we didn't have an airplane, go seventy-five miles back down the road and turn left. The old man thought that was really funny."

We entered Black Gap and descended on a rough road toward the river at Maravillas Canyon. "This is about as remote a place as you can find in Texas," Spurr said. Up ahead we saw a campfire. We could hear the river. The first rapids of the trip was fifty yards away.

Most of the others were standing round the fire. They were playing guitars and harmonicas, singing, talking, drinking whiskey. But always we could hear the river like a wind blowing.

"You done much canoeing?" Caldwell asked me.

"None."

Caldwell nodded. What I didn't know at the time was that he had read a Sierra Club report on the trip we were about to take. It dwelt on the difficulties and dangers of the river, warned that under no circumstances should the trip be attempted by a lone canoe, and said no one should paddle that stretch of the Río Grande who was not an expert canoeist in excellent physical condition.

If I had seen that report, there might not have been a story like this.

The Río Grande rises at the Continental Divide in southern Colorado and flows 1,800 miles into the Gulf of Mexico. It goes south down the center of New Mexico, enters Texas at El Paso, and turns southeast to form the border between Texas and Mexico. At the Big Bend, the Río Grande turns and runs north, northeast, and east for more than 200 miles before dropping southeast again. Most of our trip would be north and northeast. It seemed to me it would be harder to paddle north than south, but what did I know? I was assured it wouldn't make any difference unless a good north wind came down into our faces.

Long stretches of the river are often dry enough to walk across. Farmers in New Mexico irrigate from the Río Grande. Santa Fe, Albuquerque, Las Cruces, and El Paso, among other cities, take water from it. The Rio Conchos flows from Mexico to replenish the Río Grande at Presidio, but Mexico has built a dam on the Rio Conchos to irrigate sections of the Chihuahua Desert. The Mexicans pretty well control the level of the Río Grande for hundreds of miles through the Big Bend. After the river turns south again, past Langtry, another big dam at Del Rio creates the Amistad Reservoir, an enormous, twisty lake that looks like a tidelands bay.

Some of the canyons on the river have never been named on official documents. The area we were to go through is usually called Reagan Canyon, or Bullis Canyon, although in fact several canyons enter the river there. The walls are steep, and there is seldom a place to climb out. Where the canyons are less vertical, an occasional smugglers' trail may be seen. There is a steady, illegal business in smuggling the candelilla plant into Texas for the making of high-grade candle wax. Now and then you come across remains of a camp marked by the presence of fifty-gallon drums used for boiling down the wax. The occasional goat herder's camp is always empty, although the coals may be warm. Marijuana and peyote no doubt come through there sometimes, but it is difficult country for a smuggler to cross.

Temperatures in the Big Bend go up to 140 degrees in the summer and down below freezing in winter. This was April, and I figured it would be hot all day and cool at night. But the cold look of the rainy morning back in Austin had persuaded me to borrow a long underwear top. God bless it. The first morning at the camp on the river, I was huddled behind a truck with a coffee cup shaking in my hands. My sleeping bag lay crumpled in dark, wet grass. I was wearing everything I had brought with me. Palms red from the hot cup but fingers blue. We were camped beside a huge midden, a mound of dirt, stones, and cooking utensils built up by Indians over centuries. Anders Saustrup walked past in a T-shirt, suspenders, and baggy pants, brushing his teeth.

"What the hell is this with the T-shirt?" I said. "Don't you realize it's about to snow?"

"It's not cold. It's very nice weather. Beautiful weather, in fact," said Anders, fog blowing out of his mouth.

Anders was born in Denmark. What business does a Dane have telling a native-born Texan whether it's cold or not? This might have been a pleasant spring morning on the Arctic Circle, but for this time of year in Texas, it was cold. I could hear that first rapids roaring. Caldwell came by wearing a yellow rain suit. I asked if he thought it was cold. "The water sure will be," he said.

My first canoe partner was Bill O'Brien, a young, hairy-faced architectural engineer from Fort Worth. He is a son of Davey O'Brien, who was an All-American quarterback at TCU and set passing records for the Philadelphia Eagles thirty years ago. Bill went to the University of Wyoming and likes to climb mountains. He didn't let on if he was worried we might dash into the rocks.

"After the first two rapids, you'll know what to do," said Jenkins Garrett. "Just remember when you run into cane and salt-cedar branches that grow over the river, don't pull away from them and upset the canoe. If you hit something in the water, lean forward, downstream."

In the morning light, the air was so clear that mountains across the river in Mexico looked fake. The dry air does tricks with distances. Canyons that appear only 500 feet high will in truth be three times that high. A wall you think you can hit with a rock you might not be able to reach with an arrow.

We put into the river just up from Maravillas Creek, which is 100 miles long, has a bed that would accommodate the Hudson, and is usually dry. Bill and I looked at the narrow, boiling channel of the rapids. "Might as well," he said. We got up a bit of speed, entered the current, and whanged into a rock. There was a scraping sound like tin tearing. The current began to swing the canoe broadside to the flow of the river. "Use your paddle like a lever," Bill yelled. I stuck my paddle between the boat and the rock and yanked. We popped loose from the rock, shot down the channel, crashed through some overhanging cane, and were past the first rapids. It was not one of the monster rapids of North America, but I will remember it fondly.

The second rapids, we raked bottom rocks. The third, we went too far left, and I shoved at a boulder with my hands as we slid quickly past. It was not a classic move. But anything you need to do to keep a boulder from knocking you into the water has to be acceptable.

By now it was warm enough to peel off my windbreaker, wool shirt, and long underwear top. The water moved us along with easy paddling. The land, called Outlaw Flats, was fairly level for a while before it climbed toward the mountains. Up ahead in Mexico was a sheer, flat-topped butte that shone red in the morning sun; it is known as El Capitan and is supposed to hold a clue to a lost mine.

Several little girls and a woman were fishing on the Texas bank. Were they, too, intrepid explorers? A man and his son had pulled their outboard onto a gravel bar a mile farther on. "You turn over yet?" the man yelled in greeting.

During the day we stopped and climbed a rocky slope. Curtis Tunnell, the state archaeologist, pointed out broken Indian tools on a large midden. Round mortar holes had been dug into the rock for the grinding of grain. Flints lay on prehistoric scraping sites. Buzzards floated above the river. Marshall Johnston, a University of Texas botanist who had been working for months in the Chihuahua Desert, which is nearly as large as all of Texas, pulled up a wild tobacco plant with yellow blossoms. Creosote bushes and candelilla grew all around. Dr. Johnston broke open a plant called leatherwood, or dragonroot, which Indians used as eye medicine. It pours blood when uprooted.

Then we entered the canyons. First the wall rose on the Mexican side, and we hit some rapids. Then the wall of Reagan Canyon soared on the Texas bank. For the next forty miles, we would be in the canyons, and the walls would get higher and closer as we went downstream. When we landed to make camp, I dragged my two US Marine surplus waterproof packs up the bank onto a grassy bluff and began to unload them. Packing is a tedious chore, especially when done in the cold early morning. The straps make your fingers bleed. Unpacking is a lot better. When you dig toward the cognac bottle and the sleeping bag, you feel you're getting something done.

I spread my air mattress and sleeping bag and looked at the stuff I had brought. Knife, mess kit, spoon, cup, water jug, canteen, three paperback books, two pairs of Levi's, sneakers, windbreaker, two T-shirts, one wool shirt, long underwear, tape recorder, batteries, life jacket, straw hat, towel, two Flair pens, a notebook, three cassettes (including, accidentally, an old tape of Janis Joplin singing in Austin at Kenneth Threadgill's birthday party where a girl got bit by a rattlesnake, and another old tape of Tom Landry talking about God and football).

And food, of course. Kennard and I were splitting rations. We had cans of chili, cans of Salisbury steak, cans of stew, a bag of rice, many boxes of raisins, milk chocolate, vegetable soup cubes, powdered potatoes, onions, Vienna sausages, potted meat, and crackers. I looked at that mound of food lying there, patted my sleeping bag, and knew a great contentment.

Then I looked around the camp. My God, it was Brasilia! Orange and yellow and green and blue nylon tents had sprung up everywhere. Inside the tents were air mattresses and puffy sleeping bags and hunks of foam rubber and candle lamps for warmth and light. All over the place, little Swiss cooking stoves were burning.

Bill O'Brien was preparing a hot meatloaf dinner with vegetables. Jenks Garrett and his son Jenkins Jr. were dining on soup, tea, lasagna, and banana pudding. Dr. Spurr and Clifton Caldwell had opened a crate packed with dry ice and removed a couple of filet mignons for dinner. Except that he scorned the use of a tent, Dr. Spurr was elaborately equipped for the trip. I asked him at different times for tweezers, a hand lens, suntan lotion, a saw, a can opener, a Brillo pad. He had them all. He even had packets of sugar from the Coconut Grove, Ambassador Hotel, 1968 Rose Bowl. The only thing I asked for that he didn't have was a piece of watermelon.

But where had all this stuff come from? How had they crammed it into the canoes? Well, a whole pot of lasagna with plenty of meat fits into an envelope now.

The cooking stove folds into nothing much. You can almost stick a new sleeping bag into your coat pocket. A tent doesn't take up as much room as a pillow. But I had not been into a sporting goods store in a long time, and my old sleeping bag occupied as much space as Alex Karras doubled over.

In the middle of the night, the wind struck. Tents clapped and wires whined. The wind itself sounded like rushing water. "The Mexicans have let water out of the Rio Conchos!" someone yelled. But no, it was just a blue norther. It was what a friend of mine would call semi-miserable. In fact, it was halfway an ordeal. It was cold to begin with, and the wind wouldn't let up. As we went down the river again, the wind stayed in our faces. We had to dig water to move. I was thinking I wouldn't do this again for $1,000.

In the afternoon we came to Arroyo San Rocendo, the biggest canyon entering the Río Grande from Mexico. We had passed the Asa Jones pump house, a cabin stuck against the top of a steep cliff, with broken water pipes sticking down toward the river. Bill O'Brien climbed to the top, just as he later scaled a cliff to rescue a baby goat trapped on a ledge. After the pump house, we heard the rumble of rapids around a sandstone corner. At San Rocendo is Big Hot Springs Rapids, named for the hot springs on the Mexican shore.

They say it is not advisable to run Big Hot Springs. We got out and lined our canoes down through the rocks to a pool between two sections of the rapids. It was hard, wet work, crawling over slippery boulders, dragging canoes and equipment. When the last canoe was in the pool, we were tired and shivering.

I found a place that was sheltered on three sides by thickets and a cliff. Kennard set up his tent to block the wind from the fourth side. We built a large mesquite fire. Down by the river, a hot spring opened into a natural rock tub about fifteen feet across. We soaked in the spring for a while. For dinner we heated cans of chili, chopped a couple of onions, and cooked some rice on the fire and then stirred the mess up in a pan. It was as good as anything I ever tasted.

For the first time on the trip, I used enough breath to blow up my air mattress; I wrapped my life jacket in a towel for a pillow. Stuffed with chili, rice, and onions, smoothed out by a little bourbon and a cigar, I lay in my bag just outside the firelight, listening to the talk, hearing the river and the wind. The stars were down in my face, all right. Orion, the Pleiades, Arcturus, the North Star, the Big Dipper. Moonlight spread over the canyon wall high up. Whoever said this was an ordeal?

I changed over to Bob Armstrong's canoe the fourth day out. We were going to catch up with some canoes that had gotten far ahead. Bill O'Brien wanted to hang back with the scientists. Armstrong was a little bothered because I weigh a lot more than he does, and also because he didn't want to turn over with his $1,400 worth of camera equipment. But he kept up a cheerful attitude about it.

"I guess you know how to reach and pry," he said as we set out alone.

"What's that?"

"To reach, you reach out with the paddle and draw it toward the boat. If you reach to the right, it swings the front end to the right. To pry, you push out with the paddle, and the boat moves in the other direction. If you don't mind my asking, how did you manage to come forty or fifty miles without knowing that?"

Up ahead was a noisy rapids. Armstrong stood in the rear of the canoe to study the flow. I thought you were never supposed to stand in a canoe. The good canoeists appear to do it whenever they want to. "Hit this one on the left and go like hell," Armstrong said. The canoe leaped ahead. Armstrong cried for me to pry on the left, and I did. It was like a miracle. This boulder that I would probably have poked with the paddle or shoved desperately with my hands, this boulder flew past inches away with a satisfying hiss and gurgle. Then we were bouncing in haystack waves and spray. Then we paddled hard in an eddy before coasting in a current.

"See what I mean?" said Armstrong.

It had taken me several hours the first day to realize the person in the bow could help at all, steering in the rapids rather than merely providing locomotion. The person in the rear is the captain. He does most of the steering, and if the person in front does not stay alert and keep glancing back, the captain is liable to rest too much. But now this new knowledge about reach and pry gave me power. So an hour later, we cracked into a rock and turned sideways. The canoe filled with water. We jumped out and fought to keep the boat from going over. You figure a canoe full of water weighs about a ton. Put the force of the current against it, and you can see why it is nice to have several people around to help.

We wrestled the canoe to shore and began bailing. Armstrong hammered out the dent. I had learned one lesson I didn't know I had learned until that night. The lesson is, no matter how cold and early it is in the morning, don't be sloppy in packing your waterproof bag.

Some things have blurred in my mind, but I remember a few places very well. I remember castle rock formations, keyholes to the sky 1,500 feet above our heads, side canyons hardly wide enough for a man to walk into. I remember climbing to a cave where the ceiling was black with centuries of cooking smoke and the floor deep in stones and scraping tools. There was a Campbell's soup can near the entrance.

Most of the rapids are no longer distinct to me. I can't even recall at which rapids the notebook escaped from my pocket and tumbled into the current. We found it 200 yards downstream. At another rapids I knocked off my eyeglasses while changing hands with my paddle but reached back with my left hand and grabbed the glasses as they disappeared under water. All my life I have been dropping things with my right hand and catching them with my left before they hit the floor.

Into the wind again. All day long. Hands have swollen and their backs split open. Neck and shoulders are riddled with needles. Keep head down, stare at water. Think about Oxford vs. Cambridge on the Thames. Terrible idea. Clang, bang, hit a rock, the hell with it. We run a rapids near a sandbar, and the wind blows sand into our faces. You can run a rapids and get a dirty face? Armstrong remarks that adventure and fun are not necessarily the same. For a mile ahead, I can see whitecaps whipped up not from current but from wind. I discover something. Each stroke appears to move us three feet. That means 1,760 strokes will move us through these whitecaps. If the wind keeps up for the thirty miles left to go, that's only 52,800 strokes to home, boy. Let's hit it. That's two . . . three . . .

"If you start counting strokes, you'll go crazy," Armstrong says.

In all, the expedition examined more than sixty historic and prehistoric Indian sites that had never before been officially recorded. Archaeologist Curtis Tunnell says Indians occupied the canyons for at least 12,000 years. About the only litter they left was burnt rocks, pieces of flint, dried bones. At one place the floor of a cave is deep in buffalo bones. It is near a cliff off which the Indians used to stampede the beasts. When you sift through the floor of the cave, you find a 4,000-year gap between layers of buffalo bones. That means either the Indians forgot how to stampede buffaloes for a long time or else the buffaloes went away for 4,000 years. It is less than one hundred years now since the last great buffalo slaughters of the West. So maybe buffaloes will come back again sometime.

Of the 6,000 species of plants that grow in Texas, about fifty are found only along the river. Each time one of those species dies out, it disappears from the earth. The Rare Plants Center puts exotic plants of this sort in courthouse squares, garden club plots, and state parks, as well as greenhouses. "Of course, the only rational way to preserve the plants is to preserve their habitats," says Marshall Johnston, director of the center. He took more than 200 plant samples on the river and in the canyons. To protect the canyons, the state could buy scenic easements along the river, or the Department of Interior could declare the river a wild scenic area. But something else that might happen is that a third Río Grande dam may be built at Sanderson Canyon. If it is, everything we saw will be gone except the tops of the canyons.

On our last night on the river, after laboring into the wind all day, we camped on a knoll and waited for the wind to die after dark. But it kept on blowing. Caldwell and Spurr fried the last of their steaks and shared them. I found a spot where the wind was muffled by a canebrake and the rock wall. I settled into my bag, and then I heard a little scrabbling noise in the cane. Borrowing a flashlight, I saw I was lying beside a tunnel about five feet high that had been trod through the cane. Wild pigs, maybe. Deer, coons, coyotes, no telling what all. I moved over two feet and went to sleep happy and incredibly comfortable.

I read the Sierra Club story about the ferocious rapids and the need for physical conditioning. Caldwell and I talked it over. We decided the rapids and the paddling had been strenuous but not what you would call supremely difficult.

"I guess we're finished with the bad rapids," Caldwell said.

"Only one really tough one left," said Armstrong.

"I don't see it on the map."

"That's why it's known as Horrible Surprise Rapids," Armstrong said.

For the final few miles, the wind lowered, and we paddled lightly. Terns flew in formation above our heads. Thousands of swallows skimmed the river, dipped their beaks in the water, and collected mud from the bank to build nests against the cliffs. The land was spreading out on either side. And there it was ahead of us: the Texaco sign nailed to a tree that marked the take-out place, Dudley Harrison's camp.

Only one more rapids. We drifted into some rocks and got out to look. The current swung close against a rock outcrop. Spurr and Caldwell got into their canoe and went into the rapids. They clattered against the outcrop. Spurr's paddle left his hands and looked glued to the wall for an instant. He grabbed it again, and they headed to shore. Armstrong and I had a choice of running the rapids or walking the canoe through a few feet of very shallow water. We walked.

We drove in Caldwell's truck for an hour across dusty brown land, scaring up a few sheep that took off toward the mountains. We stopped at a general store in the town of Dryden. The owner wore a baseball cap. "Wouldn't be surprised if you fellas got kind of cold on the river," he said. "Had a big freeze the last few days. Wiped everything out. Hell, it snowed over in Alpine."

We ate at the Big Bend Cafe in Marathon. Caldwell placed what he said is his usual order at a place that serves Tex-Mex food—six enchiladas and three tamales. They didn't have any tamales, but they brought the enchiladas stacked up on the plate like a mound of pancakes. I had three enchiladas, three tacos, tortillas, butter, and a little bowl of jalapeño peppers. As we were leaving, the woman behind the counter asked if we were some kind of a scientific outfit. We said yes ma'am, we were about halfway scientific.

"Then you must've heard about it," she said. "Down the road south of here, they just dug up a sixty-foot-long monster skeleton with a big fang buried in its neck. You didn't hear about it? Well, go down there right now and look at it. Tell them Sally at Marathon sent you."

The Pecos River

We came 12 miles over very good roads through the mesquite brush to the Horse Head Crossing on the Pecos River, a nasty, dirty, muddy, ugly stream. Everything within two or three miles around is burned up with alkali, and the dead cattle lay thick on the banks of the river. We dip up the water and put it in the barrels for the dirt to settle to the bottom, then use the water for cooking and drinking. They have to take the horses two miles from camp to get grass.

—Ruth Galloway Shackleford, 1868

The Pecos is a long river, a strange river, a thousand miles of twisting canyon from the pine-clad mountains of New Mexico to the gray, bleak bluffs of the Río Grande on the Texas border. . . . The mountainous breaks, the alkali flats, the vast stretches of shifting sands, the treeless plains rolling out to far away hills—the Pecos world, despite narrow strips of irrigated land, will not be plowed up or, save around isolated oil fields, transformed by the structures of population.

—J. Frank Dobie, from *Coronado's Children: Tales of Lost Mines and Buried Treasures of the Southwest*

Ruth Galloway Shackleford (1833–1870) was born in Missouri and migrated to California with her husband and children after the Civil War. Her journal entries were later published in *Covered Wagon Women*, vol. 9: *Diaries and Letters from the Western Trails, 1864–1868*, compiled and edited by Kenneth L. Holmes.

J. Frank Dobie (1888–1964) published the bestselling *Coronado's Children* in 1930 and is often credited as the father of Texas literature. He was also a courageous fighter for civil rights, the environment, and intellectual freedom, proclaiming, "I have come to value liberated minds as the supreme good of life on earth."

Larry McMurtry (1936–2021) was the author of numerous novels, nonfiction books, and screenplays, most of which focused on the American West. Several of his novels were adapted into major films, including his Pulitzer Prize–winning *Lonesome Dove*. McMurtry won an Academy Award as the coauthor of the screenplay for *Brokeback Mountain*.

Texas is rich in unredeemed dreams, and now that the dust of its herds is settling, the writers will be out on their pencils, looking for them in the suburbs and along the mythical Pecos. And except to paper riders, the Pecos is a lonely and a bitter stream.

—Larry McMurtry, from *In a Narrow Grave: Essays on Texas*

Thoughts along the River

by Suzanne O'Bryan

*I*n spite of the truths that plague the Pecos, my days and nights of living near the river several miles south of the famous crossing at Fort Lancaster provide a life very different from the Natives of 9,000 years ago, or that of the Comanche and Apache who hunted and gathered for their livelihood, and more recently from the difficulties experienced by my O'Bryan and Johnson ancestors.

Today fences have been strung where herds of buffalo and cattle, a little over 150 years ago, freely wandered the mighty open range. Sheep and goats now climb the hillsides, and the vegetation has been altered drastically—from what was once grassland to mesquite, cedar, and scrub. In many places the river's boundaries have shrunk significantly from its once thirty-feet-wide expanses to a shallow stream or dry bed. The Pecos continues to be brown and muddy and is still inaccessible in most locations due to its steep walled banks. I cannot help but think about my ancestors who attempted to make a living on the Pecos River and most probably have watched the sun and moon rise and set behind these same hills.

This is the same Pecos River of historical lore that today provides me a place of solace and contemplation. It allows the opportunity for thoughts to flow beyond the present physical world. At the river there is a sense of time passing and also a sense of time standing still. There is the sense of the cycle of Life—that is, of transition, of life, death, and rebirth—for no matter how many transitions the Pecos has encountered, the river continues to flow onward for hundreds of miles from its origin in New Mexico until it joins the Río Grande.

Suzanne O'Bryan is an artist and writer based in Alpine, Texas. Her memoir, *Thoughts along the River* (Chengalera Press, 2004), is about her life as a single woman ranching along the Pecos River.

The Pecos
River of Misery and Mythology

by Andrew Sansom

We camped in a roadside park on Interstate 10 near its crossing of the Pecos River on a chilly Friday evening. My previous experience with the Pecos had been at its headwaters north of Santa Fe in New Mexico's Sangre de Cristo Mountains fishing for big rainbow and brown trout in crystal-clear waters. Here at I-10, the river bore no resemblance to that sparkling flow due to impacts both natural and human-made along its nearly thousand-mile journey to the Río Grande. These forces, from extensive withdrawal for irrigation in New Mexico to intense sedimentation, have reduced the pristine mountain stream to a putrid trickle in Texas.

My friend and colleague Duncan Muckelroy, who at that time was superintendent of the Guadalupe River State Park, had called to inform me that the Pecos was running high due to recent rainfall in its watershed. The river, which typically barely flows through this stretch of the Chihuahuan Desert, would thus be in ideal condition for a weekend white water adventure. I'd been running a lot of rivers in those days but had never gotten a chance to explore the Pecos, a river rich in myth and history.

Shortly after daybreak on Saturday morning, Duncan and I drove to the historic river crossing outside of Fort Lancaster. We were joined by his sons Coby and Lance along with my son, Andrew. We eased our canoes into the rushing water and began one of the more memorable and calamitous canoe trips of my life.

Most of the Pecos's river miles are in Texas, although by the time it gets to the Lone Star State, its flow is not only dramatically diminished; its sediment load is so high that its water is foul and so dirty that maps of the nineteenth century referred to the Pecos as the "Puerco," meaning "pig" but also "foul and nasty." Actually, although there are a number of theories as to the origin of its name, the most likely is that it was derived from a native pueblo near the headwaters in New Mexico.

In Texas, most of its length lies in what has been called the "despoblado," or "empty land." It is here that a large and rich portion of Texas literature and folklore originates. Western writers have often focused on the bleak landscape, seeing the Pecos as the place "where the west begins." Among them is Zane Grey, in his *West of the Pecos*:

"Up and down the Pecos for miles, the strange river had worn a deep channel through dull red soil, and the places where cattle could get down to drink were not many . . . This wild Pecos country, bare grass spots alternating with scaly patches, greasewood and cactus contrasting with the gray of rocks, winding ridge and winding canyon all so monotonous and lonely, rolling endlessly down from the west to the river, trolling endlessly up toward the east, on and on, a vast wasteland apparently extending to infinitude."

It is clear that the Pecos has always been a formidable barrier, or "barricade," that forms the southwestern boundary of the Great Plains and the Comanchería. Bison would not cross, and men did only at their own peril. As early as 1583, Spanish explorers descended the river and, upon reaching the region now called the Trans Pecos, named it the "Rio de los Vaca," or "River of Cows," due to the huge herds of Buffalo that appeared on its Eastern banks.

In 1866, Charles Goodnight and Oliver Loving drove the first herd of cattle to the Pecos, creating a trail through New Mexico and ultimately to Colorado and Wyoming. They reached the Pecos at an infamous point on the river known as Horsehead Crossing—due to the large numbers of equine skulls on its banks. It was a blistering summer day, and their herd of Texas longhorns had walked nearly eighty miles without a drink. The animals were so thirsty, they became "wild for water," wrote historian J. Evetts Haley. When the cattle "reached the river, those behind pushed the ones in the lead right on across before they had time to stop and drink." Goodnight and Loving lost one hundred head that day.

On that first cattle drive up the Pecos, Goodnight and Loving contended with more than thirst, including an infestation of rattlesnakes and a Comanche attack. Later, in 1885, a horrible winter pushed thousands of free-ranging cattle south toward the Pecos, where they fell in such numbers that the river was dammed with their carcasses. There were so many dead cattle in the river that cowboys drank coffee "strained through gunny sacks to get the maggots out of it," wrote Patrick Dearen in *A Cowboy on the Pecos*.

According to Haley, Goodnight came to hate the river, calling it "the grave-yard of the cowboy's hopes." He described the Pecos region as "the most desolate country I have ever explored."

Our party was now running this same river in flood stage. Duncan and I shared a canoe, and at first, the journey was exhilarating. The weather was cooperative, and the landscape was stark and foreboding but beautiful at the same time. The river was flying . . . and so were we. Our takeout would be Pandale, fifty-eight miles downstream. There was no turning back.

Then everything went to hell. Racing along in the Pecos floodwaters, Duncan and I entered a very steep box canyon. The sheer-cliffed walls pressed close in on us. We had hardly entered the narrow gorge when we saw a ninety-degree turn to the left. Digging in, we churned through the bend and avoided slamming our canoe into a cliff. As we flew around the blind turn, we suddenly saw a deadly obstacle ahead: a single strand of barbed wire was stretched across the river—just about neck high.

Many authors have written about the Pecos marking the beginning of the West, but it is surely the larger-than-life characters, real and imaginary, who have cemented its place in literary history. The most notorious of these was the mythical cowboy Pecos Bill, who, legend has it, as an infant, fell out of a covered wagon heading west near the river and was raised by coyotes. Pecos Bill used a rattlesnake as a lasso, rode mountain lions instead of horses, and is said to have roped and ridden a tornado. Dynamite was his favorite food.

Somewhere between myth and reality was Judge Roy Bean, actually a real person but one whose story is a rich blend of tall tales and truth. Judge Bean opened the Jersey Lily Saloon at Langtry, which lies near the confluence of the Pecos and the Río Grande. Apparently inebriated a good part of the time, he was appointed Justice of the Peace and thus became known as the Law West of the Pecos.

In the kitchen of one of my favorite places, the Appurceon Ranch in far South Texas, hangs a painting of Judge Roy Bean's most famous exploit. At the time, prizefighting had been outlawed in much of the United States and parts of Mexico, so the Law West of the Pecos staged an illegal world championship boxing match between Bob Fitzsimmons of Australia and Peter Maher, the Champion of Ireland. The highly publicized fight took place on a sandbar in the Río Grande. It lasted less than two minutes, but it made the judge famous and introduced the Law West of the Pecos to the outside world.

On the river, we were now barreling toward our own Law of the Pecos—a strand of barbed wire that seemed intent on decapitating us. Duncan and I desperately tried to slow or at least turn the speeding canoe. As we steered through the raging water, we capsized. Abruptly, less than an hour into our trip, I found myself pinned under the canoe, engulfed by the river.

Fortunately, we both wore life jackets and were swept along with the boat in the current. At that point, choking for air and freezing in the cold water, I made a disastrous mistake. In a panic, I reached up and grabbed the gunnel of the canoe, which floated upside down above me. Almost immediately, the canoe slammed into the canyon wall, and my thumb was smashed against the limestone cliff.

After being hurled downstream a mile or so, we managed to beach the canoe. We lay gasping on a sandbar, and I could see my thumb rapidly swelling. We still had dozens of miles to go before an overnight camp, and then a second day on the river before reaching our takeout at Pandale. After bailing out the canoe and changing into fresh clothes from our drybags, we set out again on the river. With each pull of the paddle, my thumb grew bigger and blacker.

I'd read and heard stories of Pecos country referred to as hell, death, and violence. I knew that Texas's preeminent storyteller, J. Frank Dobie, had once offered a diabolical definition for "Pecos": "Pecos, as verb: to throw into the Pecos River, hence, to kill by drowning." That morning, I became a believer.

Later in the evening, as we made camp, I swallowed all the aspirin we had in a futile effort to stem the excruciating pain. As I lay on another sandbar and tried to sleep with my throbbing thumb, I felt like I had almost been "Pecosed."

On our second day of paddling, we drew closer to the cave shelters of the Lower Pecos. Hauntingly, Texas's most storied river and human expression has its origins in the mists of antiquity. Thousands of years ago, the indigenous inhabitants of this region roamed the hostile terrain. The great cave shelters along the river upstream from its confluence with the Río Grande became the studios for the most compelling manifestation of ancient pictorial expressionism in Texas. Here, at places like Seminole Canyon State Park and the White Shaman Preserve, sensational rock art illustrations provide us with a mystical insight into the lives, fears, and aspirations of an early society struggling to survive and to express its humanity.

Eerily, the huge murals on the cave walls of the Lower Pecos, which depict animal transformation and the journey of the soul into the firmament, appear as the earliest beginnings of a storytelling continuum that persists to this day.

Part of that story today, unfortunately, is that fighting continues along the Pecos as Texas and New Mexico struggle over the increasingly precious water. For nearly a century, with differing cultures, hydrologic conditions, and water policies, but increasing water needs, both have claimed competing rights to the river.

In 1948, representatives of Texas and New Mexico signed the Pecos River Compact, designed "to ensure that the State of Texas receives its equitable share of water from the Pecos River and its tributaries." Texas's proposed share was allocated by the Pecos River Compact Commission established by Congress. Despite those intentions, by 1970, Texas had identified at least nine disputes alleging that New Mexico had violated the compact. More recently, in 2013, the dispute has become increasingly heated as Texas filed suit against New Mexico, asserting that our neighboring state was not delivering the yearly water allotment guaranteed in the compact.

And so the struggle for Pecos River water continues and has implications for our own water commitments to Mexico, for the Pecos helps supply the Río Grande. The quality of water in the river is still poor, and increasingly its banks are lined with Tamarisk, an exotic plant that sucks up enormous amounts of its flow. Increased oil and gas development has brought "energy sprawl" and its attendant problems to the region. Yet despite these new and continuing impacts, the landscape West of the Pecos maintains its stark beauty, its allure and romanticism.

Which was hard for me to see after a painful descent of fifty-eight miles down the river. I lay on the limestone shoreline at Pandale and waited for Duncan and the boys to pick me up and drive me back to civilization. By this time my thumb had swollen to the size of a tennis ball and was later determined to be broken.

My thumb is still crooked today, and though many years have passed, every time I look at it, I am reminded of my own tale of adventure on the Pecos River.

The Lost River
of Divine Reincarnation

by S.C. Gwynne

A moment ago the world was a sunny, happy place, full of giant herons gliding like pterodactyls on desert winds and schools of uncountable gar and bass swimming in turquoise pools so clear, you could see crawfish walking on the bottom in ten feet of water. A place of exquisitely tortured limestone, river boulders the size of houses, humped black canyons framing pale autumn skies.

But that is all gone now.

In its place is an entirely different reality familiar to civilized people who have taken small boats into wild rivers. Four of us, in two canoes, have entered a stretch of white water that we have grossly underestimated. Only one boat has made it through. The other is pinned sideways on a rock, transformed suddenly from a reasonably efficient craft into a fixed part of the river, a small waterfall with tons of water now cascading over it. The sixteen-foot, nine-inch polyethylene Old Town begins, ominously, to bend along its thwarts. There is no budging it. Not even a millimeter.

While watching our expedition mates cling to their canoe, Bill, my sternman, and I now have the leisure to contemplate this predicament.

We would seem to have only one option, and it is not encouraging: abandon the canoe and all of its gear, empty our craft of most of its equipment, and run the remaining rapids with four men in one boat. There is really no other way into or out of these steep rock canyons. Paddlers with worse problems—like severe injuries or the loss of their vessels—are rescued by Border Patrol helicopters, if agents are not otherwise occupied chasing drug runners, coyotes, and other border crossers who tend to crop up in this part of the world.

Our problem lies in the fact that we are, in continental American terms, in the middle of nowhere. More precisely, we are on the Lower Pecos River, in West Texas. You have probably not heard of this particular stretch of the Pecos, the

S.C. Gwynne is an Austin-based journalist and bestselling author whose books include *Empire of the Summer Moon*, which was a finalist for the Pulitzer Prize. Originally published in *Outside* magazine, August 2011. Published by permission of S.C. Gwynne.

final sixty miles of which runs down to join the Río Grande on the Mexican border near the town of Del Rio. Most Texans are aware of it only as they encounter it from the Pecos High Bridge on Route 90, where the river, widening before it joins the Río Grande at Lake Amistad, cuts through a breathtaking limestone canyon. Travelers get out of their cars and take pictures, stunned by one of the most spectacular views in the desiccated wilds of West Texas, wondering where this wide, muscular desert river has suddenly materialized from. And then they move on to San Antonio or Los Angeles or wherever they are headed. Most people who do know the Pecos River know its New Mexican section, 800 miles or more upstream, which originates in the snowy upper elevations of the Sangre de Cristo Mountains. This is not that river, in any sense, as you will see. No more than forty people run the Lower Pecos each year. In many years, far fewer.

There are good reasons for this. The Lower Pecos is surrounded on all sides by private land and is inaccessible to weekend enthusiasts and other river runners who do not have a lot of time on their hands. You are allowed to put your boat in at exactly one place, a tiny cluster of cabins known as Pandale Crossing, and take it out at exactly one place, the high bridge on Route 90— and there are sixty difficult river miles and seven days of paddling in between. There are hardly any people or towns out in this rough, empty stretch of Chihuahuan Desert. On nighttime satellite maps, this part of West Texas is one of the darkest areas in the Lower 48. There are no public lands here, no national parks or national forests or friendly rangers, no park roads or convenient facilities. The river pierces country dominated by enormous ranches— 20,000- and 30,000-acre spreads—that make it a sort of private wilderness and all the more wild for it. It is a place, alternately, of cataclysmic floods and extreme droughts.

For all its obscurity, the Lower Pecos flows through one of the loveliest and most pristine landscapes in America. Spring-fed and limestone-bottomed, the river has a clarity matched only by its wild tropical color schemes, which would remind you of a Corona beer commercial except that the colors are far more varied. It is both a white water river, with dozens of rapids from Class I through Class IV, and a giant aquarium—jammed with spotted gar, catfish, perch, bluegill, and carp—where you can watch a large-mouth bass wheel, rise, and hit your fly. The country around it is a sort of museum of Native American history, home to one of the greatest concentrations of ancient rock art in America.

And so it is surprising that, out beyond the 100th meridian, where vast commercial cultures have arisen to service affluent Americans desperate for a run down big, remote, mythic rivers, no one knows the Lower Pecos. Our predicament in the rapids is relatively simple, in one sense: we're the only ones here.

⁓◯

Our trip began on the first day of November, in bone-dry, brilliantly clear, 80-degree air, the sort of Texas weather that makes you glad you are alive and makes people from Milwaukee and Chicago wish they lived somewhere else. The cruel summer heat—110 and above—had gone away, and the northers had not started to blow yet.

We had driven 250 miles west from Austin, through the limestone canyonlands and live oak savannas of the Hill Country, the land a young Lyndon Johnson civilized with hydroelectric power. This is in fact where the Big West begins. As you pass the town of Junction and cross the winding Llano River, you realize, looking at the high mesas and rock outcroppings and ashe juniper forests, that you have finally left all of that forested trans-Mississippi land behind. Now we were in something completely other, a spectacular collision of three ecologies: Hill Country limestone river bottoms, Chihuahuan Desert uplands, and what botanists call Tamaulipan thorn scrub.

Who are we? A motley assemblage of middle-aged men, all looking for a bragging-rights adventure in the great American West. Maybe that sounds vainglorious. But middle-aged men tend to think that way. The clock is ticking down, and for most of us, the remoteness of this expedition will test the limits of our abilities. I am fifty-seven years old. There is my friend Jeff, fifty-four, an investment banker from Dallas specializing in bankruptcy, with whom I used to drink inordinate amounts of Scotch and play Jerry Jeff Walker songs on guitar until 5 a.m. before going off to work, bleary-eyed, at a bank in Cleveland. There is Bill, also fifty-four, my paddling buddy from Austin, a chiropractor with great medical knowledge and an obsession with outdoor gear, with whom I have kayaked many Class III rivers in Texas and the Northwest. And then there is Paolo, forty-one, our photographer. He is here for professional reasons. Paolo scales thousand-foot rock cliffs and ice-climbs in temperatures thirty below zero. He has swum with sharks and biked a thousand miles through Mexico. Paolo is not like us.

Our group has descended rivers before, but nothing like the Pecos, which has a reputation for being murderous on marine hardware. In 1590, the Spanish explorer Gaspar Castaño de Sosa and his expedition tried in vain for two weeks to find a place to cross the river and were thwarted by the rough and difficult country with "many sharp rocks and ravines." He also noted that the rock had managed to ruin twenty-five dozen horseshoes. In the sole guidebook to this section (*The Lower Pecos River*, by Louis F. Aulbach and Jack Richardson, 2008), the Pecos is described as a place where your boat is in almost constant collision with rock—limestone that is pitted and harshly abrasive and that chews the vinyl off the bottoms of boats. Canoes are routinely pinned or broken. Indeed, after calling a dozen outfitters, the only one who would rent us canoes for the Pecos was a guide we knew on the Devils River, another immaculate limestone-bottomed stream in West Texas. What he gave us—severely battered and cracked Old Towns with keels that had been re-epoxied so many times, they looked like abstract art—seemed like a bad joke.

We traveled an hour north from the border town of Comstock to the launch site at Pandale with our shuttle driver, Emilio, who charges $325 for the drop-off and the pickup by boat at the other end. There is no bridge at Pandale, just a place where a bridge once was and a road that can be crossed only at low water. We stuffed the canoes well beyond the gunwales with drybags and coolers and water and fishing gear, planning to be out six nights and seven days camping along the river's banks. Landowners here are tolerant of this, partly because they know how murderously difficult it would be to climb out of the canyon and trespass any further. As we launched, the river was running at 180 cubic feet per second (cfs), slightly below its average, which meant we would be encountering a good deal of shallow water and many sets of rocky rapids, especially in the first twenty miles.

We were soon careering down the first set and leaving the known world behind. One of the best things about the Pecos is its intimacy. The river is generally quite narrow, usually only twenty to thirty yards wide, bounded on both sides by ocher-colored limestone cliffs with deep black stains. As we moved downstream, there was a clear sense of descending as the canyon walls loomed higher. The river itself becomes much deeper, stronger, colder. The farther down we went, the more we seemed to be in the canyon's close embrace, enfolded by it and contained within it as though in some sort of bejeweled box amid the dun-colored hills, canyons, and mesas of the open desert.

There is another side to this intimacy, too. On the Lower Pecos, at these flow levels, we are often less on the river than in it.

Jeff and Paolo were in one boat, Bill and I in the other. As we plunged into our first sets of rapids, we were surrounded by thickets of cane, which grow fifteen to twenty feet high and create dark labyrinths in the river. The effect was a sort of Mr. Toad's Wild Ride as we whooshed through five-foot-wide chutes cloaked by cane thickets so dense, we couldn't see through them. This was complicated by the fact that our boat teams were often working at cross-purposes, the bowmen (Jeff and me) screaming "Right, right, right!" while the men in the stern, distracted by the roar of the river, steered resolutely left, directly into whatever it was that the bowmen wanted them to avoid. Two- and three-foot standing waves broke regularly over the bows, soaking us and filling the already overladen boats with water. This lent a certain comic aspect to our descent.

"I was trying to point that rock out to you," I said to Bill after we had hit one with a sickening thud and shipped on enough water to turn our canoe, aerodynamically speaking, into something more like a waterborne sofa.

"I still haven't seen it," Bill replied placidly. "Maybe we need to work on hand signals."

There are other forms of intimacy with this river. Rapids that we couldn't run had to be lined, an often difficult process using bow and stern lines to lower your gear-stuffed canoe through rapids. Throughout that first day and into the second, we were often out of our boats, hauling them over the shallow river bottom. In one notorious four-mile section, known as the Flutes, we dragged our boats over thousands of peculiar sculpted rock formations that sat just below the surface. Bill and I quickly discovered that our canoe leaked, and each time we lugged its overstuffed hull across all that rough limestone, we imagined the cracks getting bigger and bigger. We tried to patch them with duct tape where we could.

But these are minor inconveniences. For every rapid we had to line or drag, there were ten that were both rollicking and relatively easy to run. On one occasion, a few miles in, we found ourselves in an ever-darkening, cane-bracketed chute that became, alarmingly, narrower and narrower. Four feet wide, three feet wide, two feet . . . A dead end would have been a small disaster, a sort of blind alley with no way out and the straining effect that all paddlers fear. Bill and I lost sight of Jeff and Paolo, who'd somehow found the main channel. The cane closed around us, and the canoe began to turn sideways as the two of us, truly alarmed and cursing both the cane and the rather large spiders that were now running rampant over our faces and the boat, prepared to bail out. Just at that moment, we suddenly, and unaccountably, punched through the brush into the main channel.

"Hey, where'd you guys go?" yelled Paolo, a hundred yards downriver.

"To the land of the cane spiders," Bill replied. "Sorry you guys missed it."

That the Lower Pecos exists at all is a small miracle. Like so many other western rivers, the Pecos was the victim, from the late nineteenth to the mid-twentieth century, of a series of grand and misbegotten attempts to harness it, dam it, and use its water to create the sort of irrigated paradise that the usual assortment of eastern land companies, tubercular millionaires, European financiers, railroad touts, reclamationists, industrial magnates, mining capitalists, and dry-land dreamers believed the West would become. They were wrong, of course, but it did not stop them, collectively, from damming up a great river.

The Pecos in its legendary, historic state was a waterway that flowed deep and strong from its origins in the mountains, through eastern New Mexico and West Texas, joining the Río Grande—a river it roughly parallels—on the Mexican border. It happened to cross the Southwest precisely at the point where the land turned from simply harsh frontier into a gigantic, canyon-scarred, and lethal landscape that all westering settlers feared. The Spanish considered the country of the Lower Pecos difficult if not impassable. The phrase *west of the Pecos* refers not only to the folkloric character Judge Roy Bean ("the Law West of the Pecos"; see Newman, Paul), who operated out of the town of Langtry, but also and more tellingly to the great emptiness that lies just beyond it, a rugged, dry, and mountainous land that would kill you with thirst or starvation or, if you were less fortunate, by torture and evisceration at the hands of Comanches and Apaches. For most of the nineteenth century, the Pecos was one of those western rivers that, whether you were driving cattle, running a wagon train, marching blue-coated soldiers, or riding with a Comanche war party, you had to cross. It was the gateway to the Southwest, to the great lands of the old Spanish empire, to California. The river was famous for its swift currents and its quicksand, and if you made it through the most logical ford—the low-water Horsehead Crossing, between present-day Odessa and Fort Stockton—you considered yourself lucky.

All that changed in the late nineteenth and early twentieth centuries. The agent of that change was water. Five dams were built between 1888 and 1988, first by private firms and then by the federal government, to capture the Pecos's water and divert it to agricultural use. The most famous and massive of these irrigation schemes, the Carlsbad Project, happened in and around the town of Carlsbad, in the southeastern corner of New Mexico. Water was impounded and diverted in a series of canals and pipes to the barren lands around the river, turning them into fertile fields. If you fly over the central and southern parts of eastern New Mexico today, you can see the effect: a belt of bright green land spreading like a stain into the desert.

Almost all of the river's water was impounded by New Mexico, but what that state did not take, the Texans did. At Red Bluff Dam, just south of the state line, Texas impounded most of what was left of the Pecos, leaving a small, alkaline, salt-cedar-choked stream to make its way pathetically south toward the Río Grande. This is the way many people think of that river: dammed and tamed in New Mexico, a trickle in Texas. If you saw what emerged from Red Bluff Dam, you would consider the Pecos a dead river, or nearly dead, anyway, certainly compared with what it used to be—one of many victims of the reclamation craze.

But as the river cuts southward through deepening limestone canyons and ever more inaccessible land, something remarkable happens, unseen by most people. Liberated by the sheer ruggedness of its country, the Pecos rises again, replenished by a sudden and enormous flow of crystal-clear water that enters from spring-fed creeks. The biggest of these is Independence Creek; fed by some of the largest springs in the state—including Caroline Spring, which pumps 3,000 to 5,000 gallons a minute—it joins the river just south of Interstate 10.

The effect of all this on the attenuated Pecos is astonishing. Suddenly, and with a whoosh of brilliantly clear water, which my companions and I can feel as we go downriver, a great western river is reborn. The sheer volume of what is being pumped into it—an additional 40 percent of the Pecos's flow—defeats all the attempts, upriver, to contain and reduce it. Thus re-created, the river runs gloriously through its cloistering canyons to the Mexico border. If it is a waterway of great beauty—and it truly is—it is also unforgiving, the scene of some of the worst flash floods in America, draining such a huge watershed via Independence Creek that it is not unheard of for paddlers to be hit with a twenty-foot wall of water under blue skies. In 2007, water-flow levels hit 25,000 cfs in canyons where the norm is 200. At its record high in 1954, the Pecos hit 948,000 cfs and drowned several people on its shores.

On our second night out, we pull in to the campsite at Everett Springs, exhausted by a ten-mile run that involved a good deal of complete immersion in the Pecos: wading, pulling, dodging strainers. The place is a sculpted, smooth grotto. On one side is a steep rock wall, on the other a little Eden of willow, oak, mesquite, cedar, chinaberry, and mountain laurel. At least eight springs gush from the steep rock wall. One of them is wonderfully warm. Another, emerging ten feet up the rock face, is enveloped in an enormous, lush beard of moss and ferns and lichens. I stand beneath it, feeling the water run over my body. The springs flow down our little canyon, burbling in a three-foot-wide, two-foot-deep stream through clear pools in the curvilinear stone.

"How would you rate this camp?" I ask my friends as we're setting up the tents.

"Top three—ever," Jeff and Bill both say. I say top two, maybe the best ever.

Paolo says nothing at first. I assume this is because, for all I know, he has probably already run the wildest river in the Gobi Desert. "Not bad," he finally offers. "Really pretty, amazingly nice." (Later, at Painted Canyon, he will up this to "crazy beautiful.")

We slip into what will become our routine. Jeff and Paolo take off with their fly rods, ribbing each other about who is catching the most, or the biggest, fish. ("Oh, look," Paolo says, "Jeff has caught some giant bluegills," meanwhile showing off his splendid green-black haul of largemouth bass.) Bill occupies himself with tent gear and water purifiers. I busy myself with setting up the fire. Later we make fish tacos with fancy tartar sauce we brought, spotting armadillos, a javelina, and white-tailed deer as we eat.

We fall asleep to the murmur of the spring, or at least we try to. Jeff, as it turns out, snores loudly—it sounds something like the London Symphony Orchestra tuning up—so Paolo has decided to sleep outside. He is not entirely certain this is a good idea.

"What do you think there is out here?" he asks, gazing at the raw desert all around us.

"Snakes, black widows, tarantulas, scorpions, centipedes," I begin to answer.

"Centipedes!" says Jeff from inside his tent. Apparently, he is not fond of them.

"Oh, that's very encouraging," says Paolo. Nonetheless, he sleeps outside, that night and for the rest of the trip.

At each of our campsites, signs that human beings lived in these limestone caves and overhangs for thousands of years are everywhere. There are mortar holes, seams of worked flint, and strange incisions in the rock made in parallel lines. There are also hundreds of rock paintings. With a little help from an informed source, we find one of them. About halfway down the river, we pull the canoes out onto a bleached gravel bar; Jeff uses his machete to hack through fifty feet of river cane, and we follow him into a small side canyon that was invisible from upstream. We scramble up a steep slope, at the top of which is a 100-foot-long rock shelter. Running for most of its length is a brilliantly preserved 4,500-year-old painting, depicting in black, red, and yellow pigments what looks like a collision of the real and magical worlds. In the middle stands a black shaman, five feet high. He is elongated, ornamented, and surrounded by sinuous, snaking lines. To each side of him, lesser beings proliferate; you can see spears and clubs, dead people. There are arcs and squiggles that seem to define and limit power; there are odd flying creatures. On the far left is a plump panther, prompting the name by which this cave painting is sometimes known: "Piggy Panther." The painting manages to be surrealistic, primitive, abstract, and completely real. It's like stumbling upon a Vermeer while walking in the woods.

The next day we find petroglyphs. We make camp at Lewis Canyon, on yet another tiered, sheltered white limestone shelf, climb to the top of the cliffs, and find ourselves standing on two full acres of rock art—carvings on a flat limestone surface. There are hundreds of glyphs, many of them pure abstractions. There are handprints and bear paws and swirls that look like targets; there are carvings of atlatls everywhere.

After dinner, we apportion our whiskey—a few ounces apiece—and lie back and gaze at one of those startlingly clear star shows you get only in the darkest parts of the electrosphere. Bill, in his wisdom, offers an elegantly simple explanation for what we have just seen: "They were just drawing what they saw," he says, "and you have to believe they were seeing the same thing we are seeing. They were drawing the gods of the night sky."

In our planning for the trip, we made one miscalculation, and it was a serious one. By day four we are running out of water. This may seem odd, surrounded as we are by a diamond-clear river. But that's one of the prices we pay for dams. South of Red Bluff Dam, the river flows over alkaline beds, which means that even though we cannot taste them or see them, the river is full of alkali salts. The water can make you sick. Bill's high-tech water purifiers do not work against this.

In the lower part of the river, there is exactly one freshwater source, known as Chinaberry Spring. As we come within range of it, we have exhausted our water. Chinaberry is no ordinary spring, in the sense that it does not emerge from a rock in an easily visible place. Bill has tried to plot its location using his GPS and topographical maps, but he can only approximate, and our only tangible clues to its location in a sixty-mile run through an enormous desert are (1) a chinaberry tree, of which there are tens of thousands, and (2) as Aulbach's guidebook describes it, a sound of "a gurgle of running water" back in the cane. That's all.

Amazingly, Jeff and Paolo both manage to identify the tree. Then probing along the cane thicket at the river's edge, they hear a very faint sound of dripping. But the sound is coming from deep inside the cane. We all pull our boats up, and what follows is that peculiar existential moment when someone has to be chosen to do the dirty work. Jeff, the owner of a machete that has done yeoman work on our trip, volunteers. "How many centipedes do you think are in there?" he asks. (Even though we have seen only one centipede and have only a vague idea of what one could do to you, they provide a sort of thematic unity to the trip.)

"Probably not more than a couple thousand," I answer cheerfully. "Your main worry is probably snakes."

And so Jeff gets out, wades through the muck, and begins to hack his way through dense thicket until he has completely vanished from sight. The rest of us wait, anxiously, in our boats. Above us looms a 300-foot cliff.

"You guys are going to owe me big," comes the voice. He is now up to his waist in mud and in almost complete darkness.

"Can you see it?" I ask, not really believing for a moment that he can.

"Yes," he says at last. "Yes, I can see it."

What he sees is the sort of trickle that would be barely enough to brush your teeth, and it is bubbling out of the mud at the base of the cane, about a foot above river level. It's a sort of miracle. Jeff has to whack away the mud and the cane to even get to it. He fills a five-gallon jug with the water and emerges, and now it's my turn to fill the second jug. I wade into the muddy darkness and behold the tiny trickle. I fill the rest of the jugs while Paolo attempts to shoot this weird, dark endeavor. But we have our water.

In the last two days of the trip, the river bears little resemblance to the one we started out on. Everything is bigger, from the water, which is now often twenty feet deep, to the black cliffs, which rise 200 to 300 feet above us. The current is much more powerful here. We seem to be almost constantly in strong rapids that demand our full attention. In Waterfall Rapid, a Class III with a nasty hole, we decide to line the boats—mainly because the prospect of losing one or both of them is starting to seem less and less desirable. Bill and I go first. It's an immediate disaster. The boat flips, smashes into a rock, rolls over, then labors on its side, like something dying, through the rest of the rapids. This places Paolo in a professional dilemma. He is just downstream, shooting this marvelous scene of canoeing gone wrong. Should he do his job or save the boat? He curses, shoots a few more frames, then hustles down the rock bank after the boat.

Now it's Jeff and Paolo's turn.

"What do you think went wrong?" Jeff asks his partner.

"Operator error," says Paolo. "This is a piece of cake."

Moments later their boat is fully capsized and engulfed in white water. For the next hour, we retrieve gear and bail and repack the boats. Our last night is spent at the most beautiful place we've seen yet: Painted Canyon, on a high limestone shelf at the head of a long Class III rapid. Here the river has carved a small lagoon with thirty-foot walls and brilliantly green water. The lagoon is also full of fish. The spotted gar are three feet in length, with long snouts that make them look like barracuda. We swim, diving deep into the emerald pools. We eat catfish and bass and bluegill, marinated in olive oil, garlic, and salt and pepper and then pan-fried. We go to sleep in warm desert thermals and wake to a perfectly still morning in what seems to be the very heart of the American West, a place as it once was, when Stone Age hunter-gatherers ground their food in the rock holes we see all around us. I am exhausted; I ache and have bruises and cuts all over my legs. But that night as I watch the stars, I have an odd momentary realization that I'm not thinking about anything but those stars. Everything else has disappeared.

The end looms. Six miles downstream we are supposed to meet Emilio and a friend, who will tow us out the remaining ten miles to the take-out at Pecos High Bridge. We were sternly warned about these final miles, where the river begins to join Lake Amistad, created by the damming of the Río Grande. Here the wind can blow forty miles per hour for days at time, a southerly blast from Mexico so strong that you cannot paddle against it. It can be a cruel and bitter ending to a good trip.

It's in this last stretch of river before our meeting spot that we enter something called Big Rock Rapid, where we pin the canoe. Pinning is a unique, unsettling experience. It does not even seem quite plausible. One moment you're paddling a relatively maneuverable boat; the next you're contemplating a sunken, immovable piece of wreckage. We spend a good hour taking everything out of the canoe, watching for signs that it's going to break in half. Somehow it holds. Once it's empty, though, it seems just as stuck under all that water as it did with 300 pounds of gear in it. At this moment, spurred by our mishap, I realize, for the first time, really, how much can go wrong, even on a doable river like the Lower Pecos—a notion that probably wouldn't have occurred to me at all at the age of thirty or even forty but very definitely does at fifty-seven. The Pecos at this water level is not a terribly dangerous river. And yet in these wilds, injury or even death can be quite a casual thing: a foot stuck under a rock in high rushing water, a slip on one of the rock cliffs we climbed, a rattlesnake bite, or just a garden-variety heart attack. I silently vow never to run this river again with fewer than four boats.

Paolo, of course, has the solution. He tells us all to pull upward on the upstream gunwale, and miraculously the boat buoys up and floats off, swamped but intact, beyond the rocks, to the pools at the bottom of the rapid.

All that remains is our tow out. Emilio and his friend meet us in an old pontoon boat with an even older outboard motor. We pile the gear on, strap the canoes alongside, then motor for two and a half hours into a stiff headwind. Our destination is that magnificent Route 90 bridge, the one with the stunning view of the Pecos River Gorge, where people take pictures and wonder, as I used to, where in the hell that river came from. And it is gratifying that, after a week on the water, I finally know the answer.

The Upper Colorado River

Headwaters of the Colorado and Colorado City

by Margie Crisp

Headwaters of the Colorado

Sixty miles from Lubbock and south of the town of Lamesa, I turn east onto gridded section roads to look for the edge of the Caprock Escarpment. The landscape is so vast that ranches are described in square miles, called sections, not acres. The roads surrounding Lamesa form such perfect right angles and parallel lines that a map of the area looks like graph paper. Driving the dirt and gravel section roads is easy (though no one has wasted money on road signs), but my truck erases all behind me in an enormous plume of dust. When I stop to check the map, the cloud envelopes me so that I am blind and blanketed with a layer of fine grit. With my finger firmly planted on the map at my presumed location, I creep across the county map along the ruler-straight roads. Every inch of land is plowed except the road base, bar ditches, and oil pump sites. Bales of harvested cotton squat at the edge of roads. Dirty fluff is drifting like old snow in the ditches and catches in the weeds straggling at the verges. The late afternoon light breaks through

Margie Crisp is a nationally exhibited artist and writer who lives in Elgin, Texas, with her husband and fellow artist, William Montgomery. Her first book, *River of Contrasts: The Texas Colorado*, which she also illustrated, won the Texas Institute of Letters Award for Best Nonfiction. Excerpted from *River of Contrasts: The Texas Colorado* by Margie Crisp. Texas A&M University Press, 2012. Published by permission of Margie Crisp and Texas A&M University Press.

the flannel of the clouds to lie long and bright against the fingerprint whorls of plowing. At a slower pace, the area becomes surprisingly beautiful. The hypnotic rhythm of the contour plowing becomes a fugue—graceful sweeps of converging lines dissolving and reappearing as I move over the subtly rolling swells. The patterns merge and repeat in variation until I feel like I am in the midst of a giant tapestry of dark wools and silks, a subtle but infinitely varied design in umber, sepia, and gold.

With no more warning than a barely perceptible curve in the road, I am at the top of the Caprock Escarpment. I feel like I have discovered the quintessential Texas landscape: hidden in plain sight, a breathtaking geological formation of such magnitude that it is impossible to comprehend until I am standing at the edge of its palisaded cliffs and looking over land both wildly beautiful and devastated. The earth falls away and reveals itself in eroded ridges of bright red Triassic clay bluffs and secretive draws where the waters collect to form the small beginnings of powerful rivers. The springs and seeps at the edge of the Caprock Escarpment give rise to not only the Colorado River but also other Texas rivers, including the Concho, the Brazos, and the Red River. The slopes below me are clothed in mesquite, cedar, prickly pear, yucca, bunch grasses, and broom weed. The scrubby vegetation is a relief after the endless miles of raw soil. Cattle graze between the oil pump jacks that are mindlessly diligent, pivoting up and down, creaking and groaning. Calves step delicately over the pipelines crisscrossing the land between pump jacks and tank batteries that perch on slopes sliced, smoothed, and leveled. Roads overlay the basin with a net of white gravel that binds oil, land, and water together into an uneasy alliance.

Don and Martha Stewart, the owners of the tract of land designated as the geographical headwaters of the Colorado River, cheerfully insisted that I drop by their home in Lamesa that morning for a cup of coffee and a chat.

In the early years, the river ran and flooded with regularity. Now it rarely has water unless they get a good rain. Don says that over thirty years of taking more out of the Ogallala Aquifer than gets puts back by rain has taken its toll . . .

Three draws on the Stewart property drain off the Caprock Escarpment into the river. The gradual slopes create a gentle basin—unlike the dramatic drop-offs to the north and south. The rolling terrain is dressed with thick grasses, scrubby cedar, and broom weed that Don refers to as "turpentine weed."

I walk down to the dry bed of the river. Is it a river if it has no water? Isn't a river defined by its flow and by the passing of time?

What I discover is that deep in the washes, in the dry beds, life is thick. Out of the hand-numbing and nose-reddening wind, birds sing and flowers bloom . . .

I follow the wash downstream and come to what the Stewarts designate the first "permanent" water on the river (though it is actually on the neighboring Miller Ranch). The small seep, or spring-fed pool, of silty water is about seven feet deep and ringed with faded brown cattails and bright green sedges with a pale, gravel caliche bluff eroding on one side. An unidentified but clearly indignant duck flies noisily away, and a great horned owl silently drifts from the bluff to a leafless tree on the opposite side of the draw as I approach. A spooked least bittern squawks irritably as it flies past me.

Below the little marsh, the stream narrows again and burbles over smooth round pebbles. Each small stone near the water has a ring of white mineral crystals. The stems of grass and sedge all have feathery coats of crystals, and there is a white crust on the drying clay of the bank. I'm too chicken to taste the water or touch the crystals to my tongue to see if they are salt or alkaline. The presence of the oil pump jacks, signs warning about poisonous gases, and mysterious black plastic pipelines running chaotically across the river make me nervous. Early explorers' accounts of the upper Colorado River often intimated that the waters were brackish or salty, and according to the *Springs of Texas* by Gunnar Brune, much of the original spring water issuing from the Caprock was heavily mineralized. Frank Beaver told me that the river used to run clear but always had an "alk-y" taste. The Rolling Plains area is rich with minerals; Permian gypsum and natural salt deposits leach into groundwater. Long-term drought has exacerbated the problem by concentrating chlorides and sulfates in the remaining surface water.

In addition, this area has the added burden of chloride pollution from the oil fields. Underpinning most of the headwaters basin, the Jo-Mill field in Dawson and Borden counties is one of the seven largest-volume fields in the Spraberry-Dean Sandstone oil fields, part of the rich Permian Basin. When wells are drilled into the tightly packed but porous sandstone of the fields, oil, natural gas, hydrogen sulfide gas, and brine (heavily concentrated saltwater) flow upward. The wells pump up oil and brine and then put the mixture through a separator. From 1954, when the first well was drilled, until 1969, the oil companies discharged the brine into open, unlined dirt pits. The heavy, concentrated saltwater and toxins seeped through the sand and gravel into the freshwater aquifer; during heavy rains, the pits would overflow and wash directly into the river and its tributaries, poisoning the soil along the way. On the Stewart ranch, Don pointed out the site of the settlement pits that contaminated their well water. Although Exxon filled the pits decades ago, the area is almost bare of plants, unlike the tangled grasslands surrounding it. Since 1969, the brine and chemicals used in the drilling process, including highly toxic barium, arsenic, and cadmium, are put in tanks and transported by truck for disposal at approved sites. Yet chloride contamination is an ongoing problem because abandoned, unplugged, or improperly plugged oil wells provide an easy route for brine, oil, and chemicals to migrate into aquifers. In addition, wells with deteriorating metal casings allow brine and oil to seep into surrounding soil, groundwater, and the river.

A pump jack labors above me, and a crude oil pipeline crosses the riverbed, suspended over the eroded banks. I clamber up the bank to go over the pipeline with pounds of sticky clay layered on the soles of my boots. With every step, I accumulate more pebbles, sticks, and dirt until I have a two-inch-thick platform glued to each foot. I skid back down to the river and skate over to a ledge. While reaching for a rock to pry off the goo, I see, in the soft, orange clay by my hand, bobcat tracks. Each print holds minute and exact impressions of fur and the texture of the skin on the paw pad. The sun glints off the river, and I see a shining trail of water-filled tracks trotting downstream.

I stand on the shoulder of Mushaway Peak in northern Borden County looking south across the headwaters basin of the Colorado River. To my right, the Caprock Escarpment rises long and low, indigo blue against the pale wash of early afternoon sky. Before me, the rolling terrain is sculpted by the creeks that join like the fingers on a hand to form the Colorado River: Gold Creek, Tobacco Creek, Glen Creek, Rattlesnake Creek, Plum Creek, and Grape Creek. Ignoring the few barbed-wire fences and power lines, I begin to mentally erase the tangled brush and the drought-burned pastures before me and dress this landscape in the thick grasses and wooded streams that made up the natural prairies in the eighteenth century and earlier. Grasslands that grew thick and stirrup-tall in good seasons were interspersed with pockets and islands of mixed woods. Numerous historical accounts describe the streams east of the plains of the Llano Estacada as having rich galeria forests along the stream bottoms. Del Weniger, in *The Explorers' Texas*, recounts how, in 1854, J.H. Byrne, part of a western railroad expedition, describes the stream banks as "thickly covered with timber-mezquite, hackberry, wild china, plum, willow and scrub oak." Other explorers remarked on the beauty of the area, saying, "These rivers are very beautiful because of the large numbers of trees near them, good and palatable water, good watering places, and grass that grows abundantly near the water." With trees arching over the streams, these graceful "gallery forests" threaded the length of the Colorado and its tributaries through the grasslands.

The terminology of the open sea seems natural to this place of open treeless plains and former rolling prairies: waves of grasses and islands of trees, swells of land surging and lapping at the base of the Caprock; I find myself swaying slightly to the imagined currents.

Onto this reconstructed landscape, I imagine the brown wave of a herd of bison cresting the far ridges. Brown shapes fan out over the horizon as they graze, moving slowly and inexorably along. I reject a Hollywood-inspired stampede and substitute a creep-like brown molasses across the prairies, as immense herds move slowly north with the spring. Droves of white-tailed deer browse through the gallery forests and on the verges of the grasslands. Herds of pronghorns, our native "antelope-goat," stay separate from the bison, but they wheel and take flight like flocks of birds, speeding over the grasslands as packs of wolves circle the edges of the herds looking for prey. Fire roars across the landscape, burning out the trees and shrubs sprouting in the grass-lands, leaving fertile ash for the grasses and herbs that will reemerge in the seasonal rains.

Colorado City

In 1952, when the dam for Lake J.B. Thomas was completed, people in the member cities of the district—Snyder, Big Spring, and Odessa—celebrated. The Colorado River Municipal Water District not only built the dam; they also drilled a well field in Martin County for groundwater and installed over 115 miles of pipeline to deliver water to their customers.

The first indication that things might not work out as planned was the lake's refusal to fill. A year after the dam was sealed, Texas was in the throes of a mas-sive drought: the drought of record for the state. But the drought-busting rains of the early 1960s produced more than enough rain to fill the lake. Water sheeted off the hills, trickled into washes, flowed through streams, and rushed down the riverbed. The rainwater washed across the drought-ravaged rangelands carrying soil and debris into the reservoir, foreshadowing the tons of silt that continue to plague the lake. Lake J.B. Thomas has only been full three times in its more than fifty years—and all three of those times were between 1960 and 1962. During the time when folks believed that the lake would not only fill but also stay full, a real estate boom sprouted vacation properties along the bluffs ringing the perimeter. With the current lake measuring less than 15 percent of capacity, the few remaining homes overlook a lakebed choked with salt cedar, seep willow, and grasses. Constant demand, limited supply, extended droughts, and a serious overestimation of runoff amounts have kept the lake less than one-quarter full—or three-quarters empty—for most of its life. As an important source of water for multiple cities, its existence is crucial, but with evaporative rates averaging six feet per year and chronic problems with silting in, its future as a water supply looks bleak.

I pass poorly maintained pump jacks spewing black oil that coats the ground and coagulates into evil-smelling pools. Glossy black moats surround rusty tanks striped with leaking oil. I turn off onto a side road that, according to the map, dead-ends at the lakeshore. Off to my right, I see what looks like a water intake station. It extends off a bluff, a glass cube supported by tall concrete pillars that plunge into a wooly sea of grasses and brush. To my left, a groaning pump jack is perched on a pimple of land, grinding away and emitting sulfur fumes. A dressing of black oil oozes along one side. Fifty years ago, the pump jack would have been surrounded by water; now it is surrounded by a rank thicket of salt cedar, seep willow, grasses, cockleburs, and other brush. A ribbon of tall, bright willows parts to reveal the river: orange, opaque, and lazy. A concrete apron slick with moss and algae forms a low-water crossing. Tangles of fishing line and bright red and white plastic bobbers swing from the branches. In the deep, quiet shadows, it is cool and green. According to the map, I am currently underneath twenty feet of water in the center of the lake. I need a new map.

My truck surfaces from the green shadows of the willows into the scalding sun, and I head back up onto the bluff. Vacation cottages and mobile homes, circa 1960, line the edges. A few maintained homes and occasionally a newer house pepper the rusting and decaying rim of buildings. Concrete boat ramps end in tangles of cockleburs, willows, and more feathery salt cedar. In the distance, I see the turbid orange-brown of the lake.

A thin dribble of water flows from the dam into the riverbed below Lake J.B. Thomas. By the time the river reaches Colorado City, it has gained enough water to have a modest presence. Yet the river seems to be entirely ignored by the town: there are no parks along the river and no public access; without the bridge signs on the highways, I'd never have known the river was there at all . . .

In the cool of the morning, I explore Colorado City. Dusty yards with scattered children's toys and gently degraded houses lend an air of benign neglect. Cresting a low hill, I look down into the river bottomland where floodlights blast the early morning away. The shining razor wire and chain-link fences of a prison are a stark contrast to the town.

Behind Main Street and over the railroad tracks, I find a street running along the backside of the downtown near the river. A couple of houses look barely inhabited; the rest are falling down. Through broken windows and missing doors, I see layers of wallpaper peeling off the board walls. Asphalt shingles, asbestos tiles, and wood siding slough off the outside of the dry, disintegrating buildings. Empty cotton trailers with ragged bits of fluff clinging to the wire sit in overgrown yards. I pull onto a track crushed into tall weeds and park next to an empty metal warehouse.

A field of head-high weeds surrounds the buildings. I push my way through towering giant ragweed and Johnson grass. The saw-leafed daisies are not blooming yet, but the sharp-edged leaves clasping the tall stalks are identification enough. Sleepy daisies huddle with petals tightly closed against the morning air. They will unfurl their yellow flowers in the bright sun and then close again at dusk.

Old sofas, cushions, and disintegrating recliners slump in the weeds; rubble heaps of bricks and construction debris litter the field, and rusting appliances peek out from behind the screen of vegetation. I slink through, stepping from trash mound to tin pile. Small game trails have formed low paths through the grass and weeds, so I crouch to scramble under tangled branches, hoping I won't come face-to-face with a rattlesnake. I can hear the frantic scrabbling of fleeing creatures as I step on abandoned sheet metal. While the air of neglect gives the place a melancholy aspect, I know that my husband would be thrilled with such a rich hunting ground. As an avid herpetologist, nothing makes him happier than an abandoned house with piles of roofing tin and siding he can flip to look for snakes, lizards, frogs, and toads. The detritus of civilization is a different sort of wildness.

To reach the river, I slip through a barbed-wire fence and into a thicket of dead willows. Salt cedar crowds the sandy banks of the river. The water is surprisingly clear. Small fish dart in the pools. There is a strong sulfur smell, similar to the hydrogen sulfide gas released by oil pump jacks.

The west side of the river has reddish-brown sandstone humps eroded into graceful and wild shapes. Overhangs and crevices carved by wind and water flow into smooth curves and glides. Morning light hits the tips of the rocks with a burst of red and gold. It ricochets off the rocks and down into the river bottom where it is caught in droplets of dew. Blooming salt cedar—feathery fronds swaying low under the weight of dew—sparkles like a net of jewels in the morning light. It is breathtakingly lovely, with pale lavender flowers clustered at the tips of pale frosted green. I take a photo of a dew-drenched branch of the non-native plant.

Just across the river, I see dump trucks busily driving up and down the bluff. I cannot see any names or logos on the trucks. I creep upstream and look out onto a stripped landscape. Bulldozed raw soil scrapes the river's edge. The stench of sulfur suddenly makes everything seem poisoned and polluted. I've seen no snakes, frogs, or lizards, and then I'm stumbling, rushing to get out of there, spooked by the trucks, the smell, and the desolation.

From the I-20 business bridge, I look down over the bulldozed area. Stretching downstream are shallow pits, viscous-looking green ponds, and a raw dirt basin with white plastic pipes protruding from the soil. Busy dump trucks rumble around the site. I do not know it, but I am looking at a Superfund site, a hazardous waste site nasty enough to garner the attention of both the state and the Environmental Protection Agency (EPA).

One of five Superfund sites in the Colorado River Basin (but the only one on the river), the Col-Tex Petroleum Refinery, built in 1924, operated for forty-five years and was mostly dismantled in the 1970s. But the owners continued to use a few above-ground storage tanks. Three of those tanks squatted next to the river and leaked oil and toxins into the river, soil, and groundwater. Adding insult to injury, on the other side of the highway (but still next to the river), they used a dammed and diverted gravel creek bed as an open pit for separating petroleum mixed with brine. A polluted seep from the old refinery contaminated the groundwater that still flows into the river.

Back at home, my husband slips quietly out of the room when he sees the Texas Commission on Environmental Quality (TCEQ) Superfund website on my computer screen. He listens to my astounded enumeration of the facts and then, while sharing my anger, leaves me to wrestle with the implications. The language used in the settlement makes my stomach clench and shoulder muscles constrict into knots. Since 1990, the oil companies, or "potentially responsible parties," have been "remediating" the area. Seven thousand tons of petroleum-soaked dirt were recycled into asphalt road base and "donated" to the county for resurfacing roads. Mediation for cleaning up contaminated groundwater is underway, and a restoration plan for the site is in motion. "Yeah right," I mutter. "Restoration probably means a field of Bermuda grass and a herd of cattle."

I click on the link to the restoration plan. I scroll down. I stop sneering. Rolling down my computer screen are the carefully thought-out and exquisitely detailed steps needed to restore the river corridor back to a healthy riparian ecosystem. I page down and find everything from diagrams noting planting densities for different zones (color coded on an aerial photograph) to tables of appropriate trees, shrubs, and vines. Four thousand feet of river corridor will have the salt cedar and Johnson grass removed. Cottonwoods, black willows, and other native trees will be planted, and the slopes along the river will be seeded with native grasses and planted with native shrubs, vines, and trees.

Instead of ignoring the damaged land—or scraping it bare—our state, in the form of TCEQ, the Texas Parks and Wildlife Department, and the General Land

Office, has arranged for the PRP (potentially responsible parties) to clean up their mess and leave the place nicer than they found it. Truthfully, the work may never happen, or it may be completed and then never maintained. But for today, there is a small fissure of optimism in my protective shell of cynicism. Three-quarters of a mile of river cleaned and restored, with erosion control, overhanging trees for cool shadows, wildlife-friendly plants, and clean water. Out of the total length of the river, it is a tiny fraction, and the effort may be akin to bailing out a sinking ship with a teaspoon. But since the river builds drop by drop, maybe, just maybe, we can save it piece by piece.

The Concho River

San Angelo was and is a green oasis, especially for travelers approaching from the semidesert west, where annual rainfall takes a sharp drop. The North, South, and Middle Concho Rivers join to form one stream that meanders off eastward and merges with the Colorado. At that confluence of three rivers, the frontier army in 1867 had established an isolated outpost that became Fort Concho. Tall trees, pecan and other varieties, cast their heavy shade upon grassy riverbanks. . . . As a Boy Scout I had once camped with friends on the river and thought San Angelo was the prettiest town I had ever seen.

—Elmer Kelton, from *Sandhills Boy: The Winding Trail of a Texas Writer*

Elmer Kelton (1926–2009) was a West Texas native who published over forty books and is considered one of the greatest western writers of all time. Among his most notable novels is *The Time It Never Rained*, about the great drought in the 1950s.

Concho River

by Larry D. Thomas

The first time "Bobo," my younger brother,
and I laid eyes on a body of water
it scared us, so scarce it was
in far West Texas where we grew up.

We resided in Midland,
midway between Fort Worth and El Paso,
a hundred long miles from the nearest
running river or manmade lake.

For an outing, to rid our bodies
of red dust, mom and dad would take us
to San Angelo, to the Concho River.
Before dad hit the brakes of the old Buick,

we'd freed ourselves of shoes, socks,
Levi's, shirts, and modesty, ready to jump
off the riverbank. The soft mud
was a blessing, oozing between our toes

like poop in a chicken coop.
Clad with but our oldest pairs
of threadbare Fruit of the Looms,
we'd dunk one another repeatedly

in the brownish-green water, splashing
and diving to exhaustion,
the Concho so much better
than the frightening waters of baptism.

Larry D. Thomas grew up in West Texas and has published twenty-two collections of poetry. He was the 2008 Texas Poet Laureate. Among his many awards are two *Texas Review* Poetry Prizes, two Western Heritage Wrangler Awards, and the Violet Crown Book Award. © Larry D. Thomas, 2020. Published by permission of Larry D. Thomas.

The Devils River

The Devils River
Undammed and Unforgiving

by Joe Nick Patoski

*Y*ou know how songs get stuck in your head?

There's one written by the great Texas composer Billy Joe Shaver called "The Devil Made Me Do It the First Time" that wouldn't go away while I was on the Devils River. The diablo connection was probably how it burrowed into my brain in the first place, but the story line was the gnawing part. The singer blames all his troubles on Satan the first time around but says, "The second time I did it on my own."

Billy Joe had the river and me down cold.

My first time down the Devils was easy to explain. I'd only been hearing about it for the past thirty years. It was the great, lost Hill Country river, a spring-fed jewel on the western edge of the Edwards Plateau, running swift and fast through that vague badlands where Tamaulipan scrub—also known as South Texas Brush Country—fades into the Chihuahuan Desert, from somewhere between Ozona and Sonora down to just above Del Rio, where it dissolves into Lake Amistad. Its almost-Caribbean hue was striking, as pretty pale as a summer sky. The translucent water brimmed with smallmouth bass you could follow with your eyes, the clarity was so sharp.

The Devils lives up to its name. It is almost impossible to see, landlocked by sprawling ranches whose owners have been known to vigorously file trespassing charges and sometimes take even more extreme measures to discourage

Joe Nick Patoski is a journalist, author, radio host, and renowned expert on many aspects of Texas culture. He's written books on Austin, Willie Nelson, the Dallas Cowboys, Selena, Texas nature, Stevie Ray Vaughan, and more. Originally published in *Texas Parks & Wildlife* magazine, July 2002. Published by permission of Joe Nick Patoski.

river use by outsiders. It is wild, empty country. Spotting wild turkeys is easier than spotting another human. Doing most of the floatable part of the river takes two days, requiring fifteen miles of paddling on one stretch. There is no room for accidents. Rescues are out of the question. Once you get on, there is no turning back.

When I moved near the Blanco, a river that has become sacred in my life, the Devils always loomed. Half the time I'd talk to people about "my" river, the Devils came up, usually in the context of local river folks pointing out that the Blanco is the second-cleanest river in Texas.

"And what might be the cleanest?" I'd inevitably ask, never challenging the veracity of the claim.

The Devils.

My love of the Blanco, that "cleanest" superlative, and a developing obsession in paddling down rivers, beginning in an inflatable Sevylor and presently in a Yahoo sit-on-top kayak, led to the conclusion that if I really wanted to know what everyone was talking about, I'd have to get on the Devils.

That was easier said than done. Not only is the river in a very remote, lightly populated part of the state, but the environment is particularly harsh, and the flow tenuous at best. It is reputed to be a homewrecker and heartbreaker that could tear lifelong friendships asunder. Too hot to run in the summer and too cold to endure in the winter, it is best attempted in fall or spring. If one could get on the river at all, that is.

In a state where property owners have historically clashed with recreational river users, the Devils is arguably the most hostile. "You didn't just risk getting shot; you might be held under fire for six hours," one retired boater claimed, in relating what happened to him twenty years ago shortly after he put in at Baker's Crossing and got separated from his canoe. Even touching the bank can get one arrested for trespassing. Ranchers like to invoke the Spanish Land Grant version of property rights, which accords ownership of a river to include its bottom.

Until 1988, paddling was downright impossible if you couldn't do twenty-five miles in a single day. That's the year the Finegans sold the Dolan Creek Ranch to Texas Parks and Wildlife Department, which designated the land as a state natural area with virtually no park infrastructure. That made it possible to run the upper 15.5-mile part of Devils from Baker's Crossing—still a physically exhausting challenge—and legally pull out to sleep, then do 9.5 miles to the takeout, where fishing guide Gerald Bailey operates a shuttle service.

I managed to complete the run in two days, but only after hours of pulling my boat over shallow stretches, getting lost in jungles of river cane, running aground on the coarse, exceptionally abrasive limestone lurking just below the water's surface, and paddling into relentless headwinds that kicked up waves in my face. Heeding the retired boater's advice, on the few occasions I actually did touch a bank, it was of an island in the middle of the river. I felt a sense of satisfaction completing the journey, even while I was convinced I'd joined the silent majority whose first time on the Devils was their last. Maybe I'd run it again, I told myself, but only after an extended period of heavy rain, when the Pafford gauge was reading at least 500 cubic feet per second, twice the normal flow.

Less than six months later, I went back on my word. Somehow, my memory had erased all the nightmarish particulars of the first trip. I forgot sleeping for twelve hours straight at the end of the first day's paddle because I was too exhausted to do anything else.

That's the only excuse I can offer for returning to Baker's Crossing in early March to do it again. This time, the flow is mostly the same from the previous October. And if conditions aren't ideal, the one thing I recall from the first trip was, there is no such thing as an ideal day on the Devils. You work with what you get. At least overnight temperatures aren't dropping into the teens, as they had two days earlier. Even Mary Hughey is reassuring. "The Devils River and kayakers get along just fine," she tells me as she collects the camping fee from Joe Hauer and me at Baker's Crossing. Canoes might drag the whole fifteen miles down to the state natural area. But not shallow-drafting kayaks.

Hughey is the matron at Baker's Crossing, the owner of the two-story mansion set by the banks of the tree-lined river and the surrounding campgrounds. A sweet lady who is training her two-year-old grandson, Casey, for a career in the hospitality industry, she makes it plain to each and every boater camping out to be on the river by nine in the morning, or she'll make darn sure they will. She gets enough heat from landowners downstream for letting people on to the river in the first place, she says, and she doesn't need any more grief.

She also raises a warning flag. While talking about lack of rain, a common topic of conversation west of the 98th meridian, I mention the ten-year drought.

"Ten years?" she says. "It's more like a thirty-year drought. The river hasn't really run since the '70s." She isn't kidding. Thirty years ago, the headwaters of the Devils were generally recognized as being near Juno, ten miles up the highway. These days, it barely holds a flow at Baker's, though there is enough moving water to lull me to sleep the instant I climb into my sleeping bag.

We are on the river before eight the following morning, and reality rears its ugly head within ten minutes, when the little riffle I ride disappears in a pool of gravel. Scrunch. I get up and pull, the first of more drags than I care to count. Somewhere in that first hour, I check the new seat I'd hooked onto my boat for back support and realize the zip pocket behind the seat is not watertight but in fact self-baling. The topo maps I'd downloaded have turned to mush. I've left my river guidebooks in the car.

My first trip in October was with David Hollingsworth, who'd run the Devils before and brought along his GPS to pinpoint our location. This time, I am the experienced one, and now I have nothing—no map, no printed material, no help, since only a handful of people live along the river—nothing but my obviously defective memory. I calm down by reminding myself I've done this before. It is only two days. Heck, I could go without water for that long if I really had to. And we had plenty of water, trail mix, and nutrition bars stuffed into our dry-bags. I decide doing it without any navigational aid would be liberating, with the understanding that mistakes would be unforgiven.

Hauer doesn't believe me when I tell him it will take the full day to get down to the state natural area. Like me on any first time on a river, he keeps thinking the takeout is just around the next bend.

"Patience," I counsel.

As long as I maintain a steady stroke, I can savor the sweet bliss of floating through a genuine wilderness practically devoid of power lines, roads, or human presence—save for the occasional hunting shack. In Texas, no less. The views are sublime: a flock of mallards skittering off the water, coots diving, a killdeer swooping just above the water line, hawks surfing thermals high above, a great blue heron lumbering out of the river cane. A bass spooks from under a shallow shelf, tail flopping above the surface, startled by my intrusion. On almost every cliff overlooking the water, I see caves and overhangs, the types that provided nomadic people over the previous 6,000 years with shelter and access to the other basic necessities of water and food nearby. There are more pictographs in the Devils, Pecos, and Río Grande watersheds than anywhere else on earth, save for the south of France.

My soundtrack is the steady splish-splash of every stroke, accompanied by distant squawks, chirps, and screes, the occasional soft flutter of flapping wings, the intermittent whooshes of wind; and that Billy Joe Shaver song. It is a splendid river. More than once, I find myself on a tight rapid or in a gin-clear pool shaded by nearby groves of pecans and oaks, thinking I was back on the Blanco, more than 200 miles east. The cliffs, the outcroppings, and the massive limestone the river cuts through brought Big Bend closer than it really is. Life is distilled to the sweet essence of river, land, and sky. But I cannot get lost in the moment. After all, this is the Devils. You never know when the water will run out or where the next crusty rock is crouching just under the surface, ready to snag an unwary boat. On some rocks, I recognize the distinctive blue streaks of my kayak, skid mark souvenirs from my first trip.

It is not difficult to focus on the dry, desiccated landscape and imagine something that during a much wetter period resembled the Hill Country. The first European to note the Devils' existence, the Spaniard Gaspar Castaño de Sosa, was not exactly impressed. He named it the Laxas, which translates as "feeble" or "slack." Explorers and travelers who followed him held it in higher regard, naming it the San Pedro and often lingering longer than planned, since it was the last rest stop before striking out west across the desert. St. Pete struck Texas Ranger Jack Hays as an uninspired name for the river when he came upon it in the 1840s, before he moved on to California. He reckoned the Devils would be a more suitable title. A military camp had been established on the river after the Mexican War. Another Texas Ranger, Capt. Pat Dolan, arrived to clear the region of outlaws in 1870, early enough to have his name attached to the falls.

That made it safe for E.K. Fawcett, who, along with a group of friends, left his mark inside a cave above Dolan Falls on July 24, 1883. As the Devils' first settler, Fawcett started grazing sheep by the falls, and others followed with goats and cattle. Eventually the grasses in the watershed were worn down to the nub, leaving rocks, prickly pear, cedar, mesquite, and the occasional lechuguilla. The browsing down explained why I heard but a single calf on the trip. Not much is left for today's livestock to eat.

Gary Garrett, the Texas Parks and Wildlife Department biologist who has studied the Devils extensively, confirms that the river is relatively unpolluted and undammed: less than 2 percent of all American rivers remain free of such impoundments, and the upper part of the Devils is the only free-running river left in Texas—and one of the most pristine in the southwestern United States. But he also makes clear that, like every river in Texas, the Devils has been impacted plenty. Its flow has declined steadily. Chloride, phosphate, cadmium, lead, and mercury have been found in concentrations high enough to be potentially dangerous for aquatic life and human health. The Río Grande cutthroat trout, once native to the region, disappeared long ago. The smallmouth bass, which attracts fishermen from all over Texas, is an exotic introduced to the river, and with the cessation of the practice of stocking exotics in the Devils, the smallmouths are just holding on, making the practice of catch and release on the river crucial to their survival. Garrett suspects the smallmouth and other exotics, including carp, black bullhead, and blue tilapia, may be contributing to the threatened status of the native Devils River minnow.

But Garrett also gives me hope. "Stewardship is at a higher level here than on other Texas rivers, and property owners are utilizing Texas Parks and Wildlife resources to learn sound land and water management practices," he says. The big ranches are staying big, thanks to attorneys and doctors who want to keep it that way, buying big chunks of real estate. The Nature Conservancy bought

10,000 acres within the watershed, including Dolan Falls in 1991, and has brokered sales of another 35,000 acres with conservation easements, meaning the land will remain undeveloped forever.

I arrive at the state natural area fifteen minutes ahead of Hauer. Usually it's the other way around. For all the exertion, we haven't averaged even two miles an hour. Back home we could do twice that distance in less time. But we aren't back home. We are on the Devils. And it has beaten us down bad. By the time Hauer crawls onto the rock shelf, he is declaring his fealty to the San Marcos River. Why come all this way to be brutalized? He is asleep before the sun goes down. I stay awake to watch the last light of day fade to dark while a couple of bats flutter erratically overhead. The last calls of a lonely mallard pierce the night. It is warm enough to sleep out without a tent and cool enough to snuggle into a sleeping bag. I don't care whether the wind whips up or if it drizzles before dawn. I am too wasted.

The second day begins with a short, less-than-a-mile paddle from the state natural area to the juncture where Dolan Creek, the most abundant of thirty-two tributaries, meets the Devils. The meager flow builds into a churning and hissing torrent, climaxing at Dolan Falls. Water gushes through four chutes carved from solid rock, adorned with maidenhair fern. I'd seen a similar setting once before, at the Narrows on the Blanco. And like the Narrows, running one of those chutes likely would have terminal results. We scout and ponder, craning our necks, and decide to portage, following the metal arrows on the rocks on the left bank.

Dolan Creek's recharge makes the last nine miles a pleasure. Rapids carry the boats instead of stopping them. Picking a path through the reeds becomes a game of chance. Pick the right chute and get easy passage. Pick wrong, get out and drag. I even find a couple of spots where I can point my boat upstream and surf.

Although we've seen a scattering of trailers and cabins, one two-story structure high on a ridge above the eastern bank that looks like a hotel or a resort is the first real sign of civilization, other than all the posted "No Trespassing" signs. It is tobacco lawyer John Eddie Williams's Rio Vista Ranch, I later learn.

We find Gerald Bailey's place with no problem. His hillside home is marked by a canoe jutting into the air. Gerald is out guiding a fishing trip, his wife tells us, but Don Kelley will be over in a minute to drive us back. Don, one of the few other full-time residents of the Blue Sage subdivision, used to be a hunter and a fisherman when he first visited the Devils, but since he moved to a house overlooking the river from a high bluff, he says he's become a naturalist out of necessity. "You can't do much of anything if you live here, other than be a screwaround, because it's so remote and far away from everything," he says while he ties down our boats and loads us into his Suburban.

I happily pay Kelley $150 to shuttle us back to Baker's once I see what passes for roads on the Blue Sage subdivision and knowing the next takeout is another twenty miles downstream on a part of the river that is more like a dammed-up lake. It takes an hour to drive the fourteen miles out to US Highway 277, and almost another two hours back to either the natural area or Baker's.

We talk about wild turkeys. I've seen more on the Devils than anywhere in my life. We talk about how rocks seem to hold heat in this part of Texas longer than anywhere else, how untamed the river gets when it does flood, and how the same landowners with the hostile reputations are actually protecting the river and the caves and pictographs by discouraging tourists. I marvel how I hadn't seen a piece of trash anywhere on the entire trip.

We talk about rain and how it almost never does in these parts.

Hauer figures he left at least $100 worth of his Perception's bottom on the caustic limestone in the river. His first time on the Devils may be his last. Me, once again I swear on a stack of Bibles that I won't do it again until there's been a really, really big dump in its watershed, which may not happen again in my lifetime.

Then again, that's what I said the last time around. Before Billy Joe Shaver started rumbling around in my head.

South Texas

The San Antonio River

We marched five leagues over fine country, with broad plains—the most beautiful in New Spain. We camped on the banks of an arroyo, adorned by a great number of trees, cedars, willows, cypresses, osiers, oaks, and many other kinds. This [river] I called San Antonio de Padua, because we reached it on his day. Here we found certain rancherías in which the Payaya nation live. We observed their actions, and I discovered that they were docile and affectionate, were naturally friendly, and were decidedly agreeable toward us.

—Domingo Terán de los Rios, 1691

The San Antonio Spring may be classed as of the first water among the gems of the natural world. The whole river gushes up in one sparkling burst from the earth. It has all the beautiful accompaniments of a smaller spring, moss, pebbles, seclusion, sparkling sunbeams, and dense overhanging luxuriant foliage. The effect is overpowering. It is beyond your possible conceptions of a spring. You cannot believe your eyes, and almost shrink from sudden metamorphosis by invaded nymphdom.

—Frederick Law Olmsted, from *A Journey through Texas,*
or, A Saddle-Trip on the Southwestern Frontier, 1854

Domingo Terán de los Ríos was appointed governor of Spanish Texas in 1691 and traveled through the region to report on conditions. His account was translated by Mattie Alice Austin Hatcher and published by the Texas Catholic Historical Society in 1932.

Frederick Law Olmsted (1822–1902), who designed New York's Central Park, was also a writer and social critic. In 1853, the *New York Daily Times* sent him to Texas, where he spent months traveling through the state, recording his impressions.

River Music

by Carmen Tafolla

Curving into its cálido colors
mirrored against its own marbled movement
this stream has always sprung simply
smoothly from the heart of song
making soft melodies ring from the leaves
from mission bells and tender voices
of children who play here between the centuries
rippling in and out of laughter

Strong as silt, they stay unchanged
unweakened even by the years
their large dark eyes still staring, boldly
begging miracles of this green liquid gem
that washes quiet through city's soul
healing, hearing, hoping

From sunpeak's sound of rest
a moment's cool peace stolen from
Payaya-speaking trees,
to midnight's festive dance of colors
shimmers on the river singing
weaving past the barges named
María and Elena
and the paddleboats' soft splash,
glimmering through and past
its sons and daughters
grown and multicolored like its flowers, barges,

Carmen Tafolla is an internationally acclaimed Chicana writer from San Antonio and the author of more than thirty books. She was named San Antonio's first-ever Poet Laureate. The first verse of "River Music" is engraved onto a sculpture at San Antonio's Elmendorf Park. From *This River Here: Poems of San Antonio* by Carmen Tafolla. Wings Press, 2014. Published by permission of Carmen Tafolla.

like its Christmas lights,
comes this river music,
comes this harmony
to make the spirit-breath
dance peaceful
and flow strong,
reflecting
the very rhythm
of you

The Mythic Narrative
of San Pedro Creek

by John Phillip Santos

San Antonio de Béjar wears its glistening halo of river, creeks, and arroyos like an ageless crown, as if this place at the edge of the arid countryside to the west and south has been blessed by time, receiving a long span of years with the grace of a thousand springs and endlessly flowing water. Maybe it is an accidental oasis, a singular place in a singular part of the world, with a singular story to tell, a story of how a city was imagined into being on the banks of the humble stream that would come to be known as San Pedro Creek.

As the place where San Antonio was born, the story of the creek and the city are forever intertwined. Without San Pedro Creek, the city's history would've looked very different, if it would've had a history at all.

An early Spanish explorer, the Fray Isidro Félix de Espinosa, wrote in 1709 of a lush valley with a plentiful spring, and prophetically noted, "The river, which is formed by this spring, could supply not only a village, but a city, which could be founded here." Nine more years would pass before his words would come true.

As in some ancient legend, a city emerged out of these waters. A city bubbled forth out of this spring-fed stream, running from long before there was anyone here to witness it—or drink from it.

If you follow the *ruta* of San Pedro Creek, you are on a pilgrimage rooted in the past, destined for the future.

300 years long, the story of San Antonio is but a brief episode in the millennial chronicle of San Pedro Creek. If this creek could speak, in whispers of song, or poetry, it might tell the story of the city that it birthed, brought to the light of history, its most extraordinary, and perhaps unexpected, progeny. Whispers of memories, echoes of song, rhythms of poesy, drumbeats and bugles, punctuated by cannonades—and long intervals of peace. Then all the bustle of building

John Phillip Santos, born and raised in San Antonio, was a finalist for the National Book Award for his *Places Left Unfinished at the Time of Creation*. He serves as University Distinguished Scholar in Mestizo Cultural Studies at the University of Texas at San Antonio. An earlier version of this essay appeared as "A Creek Tells Its Story" in the *Rivard Report*, November 15, 2015. Published by permission of John Phillip Santos.

the great city, whining saws, hammers pinging, whirring engines of industry and commerce, the wail of locomotives and engines, ebbing and flowing between the past, present, and future.

Occasionally, as if angered or overcome by the tumult of human conflicts and industry, the creek would rise up over her banks, flooding the growing settlement, sending her currents into the streets of the city, washing away whatever wasn't well-secured.

And we walk on. We flow with these waters, into the city created by these springs of ancient origin. Archaeology tells us that the creek's mother springs and shady environs were an ages-old place of shelter and succor. Archaeologists have found evidence along San Pedro Creek of settlement reaching back 10,000 years. Evidence of those first settlements, a hidden legacy, is under the earth near the corner of Camaron and Santa Rosa streets.

The path of the creek, long hidden by strata of asphalt and urban development, traces an arc through the very heart of downtown San Antonio, a route that carries much of the city's earliest history and lore, a reminder of how deeply the landscape and human enterprise have been linked in this Central Texas oasis.

San Antonio is the modern chapter in the epic history of San Pedro Creek. On the occasion of our city's 300th anniversary in 2018, we remembered that we would not be here if not for the clear running waters that are the original blessings of this *tierra*. San Antonio is a city whose existence was ordained by this graced geography, birthed in the swath of alluvial basin land nestled between what came to be known as San Pedro Creek and the San Antonio River, the one-time *Yanaguana*.

The saga of the city's creation is a chronicle of meetings between strangers, an incomparable historical drama underway in the earliest days of the New World, the meeting point between the epics of Mexico and the United States.

Intrepid Spaniards first encountered the native peoples of these lands here, and eventually the city that emerged from that fateful meeting became a *frontera* crossroads of the world—a place of *mestizaje* and transformation.

Today, it is home to people of every nation on Earth.

While there have been episodes of misunderstanding and violence, the deeper story of San Antonio is one of exchange, triumph, and hope, a tale of humanity's capacity to build *a new kind of home* out of the wilderness, *becoming a city that embodies the world*. San Antonio's long history testifies to the unique mingling of cultures and heritages that has shaped the southwestern borderlands of the United States.

Indeed, our history is a *testimonio* to the way this legacy of encounters between peoples has manifested a new kind of humanity. We are older than the

American Republic, but we are also an emerging capital of America's undeniably *mestizo* destiny.

San Pedro Creek is a pathway into the deepest currents of San Antonio's history and memory. Spaniards were tireless scribes and cartographers of their journeys in the New World. A series of maps, by the Marquéz de Aguayo, Luis Antonio Menchaca, and José de Urrutia, among many others, document the evolving place and importance of the creek in San Antonio's infancy. Later, the creek would become a dividing line between the city's Hispanic—and Anglo—American communities, between downtrodden *Laredito* on the west bank, and the shiny white American city on the east side of the creek. It was a partition that was breached as commonly as it was observed, resulting in the deeply *mestizo* culture of today's San Antonio.

San Pedro Creek harbors many such stories of San Antonio's "becoming," the myriad ways a place in the wilderness of the ancient New World became a modern American city, uniquely rooted in the deeply braided epics of Mexico and the United States. Two presidios were built near here, before the Alamo. San Fernando Cathedral, as well as other temples and sanctuaries, arose nearby. The courthouse, city hall, garrisons and jails, San Antonio's first train yards, all found their places alongside San Pedro Creek.

The creek's story unfolds like a pilgrimage tale—hearkening to such legendary paths as the journey to the Tepeyac shrine of the Virgin of Guadalupe in Mexico City, the *Ruta de Santiago* in Spain, the paths of pilgrims in Mecca. From a past of crossed swords, the waters of the creek ever flow toward concord.

When you follow the *ruta* of San Pedro Creek, you are on a pilgrimage rooted in the past, destined for the future.

San Antonio

A City Guided by Its River

by Alexis Harte

A river's inclination is to change its course—exploiting the shore's variations, throwing its energy into erosion-prone banks. As cities burgeoned around once-wild rivers, there followed a period of struggle as the two forces learned to cope with each other.

When they were no longer able to change their paths, rivers would transform their characters. Following the ascendancy of rail transport in the 1800s, many became polluted, sullen places, the neglected neighbors of iron scrap yards and industrial decay. Confined to flood channels, rivers rebelled, regularly hopping their banks with disastrous results.

San Antonio is a prime example of a city and river coming to grips with each other's inevitability. Although historically prone to frequent bouts of flooding, the San Antonio River has become the well-groomed, even-keeled pride of the city.

With its canopy of native cypress and oak overhanging a subterranean labyrinth of waterfalls, lily ponds, stone stairways, and trestle bridges, San Antonio's 2.5-mile River Walk is a triumph of landscape architecture on a grand scale—a monumental work of riparian fantasy. Today the river's character is shaped more by residents' whims (from an environmentally friendly Irish-green dye job to a yearly drain-and-scrub party) than by its own hydrologic leanings.

The River Walk's European Style cafés, shops, bars, and restaurants also make it a serious economic engine for the city, annually drawing more than seven million visitors who spend roughly $800 million. An unmistakable serenity combined with thriving commerce and ample recreation places the River

Alexis Harte is a Bay Area singer-songwriter who earlier worked as an urban forester after graduating from Yale's School of Forestry and Environmental Studies. Originally appeared in *American Forests*, Summer 2003. Published by permission of Alexis Harte and *American Forests*.

Since this article was published, the San Antonio River Improvement Project has successfully restored over thirteen miles of the waterway's ecosystem while expanding recreational opportunities.

Walk in the forefront of urban US waterfront projects and neck and neck with the Alamo as Texas's most popular tourist destination.

And because it provides a multitude of services—recreational, economic, aesthetic—the River Walk invites stewardship from an incredible diversity of San Antonio residents. Festivities surrounding the yearly scrubbing, in which locals pay a nickel to vote for the "King and Queen of the Mud," are indicative of the enthusiasm with which residents greet their care of this resource. The urbane river park of today, however, is the latest stage in a millennia-old human-river relationship.

The native Payaya people called it "Yanaguana," or place of refreshing waters. Arriving in 1691, Spanish missionaries found the Payaya living in "an oasis of wild grapes and cypress." Before laying down their satchels, the missionaries named it Rio San Antonio do Padua. With abundant water and unvarying climate (water temperature changes only five to seven degrees throughout the year), the Spanish thought it ideal for the five missions built between 1718 and 1731 in and around what is now the city of San Antonio.

Unlike Texas's fifteen other major rivers, the San Antonio has been spared a major dam or reservoir on its main trunk. Flowing southeasterly 194 miles through mostly mixed riparian forest, the San Antonio drains 4,180 square miles in six counties before joining the Guadalupe River. The Aransas National Wildlife Refuge, located on the confluence of these two rivers at San Antonio Bay, lies on the central neotropical migration path for hundreds of species of birds, including the world's largest existing flock of endangered whooping cranes.

While the San Antonio River system has long supported birds and wildlife, its relationship with humans has occasionally been less hospitable. Following deadly floods in 1921 that killed fifty and cost $10 million in damages, city leaders thought it best to simply bury the urban stretch of the river once and for all. A prominent engineering firm, Hawley and Freese, floated a fairly traditional plan that proposed constructing an upstream dam as a retention basin, straightening and widening the channel, and covering the downtown section with concrete. The city council quickly approved the plans.

With construction set to begin, the city's environmental consciousness awoke with a combination of jazz-age enthusiasm and frontier determination. Vocal opponents included the San Antonio Conservation Society, Daughters of the American Revolution, San Antonio Advertising Club, and San Antonio Real Estate Board.

Among those envisioning a river park for San Antonio was landscape architect H. H. Hugman, who waxed poetic about romantic midnight gondola rides past gas lamps. "Imagine," he told skeptical civic and business leaders, "floating down the river on a balmy night fanned by a gentle breeze carrying the delightful aroma of honeysuckle and sweet olive, old-fashioned streetlamps casting fantastic shadows on the surface of the water, strains of soft music in the air."

Despite the potent imagery, it took a few years to convince pragmatic civic and business leaders of the plan's merit. With the onset of the Depression, the city could not afford a plan that looked good but didn't tame the river's wild streak. And Hugman's somewhat dandified vision stood in marked contrast to the river's temperament outside city limits, where cattle ranching formed the main economic activity. Today hundreds of families still manage active farms throughout the region, a tradition that dates back to pre–Civil War times.

The River Walk plan gained momentum only after local businesses, grasping the benefit of a park atmosphere near their shops, in 1938 approved a small tax increase. The vote enabled the issuance of a $75,000 bond, seed money for the $3.5 million Works Progress Administration grant that followed. With funding in place, the city appointed Hugman principal architect and hired more than a thousand workers to clean and deepen the channels; construct retaining walls, elegant stairways, and bridges; and plant more than 11,000 trees and shrubs.

Many of the native bald cypress seedlings they planted then still tower overhead, but Hugman's plan was not restricted to natives. The River Walk retains a picturesque combination of perennials and subtropical trees and shrubs.

Completed in 1941, the cement-channeled River Walk bore little resemblance to the original river, and the rapid revitalization was matched by an equally swift deterioration. Financial planners overestimated the potential for revenue generation, and for the next twenty years, the area became a nest of illicit activity and petty crime.

When San Antonio was selected to host the 1968 Hemisfair, a scaled-down World's Fair for the Americas, a new generation of civic leaders began to see the River Walk's potential. A 1962 master plan called for a permanent River Walk commission, recommended improvements to lighting for safety and aesthetics, and reoriented many stores to face the river.

Now the River Walk is seen as a worldwide model for urban riverfront revival—and an early triumph in citizen conservation planning. Through perseverance and with an eye to the aesthetic potential, the original champions of a river park concept narrowly saved the San Antonio River from becoming another paved afterthought—the fate of many rebellious urban rivers in the early part of the twentieth century.

Leaving the idyllic shade of the River Walk, the San Antonio River heads southwards into trapezoidal, cement channels through the Historic Mission Reach. This once-meandering nine-mile stretch skirted through five of the original Spanish missions, including the Alamo.

Successors to landscape architect H. H. Hugman pored over the smallest details to balance aesthetics and flood prevention within the city center, but the US Army Corps of Engineers was far less imaginative elsewhere. Between the 1960s and 1980s, the Corps straightened and contained the river, removing large numbers of trees and other vegetation—standard flood-control practices in that era.

To the south, the straightened San Antonio River no longer abutted the missions themselves. The river that attracted and sustained the earliest Native American settlements and later Spanish settlers was detached from both its ecological footprint and its historical context. While effectively preventing devastating floods, the alterations were a triumph of function over form. Residents' affection for the River Walk is matched only by their distaste for the river's decrepit state outside town.

With a zeal reminiscent of the downtown river park's champions, the San Antonio River Oversight Committee was formed in 1998 to confront blight, lack of access to the missions, and loss of ecological integrity in the River's southern stretch. The committee also considered aesthetic improvements to the four-mile stretch north of the city (known as Museum Reach). Under the San Antonio River Authority's supervision, the city of San Antonio, Bexar County, and the US Army Corps of Engineers are collaborating to restore these sections to their past glory without undermining flood-control progress.

By acknowledging and guiding the river's energy—rather than trying to simply contain it—the northern and southern stretches will regain much of their natural course and character. Released from its confining channel, the river will be widened and its banks recontoured to allow for natural dispersal of floodwaters during and after heavy rains. Meanders will be created to reunite the river and the five missions.

A massive reforestation and planting effort will include more than forty native species. Besides attracting back native fish and wildlife, streamside and watershed planting will improve water quality.

A revised trail network, complete with public art and interpretative tools, will provide bicycle and pedestrian access from downtown, allowing the missions to regain their stature as a premier tourist destination. According to program manager Kevin Conner with the engineering firm Carter & Burgess, public support is overwhelming.

"Residents have weighed in on many issues," Conner says, "but mostly they want to know how soon this can happen."

My Home along the San Antonio River

by Sandra Cisneros

I live in San Antonio on the left bank of the river in an area of the city called King William, famous for its historic homes. South of Alamo Street, beyond King William proper, the San Antonio River transforms itself into a wildlife refuge as it makes its way toward the Spanish missions. Behind my house the river is more creek than river. It still has its natural sandy bottom. It hasn't been covered over with concrete yet. Wild animals live in the tall grass and in its waters. My dogs and I can wade across and watch tadpoles and turtles and fish darting about. There are hawks and cranes and owls and other splendid winged creatures in the trees. It is calming and beautiful, especially when you're sad and in need of big doses of beauty.

My favorite place is a huge cypress along the river. It's at least a century old and full of orifices for whispering or leaving offerings. Its roots are perfect for cradling in and reading a book. Once, it had a cleft in its belly, but someone cemented it up, I think because too many critters slept in there, two-legged as well as four. Well, why not? Who wouldn't want to sleep in the belly of a tree?

This is an ancient and sacred tree. Sometimes I find folks having a picnic there. Sometimes I find beer cans and condom wrappers. It seems everyone finds plenty of reasons to hang out by the tree. As for me, whenever I'm lost, I sit down on its lap and listen to what it has to tell me. After all, it is full of peace and unity and offers love indiscriminately to all.

In the spring after my mother died, a doctor wanted to prescribe pills for depression. "But if I don't feel," I said, "how will I be able to write?" I need to be able to feel things deeply, good or bad, and wade through an emotion to the

Sandra Cisneros is the author of several books, including her classic coming-of-age novel, *The House on Mango Street*, which has been translated into over twenty languages. Her numerous awards include a MacArthur Fellowship and the National Medal of the Arts. Copyright © 2020 by Sandra Cisneros. From *Have You Seen Marie?*, copyright © 2012 by Sandra Cisneros, published by Vintage Books, an imprint of Penguin Random House. And from "Favorite Place," copyright © 2014 by Sandra Cisneros, first published in *Texas Monthly* (vol. 42, no. 8). By permission of Susan Bergholz Literary Services, New York, New York, and Lamy, New Mexico. All rights reserved.

other shore, toward my rebirth. I knew if I put off moving through grief, the wandering between worlds would only take longer. Even sadness has its place in the universe.

I wish somebody had told me then that death allows you the chance to experience the world soulfully, that the heart is open like the aperture of a camera, taking in everything, painful as well as joyous, sensitive as the skin of water.

I wish somebody had told me to draw near me objects of pure spirit when living between births. My dogs. The trees along the San Antonio River. The sky and clouds reflected in its water. Wind with its scent of spring. Flowers, especially the sympathetic daisy.

I wish somebody had told me love does not die, that we can continue to receive and give love after death . . .

> *River said, "Don't you cry, mamas. I*
> *will take your tears and carry them to the*
> *Texas coast where they'll mix with the salty*
> *tears of the Gulf of Mexico, where they*
> *will swirl with the waters of the Caribbean,*
> *with the wide sea called Sargasso, the water*
> *roads of the Atlantic, with the whorls and*
> *eddies around the Cape of Good Hope,*
> *around that hat called Patagonia, the blue*
> *waters of the Black Sea and the pearl-filled*
> *waters around the islands of Japan, the*
> *coral currents of Java, the rivers of the*
> *several continents, the Aegean of Homer's*
> *legend, the mighty Amazon, and the wise*
> *Nile, the grandmother and grandfather*
> *rivers Tigris and Euphrates, the great*
> *mother river the sandy Yangtze,*
> *the dancing Danube, and through the strait*
> *of the Dardanelles, along the muddy*
> *Mekong and the sleepy Ganges, waters*
> *warm as soup and waters cold to the teeth,*
> *waters carrying away whole villages,*
> *waters washing away the dead, and waters*
> *bringing new life, the salty and the sweet,*
> *mixing with everything, everything,*
> *everything, everything."*

The Lower Guadalupe River

A Return to the River

by Clayton Maxwell

For three days in early October, the blue heron leads us downriver. In the mornings we push off in canoes through the olive green water of the lower Guadalupe, made murkier by Hurricane Harvey's visit just over a month before. We'd forget about the heron while focusing on more practical concerns: sunscreen, keeping the boat upright, alligators, spicy peanuts, cold beer. But then, with an audible swoosh, the blue wings unfurl, and the bird glides downstream to yet another cypress branch, showing off his mighty wingspan, his graceful flight. Hurricane Harvey's landfall in late August 2017 caused the Guadalupe to flow over its banks in Cuero and Victoria. And while many trees are down and furniture hangs high in the branches of others, the flood certainly hasn't washed away everything beautiful.

At least I think it's the same blue heron surprising us each morning, but maybe that's because I'm a romantic and a rookie on overnight river trips. Out on this water, a current flowing close to civilization and yet a world away from it, magical things feel possible. A river makes its own country: the past loops into the present, new confluences are made, a heron is leading us.

I am canoeing this rarely traveled stretch of the Guadalupe for three days with two seasoned river runners and their young sons because of John Graves's *Goodbye to a River*, a classic of Texas literature. I'd read it over the summer,

Clayton Maxwell is an Austin-based travel, culture, and lifestyle writer who has pedaled in the footsteps of Don Quijote, bumped her way to Marrakech in an overnight train, and survived on coconut juice for a week—all for the sake of the story. © Clayton Maxwell, 2019. Expanded from an earlier version published in *Texas Highways*, July 2018. Published by permission of Clayton Maxwell.

and Graves's voice, honest and wry, carried me with him on his 1957 three-week canoe trip down the Brazos, starting in Palo Pinto County and ending in Somervell County. Graves—Texas's roll-your-own-smokes fireside thinker and naturalist—passed away in 2013, but with lines like "We will be nearly finished, I think, when we stop understanding the old pull toward green things and living things, toward dirt and rain and heat and what they spawn," his writing is as present and vital as ever.

It's good to take into account where you come from. That's one of the messages that Graves whispered in my ear. For him, that meant really *knowing* the river and the land he grew up on, the fish and fowl, the people's stories. It meant caring about the history and the future of this wild land we now call Texas. It meant returning to the Brazos, the river of his youth. So I was going to return to mine.

I grew up in Victoria, Texas, and the stretch of the Guadalupe that flows through the town's Riverside Park was a frequent playground for my sisters and me; our parents would hold our hands as we stood in the current, toddlers dazzled by sun-lit water rushing against our legs. This muddy waterway named in 1689 after the patron Saint of Mexico, *Nuestra Señora de Guadalupe*, was my childhood taste of Graves's "old pull" toward the green and living things, the raw and the wild. I left Victoria when I was sixteen, but now I am going back, this time in a boat, John Graves–style.

"What you are doing, going to be on the river, that is what brought people here, why any of this is here," Gary Dunnam, a Victoria historian told me when I visited him just before our trip. The Guadalupe *is* the area's history, Dunnam explained. It's why the Karankawa, Aranamas, Tamiques, and Tonkawas were here, followed by the Spaniards who came and tried with mixed results to Christianize them in the early 1700s. In 1824, a strong-willed empresario named Martín De León came to the river, establishing a settlement that became Victoria. While these early settlement patterns along the Guadalupe might seem obvious to many, Dunnam's words hit me with a disappointing truth: even though I grew up here, I was ignorant of the entwined history of Victoria and the river that brought it into being.

Would I find traces of this history on the river? Or would I find alligators and snakes dangling from trees, as my mom had warned? The unknown loomed. I did know, however, that it would be foolish for me—all eagerness and no experience—to do it alone. So I asked Chris Carson and John Hewlett, two friends and ardent canoeists, to join me. With kids and spouses, work and busy schedules, we finally scheduled a three-day weekend when we could all steal away to Victoria in Chris's VW van with two canoes strapped on top and Chris's and John's young sons in tow.

On a hot Saturday mid-morning, we unload at an RV park nine miles south of Cuero. After multiple trips from van to boat, the canoes are teetering with the weight of two coolers, waterproof boxes for iPhones and GPS devices, three tents, sleeping bags and pads, big yellow dry sacks stuffed with clothes and first aid supplies, fishing poles, a camping stove, provisions from breakfast taco fixings to Chris's favorite jalapeño sausages, and a little bit of mezcal for fireside sipping.

Chris has even brought pillows. "I get a lot of hell for it," he said, "But what can I say? I'm a pillow guy." John Graves might have cringed, although his own canoe weighed 200 pounds thanks to all of what he called "unnecessaries," including a gun, an ax, and a lantern (headlamps were not an option in 1957). Graves laments that he, too, falls short of Henry David Thoreau—whom he calls "Saint Henry"—and his call for simplicity. Just hauling and strapping down all of our own "unnecessaries" makes us sweat before we've even begun paddling.

We drag John's canoe to the river, and water seeps in: a hole in the boat. Our shuttle driver has taken off in Chris's van, and we are now alone—John and his six-year-old son, Harlon; Chris and his nine-year-old son, Max; and me—at a Harvey-ravaged RV park boat launch, and John's canoe is filling up with water. It could be that our river trip will end before it even begins.

The importance of the right gear has become real: John pulls out the saving cure—Waterweld. This magical epoxy for boat holes has a cure time of an hour, so we apply it to the leak and wait. Sticky in the late morning sun, we take our baptismal swim in the Guadalupe, eyes alert for Harvey-displaced gators. Hallelujah, the river is far cooler and fresher than we'd thought; it's an elixir, a heat- and fatigue-conquering mood lifter. This river is going to be good to us.

The epoxy dries, we test the canoe on the water, all is healed. Thankful for Waterweld, we finally start paddling. Up in the bow, I have it easy. Harlon, whose nickname is Huckle for Huckleberry Finn, rests in the middle on a pile of tents and sleeping bags. John is our captain in the back. Devoted fishermen Max and Chris, with a homemade PVC contraption holding multiple rods as centerpiece to their canoe, linger behind, poles in the water. There is no other soul on this quiet stretch of river, and we are in the flow of the river now, gliding downstream with "the waxen slim strength of a paddle's shaft," as Graves writes, on "a drifting sparkling sunlit afternoon."

I am surprised by many things: the swiftness of the current, a bald eagle flashing across the sky—my first eagle sighting in South Texas—but mostly by the beauty. It's the cypresses. They line the river here, steady in their curvy wide trunks, faintly mystical with their knobby roots, which Harlon calls "dragon's teeth." The cypresses frame the river, even after Harvey. Other tree species have fallen, their trunks crossing the water or wrapped in another tree, helpless against the cataclysmic force of last month's floodwater. The cypresses, however, with their powerful roots, held fast and kept the riverbank intact.

So we paddle on. With a lift of the shoulders and a twist of the spine, our paddles cut through liquid, and we glide. As Graves writes, "I had the feel of the river now, and the boat, and the country, and all of it was long ago familiar." With all the map studying, weather prognosticating, and other preparations over, we sink into the state of observation that a river invites. Eyes on the water, the banks, the sky—there is much to notice. A kingfisher skims the river. An alligator gar, at least five feet long, jumps out of the water and twists its toothy maw right in my face. I startle, and the boat wobbles, my first rookie move so far. Wobbling can mean tipping the boat. All of Chris's camera gear, everything we need, is in these canoes. Tipping, Chris repeats often, is not an option.

We approach a swath of white water, and John shouts, "Paddle hard!" so we can avoid a strainer, river terminology for a fallen tree that might suck you under its branches. Hurricane Harvey has brought us plenty of strainers. There are even a few small rapids on this stretch of river, and as much as I love the swift ride, I likely would have capsized by now without my experienced crew. Nine-year-old Max, who's logged many hours on the water with his dad, has learned the art of reading a river, but I have a long way to go.

When the heat threatens, we make a landing and jump in. Harlon, whose spirit animal must be an otter, is happiest in the water. So when we first find a clean sandbank with a riffle flowing past, he and John demo for me how to do "a float." We make ourselves straight as logs skimming over rocks, our life vests holding us up until we get to a safe landing spot and trudge up to shore—all smiles—to do it again.

On one of our float breaks, the young boys and I crawl up a twenty-foot sandy bluff to see what lies on the edge of our river world. Fenced-off fields span endlessly, with just a few lonely live oaks shading a couple of cows. I think of a photocopy of a plat map from 1858 that Gary Dunnam gave me: it shows the small grid that was Victoria nestled up to a bend in the river. Many of the names on the riverside plats north of Victoria—José Carbajal, Silvester, and Felix De León—are members of Martín De León's extended family. These green fields may have been theirs.

Before the sun dips low, we find our camp spot, a sandy island we soon discover is black with vultures in the trees and sky. Chris slaps his paddle on the water, and the piercing shotgun sound scares them away. "Vulture Island" is now our home for the night. The boys gather firewood, Max catches spiky little hellgrammites—the larvae of a dobsonfly—that he will later use to catch catfish, while Chris, or "Cooky," gets busy with dinner, which tonight is canned bean chili.

"The day's wind and bright light and paddling has washed me with clean fatigue, and my muscles felt good, in tone . . . one felt damned good," Graves wrote. Now after today's ten miles of paddling, I get it. We've hit that sweet spot where effort turns to ease, and we can settle in to our little island. These ever-shifting sand and mud teardrops are often the only good place to camp on many stretches of Texas rivers without trespassing, and it feels like a sweet victory to have found ours—surrounded by private ranches—and make it home for the night.

"We are tapping into something that is crazy beautiful," Chris says sitting by the fire that night as the moon rises over the river, a bit of mezcal making the rounds while the boys sleep in tents near at hand. All the effort these two river-mad friends of mine go to—the hoisting and hauling and planning—it delivers keys to a rare universe, one removed from park rangers, people, private property. Their reward is cicada song layered over the murmur of water and a pocket of freedom in the middle of a river. We linger, losing ourselves in some fireside tales and a little Walt Whitman, not wanting the day to end. "We hung over the fire," Graves wrote, "with sharp animal relish until we knew we had to leave."

On down . . . That is a refrain Graves repeats throughout *Goodbye to a River*, and I see why: the thrill of finding out what's around the next bend. The river is Mother Nature's response to the human desire for novelty. What's next? It's a paradox of wanting. As much as we hate to leave something treasured behind—a good camp spot on our island, a precious moment with our kids who are growing up too fast—we also crave the current. A river is only good if it's flowing. Unhurried and with muscles only pleasantly sore, we set out, easing into our next ten- to twelve-mile day.

And with a gasp we see the blue flash of the heron, waiting for us, leading us downriver.

Today we are on the lookout for an almost 300-year-old remnant of the Spanish effort to missionize along the Guadalupe: a stone dam built in 1733 by "converts" at La Bahía to divert water for irrigating corn and melon crops. The Franciscan *padres* at La Bahia mission worked dutifully to Christianize the Karankawas, Tamiques, and other indigenous populations here for twenty-three years before packing off for a more protected spot in Goliad in 1749.

We find the weathered but still intact wall of rocks easily, land our canoes, jump off the dam, do a float. The kids investigate the smooth river rocks and bounty of purple-tinged mother-of-pearl clamshells on the beach. Did Aranama or Tamique children jump from this dam under the watchful eye of Franciscan friars almost three hundred years ago? Maybe, but such details of history, like Graves said, are often a fog.

Deep into the rhythm of our second day, I get a sense of just how much the canoe is a floating conversation capsule. Hours of what Graves calls an "obstructionless smooth glide" through sun, water, and sky make this boat a fine place for "how-I-met-your-mother" and other father/son talks that the busy pace back home rarely allows. As Chris would tell John and me later that night by the campfire, "You know what? Max and I, today on the river, I don't know if you heard us laughing, but he and I probably had the best conversation we've had in a long time. He said to me, 'Dad, I think one of my favorite things in life is going down the river.' It felt good."

After hours of rigorous paddling, including several of what Chris and John call "the power twenty" (twenty hard strokes followed by a pause), Harlon is restless and shouts for a swim break, *now*, but we are not in a safe landing spot. I hear John say behind me, calmly, "Harlon, look at me, I want you to understand something. We don't make the river; we don't have any control over where the islands and banks are going to be. We have to take what the river gives us."

So far, this river has been generous. We bivouac our last night on "Skull Island," which we named for an unidentifiable skull we find perched in the middle of it. We pitch camp near the river to hear its rippling as we sleep, what Harlon calls "the world's best sound machine." After dinner, we return to the fire. Here, away from the strip malls and highways, there is space to really consider our predecessors. "Think about that—this island has been camped on, this whole stretch of river, for thousands of years," Chris says, thumbing the smooth cuts in the Native American spear point he'd found among the river rocks earlier in the day. This quiet moment—this whole river trip, in fact—is required in order to step back out of time, to taste the bigger flow of history. By the moonlit water, it hits you in a way that placards and dioramas in museums can't touch.

On down. Our last day is a haul as we push through fourteen miles to get to our takeout (or "put-out," as I incorrectly called it—and the guys didn't let me forget). The cypresses have disappeared, and the extreme erosion, particularly after Harvey, gives this part of the river a post-apocalyptic feel. After thirty-five river miles, Chris and John are ready for the cold *michelada* I will buy them at La Tejanita Restaurant as soon as we find our exit, which proves difficult. Riverside Park is still closed from the hurricane, and the dock that should be waiting for us is not there. Weary, we find a long metal staircase leading out of slippery mud to the PumpHouse Riverside Restaurant and Bar twenty-five feet above us. The unload is a haze of aching-back effort, carrying our "unnecessaries" up the stairs. We find La Tejanita, and the *micheladas*, served in generous goblets, are delicious.

Graves's trip was about solitude, mostly. Mine has been about companion-
ship. Had I been on my own, it might have been easy to get stuck in my old childhood impressions of what my hometown river is about. I would have missed
the chance to see through the eyes of my friends and their sons—Max's face
upon catching a catfish or Harlon's laughter floating downstream—flashes of
beauty that have brought me a new, refreshed relationship to the Guadalupe.
Especially when Chris, not one to overpraise, exclaimed more than once how
damn pretty this rarely traveled stretch of river is—I felt a twinge of hometown
pride for a river I'd paid no attention to since I was a kid. And this expedition,
made over thirty years after I left Victoria, carved out space for the adult version of me on the river—one who's at ease with Guadalupe mud in her nails,
quick to laugh, happy with friends in the wild.

After thirty-five miles of river, how do I "take into account the thing I came
from," as Graves would ask? I come from a tangled history I now understand
better, one of abandoned Franciscan stone dams and long-expired land plats
with Spanish-Mexican names and the many people I now know came here
before. It is a story of deep-rooted cypress trees that can withstand roaring
floodwaters, wiggly hellgramites, and a blue heron that, I feel certain, wanted
to lead us downriver. It is looping my present to my past through friendships
deepened during three days of paddling, mud, and river floats. Most of all, the
Guadalupe has made clearer the immutable love between parent and child
that threads through generations, from my old days in Riverside Park with my
parents to today, watching Chris and John show their sons how to hook a fish,
build a campfire, just be together. Taking into account the thing we came from:
it is also these brownish-green waters, reviving even if muddy, that carry us
on down, no matter what.

Where the River Meets the Bay

by Michael Berryhill

When we wade in San Antonio Bay, a few miles from the barrier island where whooping cranes overwinter, my daughter and I play a game with mud. I scrunch down in the water and grab a handful of bay bottom and pour it into her cupped palms. "Here's some ice cream, Elizabeth," I say. "It's chocolate." Then I grub in the bottom for another handful and give her another scoop and another while she stands laughing, the mud oozing through her fingers.

On the fourth or fifth grab into the bay bottom, I almost always find the topping for her sundae: a common rangia clam. We stop and admire this animal that lives in the water only fifty yards from our front porch near the harbor at Seadrift.

Shaped like a bulging triangle, the rangia clam is about an inch thick at the caramel-colored hinge and tapers to a perfectly sealed lip subtly designed for burrowing. It is not a gaudy shell but is quite beautiful; its growth can be seen in the concentric succession of ridges in the top of the shell, which is acorn brown, growing gradually paler toward the lip. The rangia has a nice heft to it. Its shell is thick; it feels good in the hand. It's also good to eat. The nearby middens of the Karankawa Indians contain many thousands of rangia shells mixed in with oyster shells. A friend of mine cooked the clams in a big dish of pasta and vegetables, and they were quite good.

Like oysters, clams are filter feeders, and in our corner of the bay, they have a lot to filter. The water of San Antonio Bay is almost always murky, or what the scientists call turbid. Its color varies from dark green to whitened coffee to deep chocolate and is hardly ever clear, for San Antonio Bay is an estuary, one of the most important, and possibly one of the most endangered, on the Texas coast. Clear water can be great for fishing; it's wonderful to swim in, beautiful to see. But I have learned to appreciate the turbid water of San Antonio Bay,

Michael Berryhill is a Houston-based writer and editor and a Professor of Journalism at Texas Southern University. His 2011 book, *The Trials of Eroy Brown: The Murder Case That Shook the Texas Prison System*, won the Texas Institute of Letters Award for Best Nonfiction. This is adapted from "The Whooper's Table," which originally appeared in *Texas Parks & Wildlife* magazine, July 2003. Published by permission of Michael Berryhill and *Texas Parks & Wildlife* magazine.

for it speaks not of filth but of life, and the rangia clam is the very symptom of the bay's vitality.

The clams receive the nutrients and fresh water that pour out of the mouth of the Guadalupe River, only a few miles to the west of Seadrift in the upper reaches of the bay. The river and the bay live a yin-yang relationship. Without the outflow of the Guadalupe River, San Antonio Bay would be a completely different place, not necessarily dead, but radically altered, shorn of many species—including whooping cranes.

The truism of ecological science is that everything is connected. So it is foolish to think solely in terms of San Antonio Bay, as though that body of water alone is what matters. It's San Antonio Bay and Mesquite Bay and Espiritu Santo Bay and the Guadalupe estuary, and this place, this living place, this superorganism, depends on decisions made hundreds of miles from the mouth of the river. It's dependent on how San Antonio manages the water it withdraws from the Edwards Aquifer, which in times of severe drought supplies 70 percent of the flow of the river. It's dependent on how much water we take from the river to feed the developing cities of Central Texas.

Everything in the bay answers to the exchange of salt and fresh water. Fresh water and nutrients from the Guadalupe estuary create the nursery of the bay. Larvae produced in the trillions by shrimp, crabs, and fish find shelter among the grasses and feed on the microscopic particles washed there by the river and on each other. Only a few creatures from this extravagant spawn reach adulthood. The rest serve as food for all the creatures in the nursery: the shrimp, crabs, and the finfish; red drum, spotted seatrout, black drum, sheepshead, and flounder.

Farther out in the bay where the water is moderately saline, the oyster reefs are arranged in wide Vs to catch the plankton, living and dead, and the other nutrients the river pushes south. With oysters come oystercatchers, the birds with the red-orange, chisel-like beaks that make you believe someone studied them in order to make the oyster knife. Clams, snails, crabs, shrimp, trout, red and black drum, sheepshead, flounder, and spotted seatrout flourish in this bay, and with them come commercial and recreational fishermen and women. Ducks winter here, and with them come duck hunters. Shorebirds, stilts, sandpipers, peeps, terns, gulls, pelicans, herons, roseate spoonbills, egrets, wood storks, and the most famous birds of all, the whooping cranes, are drawn to the bay, attracting bird-watchers from around the world.

It would not be an exaggeration to say that the Guadalupe River has kept the whooping crane from going extinct, and that the crane's future depends on whether the river continues to deliver fresh water to San Antonio Bay.

Whooping cranes love blue crabs, and when they're plentiful, biologists estimate they make up 80 percent of the whooping crane's diet. This magnificent and endangered bird has never been numerous. Like the endangered white cranes of Asia, it has made a serious mistake in its way of living. It winters in pristine marsh, and pristine marsh is in short supply.

The whooping crane must be the most famous endangered species in the country. It is what environmentalists call a charismatic animal, like the panda and the koala. It's not hard to see why in 1937 the whooping cranes became the object of the nation's first major effort to save a species from extinction. They stand nearly five feet tall, are pure white with black wing tips, a red scalp patch and a black band across the eyes. When their wings are folded back, they give the impression that the crane is wearing an enormous bustle. Cranes have been revered in Asian mythology for millennia, perhaps because human qualities can be projected on them. They live for twenty-five to thirty years in the wild, they mate for life, are devoted to their spouses and protective of their offspring. In Chinese fairy tales and myths, people are always turning into cranes, the way Merlin turns into an owl and shamans in the Amazon turn into jaguars.

The whooping crane has been in decline for a long time, perhaps as long as 10,000 years, scientists say, because it prefers wintering in pristine marsh. Unlike its cousin, the smaller, plentiful sandhill crane, which feeds in fields and flies in flocks, whooping cranes are family feeders. A pair will stake out a territory of 200 to 500 acres of marsh and defend it against intrusion by other whoopers. Some of the birds have been returning to the same areas for years. Here they feed on mollusks, crustaceans, and, most importantly, blue crabs.

The cranes are special, but when I look at San Antonio Bay, I have to think of much more than cranes. I think of the river. I often take visitors up the mouth of the Guadalupe in my skiff and marvel at the steady flow of water in the narrow channel. Huge elephant ears, spider lilies, reeds and grasses, and palmetto palms line the banks. Masses of blossoming vines climb the trees, and here and there a magnificent cypress towers over the river. There's a shell midden six feet high, and farther upstream lie burial grounds of the Karankawa, who feasted on seafood here in the fall and winter, then moved inland in the summer to hunt deer and bison. Some anthropologists have theorized that the Karankawa were so tall because they ate so much seafood.

Because I live there when I can, I am tempted to call San Antonio Bay my bay, which is, of course, silly, since loving something is only a start. Romance is easy; intimacy is hard. Intimacy comes from knowledge, from seeing the connections. I sit on my porch with Elizabeth sometimes, and we just watch the sun shine on the water. The white pelicans paddle by majestically. In the morning we might see a crabber heading out, his little boat stacked eight feet high with traps. In the afternoon, the shrimp boats come in, trailing clouds of birds. A black skimmer swoops down to the surface of the water, scooping up a fish or a shrimp with its long lower bill. When you grow intimate with a bay, you want to learn everything about it, and every new thing raises another question and another.

This place is a nursery. Someday my little girl will bring her children here and, I hope, her children's children. They'll start out in that dark water, groping in the mud, reaching for clams. They will grow up knowing the bay better than I ever will, and because they know it and love it, they will protect it and care for it long after I and the rest of us are gone.

The Nueces River

oly Monday, April 4, we traveled in a northeasterly direction most of the day, and at times northeast by north for a distance of eight leagues. At the beginning the land was flat, and later there was a thicket of small mesquite trees; and having come out of it, we got into a larger one for three leagues. We came upon a river, which, although it carried little water, was recognized to flood its banks for almost half a league in times of rain. We named it Rio de las Nueces because there were many walnut trees. It is somewhat rocky, and all its rocks are flint and very fine.

—Alonso de León, 1689

The night drifted on. The river sparkled, it was a light-bearing streak through the country. A black-crowned heron waded with high steps in the dark shallows, intent on fish. An elf-owl slid in a long trajectory over its surface. From far out in the brush, they heard a water creature call out *rum-jug, rum-jug* in a low conspiratorial cry . . .

It was a dreaming time; the long blue Nueces curving through this grassy country with a secret life of its own, and on both sides of it, herds of wild horses stood together quietly grazing or sleeping. Wild cattle lifted their heads down in the brush alongside the river to hear the noise of the loping, scenting wolves, who ran with their noses to the ground searching for the smell of something newly born, something wounded, something old, something sick. The river fed the darting Guadalupe bass and its own gallery forest on either side.

—Paulette Jiles, from *Simon the Fiddler: A Novel*

Alonso de León (ca. 1639–1691) was governor of Coahuila and led four expeditions into Texas during the 1680s. An annotated translation of his 1689 account was published by Elizabeth Howard West in the *Quarterly of the Texas State Historical Association* 8, no. 3 (January 1905).

Paulette Jiles is a novelist, poet, and memoirist who lives on a ranch in the Texas Hill Country. Her bestselling novels include *News of the World*, which was a finalist for the 2016 National Book Award and was made into a film starring Tom Hanks. Her most recent novel, *Simon the Fiddler*, is set in Texas at the end of the Civil War.

The Nueces River

by William Jack Sibley

For years I've driven down Highway 16 to reach our small, caliche endowed ranch in Duval County. About eleven miles south of Tilden, the Nueces River moseys out of the surrounding flat scrub brush looking like a disoriented, dusty-green worm. A modest show of scanty trees and stunted undergrowth line the banks, highlighting the obvious disconnect between a semi-verdant source of moisture and the stark surrounding cactus and black brush *chaparral*.

This harsh, lonely, and familiar stretch of South Texas is where my maternal ancestors have toiled since pre–Civil War times. It's a long time for generations of one family to stick so tenaciously to the land. A land as parsimonious and tetchy as the stingy, frequently absent, flow of the Nueces. During the hottest part of the summer, the river can virtually disappear under sandbars, and you have to work hard to conjure up wet springs, past floods, wild torrents, and drenched bobcats shivering up trees to even remotely envision something presently labeled "a river."

Where the Nueces commences, deep in the heart of the Hill Country, in springs above Camp Wood and Barksdale, it's the very definition of a bluebonnet masterpiece. Cool blue-green waters, Greek isle rocky beaches, towering limestone ledges, groves of shady cedar and cottonwoods—all Chamber of Commerce exemplary. I've been swimming in the river below Camp Wood surrounded by butterflies, sunbathers, and the occasional fisherman all enveloped in the dreamy aura of summertime/water-time bliss.

In the Hill Country of my youth, over half a century ago, the water gurgling down this ancient ravine seemed as pure and iridescent as fluid silver. The legendary drought of the 1950s made water, any water, as precious and exceptional as finding river pearls scattered under your feet. For a South Texas youngster reared on dying mesquites and withered prickly pear, the near mirage of seeing an actual flowing stream of spring-fed liquid was almost

William Jack Sibley is a sixth-generation Texan and rancher with a versatile career as a writer. He's written dialogue for television's *Guiding Light*, was a contributing editor at Andy Warhol's *Interview Magazine*, and has seen his plays produced off Broadway. He's the author of three acclaimed novels set in Texas as well as a dozen screenplays. © William Jack Sibley, 2020. Published by permission of William Jack Sibley.

too much to comprehend. Where did it come from? Where was it going? Why was it here . . . and exasperatingly enough, why was it not where we lived and needed it?

All slights were abandoned with that first reckless dive into the chilly metallic green of the Nueces in August. Surfacing with electrifying vigor, one couldn't help but marvel at how truly hot and cold one could be within mere seconds. Hours spent diving for treasure, hunting for sea monsters, playing Indian scout hiding from settlers, piggyback battles with city kids from Houston and Dallas (whom we soon realized weren't quite as sophisticated as our mother assured us they were due to "urban advantages"). It was all an idyllic timeliness that seems even more unspoiled from the distance of hazy reminiscence. A river as languid, unassuming, and characteristic as a child's hair ribbon.

Yet when a flash gully-washer comes thundering down the valley, it's best to give the river its due. On an early August morning in 2018, eleven inches of rain fell in an unexpected cloudburst, causing the river to rise fourteen feet. Only minutes later, twenty-seven campers at Chalk Bluff Park, just above Uvalde, were awakened by a roaring wall of water. Campers saw a swollen river over two hundred yards wide, cars and trucks bobbing in the waves as they disappeared downstream. One visitor reported seeing a black pickup with its lights on racing backward down the draw. Another witnessed a car stranded on an island with its occupants inside yelling for help. Highway 55 from Uvalde to Rocksprings shut down completely when the river inundated the roadway. Other families scrambled for higher ground and climbed into trees, where they were later rescued by helicopter and boats.

A languid river? Perhaps. Erratically unpredictable? Undeniably so. From the upper tributaries and local landmarks—Pulliam Creek, Cedar Creek, Spring Branch, "Eagles Nest," "Paint Bluff"—all names familiar to those acquainted with the utmost origins of the Nueces—a river commences with devastating beauty and advances with sporadic devastation. A puzzle characteristic of nature's perpetual, changeable enticement.

Below Uvalde, the Nueces drops out of the Hill Country and enters the South Texas Brush Country—where it pretty much vanishes underground during the dog days of summer—a stagnant pool here, a murky lagoon there—mostly rock and sand islands left derelict in the sun. As an early eighteenth-century Spanish soldier who crossed this land observed, *"I for the first time beheld vast ramparts and towers of prickly pear that seemed to form walls and mountains in their terrible array. From the midst of many of these banks of prickly pear, young*

trees or saplings of the same (thorny) nature were to be seen from twenty to thirty feet in height. The whole country had a peculiar appearance, presenting a view of boundless extent and unbroken grandeur. Yet there was no beauty—it was a profound and cheerless desolation . . . a wilderness covered thick with chaparral and presenting an appearance more dismal than anything I ever beheld."

This land along the Nueces River in South Texas is precisely not analogous to some soft and endearing creature one might cradle to one's breast. And yet . . . and yet, as the great storyteller from this region, J. Frank Dobie, has pointed out, "Every old ranch in the Nueces country, every old road, every hollow and water hole has its story of treasure."

These lands, long a crossroads between Texas and Mexico, abound with tales of lost Spanish treasures—thirty-one mule loads of silver buried alongside the Nueces according to one legend, Santa Ana's lost payroll chest carried away by a flood in another. On the outskirts of Crystal City, a swampy lake has formed from a relic channel of the Nueces—a spooky place aptly named *Espantosa*. It was here, according to ancient folklore, that a group of Spaniards transporting a wagon filled with silver and gold decided to camp for the night. In the morning, everyone and everything completely disappeared, swallowed up by the lake—and the treasure is still there, waiting to be recovered.

Dobie himself dug for fortune along the Nueces—and he'd grown up on a family ranch in Live Oak County where the previous inhabitants were massacred by Indians—leaving generations of people who believed that buried silver and gold had been left behind. "Long before I was born men were digging for it," Dobie said, adding, "they are still digging."

As it turns out, there *was* buried treasure in the Nueces River country. Today it is called the Eagle Ford Shale. This oil boom hit in the 2010s with the shock of a subatomic paroxysm. Ground-zero Nueces River counties such as Zavala, La Salle, McMullen, and Live Oak were irrevocably changed from *mañana* environs to frenetic boom-town utopias. Suddenly just-out-of-high school graduates could make $80,000 a year careening down two-lane farm-to-market roads hauling frack water or natural gas. "Man Camps" proliferated like feedlot cow pies. In a matter of months, the Jourdanton-Pleasanton "metroplex" went from two motels to fourteen. Asphalt roads were thrashed from ceaseless eighteen-wheeler poundings. Oil rigs and nighttime gas flares became endemic as road runners and grass burrs. Beer joints flourished, schools overflowed, taxes went up, traffic fatalities soared, Wal-Mart made even more money, and the quaint notion of sleepy hamlets drowsing contentedly in the South Texas sunshine went the way of Grapette soda and Sen-Sen breath mints.

A considerable portion of my childhood was spent with my maternal grandparents on their ranch outside of George West. One of the highlights of each visit was when Grandmother Alberta would drive us down to the "park" on the Nueces River in her invincible Buick Roadmaster. "Park" is perhaps an overly generous categorization—it was basically a dirt road with trees. Lots of trees. A forest of trees choking out the sun in dappled, shady, towering untidiness. A true rarity in our rain-deprived brush country existence. Massive live oaks surrounded all, draped in Spanish moss like mourners wearing *serapes*. Hackberrys, mesquite, cedar elms, soapberry, Texas persimmon, prickly ash, *anaqua*, *coma*, *huisache*, *retama*, *ebano*, *chapote*, and of course the river's namesake, pecans, grew in wild profusion. A living, bilingual encyclopedia of South Texas river flora ran riot in nature's irrigated glory.

Splayed across the sluggish Nueces stood an ancient metal truss bridge paved with wooden planks that rattled and quaked with each vehicle bold enough to cross it. Our grandmother wouldn't permit us to even walk on it for fear of imminent collapse. The unexpected daylight gloom, the crumbly high banks of the for certain snake-infested, alligator-swarming, and god-only-knows-what-kind-of-creature-abiding-there aura only added to our youthful glee and terror. It was a grand and secretive amusement park designed to entice a child's unchecked imagination.

A bit farther upstream, my Uncle Tommy had a ranch that was once a part of the pioneer West Ranch that covered a large portion of Live Oak County in the late nineteenth century. In addition to the stately, ancient oaks dotting the river bottom, there was a sand mine that the grandchildren spent hours climbing up and rolling down each massive dune.

Some years the Nueces flooded mightily, and it appeared as if most of the ranch had vanished underwater. It was astonishing to see this usually insignificant rivulet turn overnight into a raging Mississippi on an erratic whim. Cattle would stand, sometimes for days, isolated on temporary islands. Javelinas swimming for their lives and white-tailed deer hopping high and long from concealment to reprieve to safety and shelter, over and over again. It was a textbook demonstration of nature unburdening and replenishing through astonishing spectacle.

The Nueces meets up with the Frio and the Atascosa Rivers in the aptly named Three Rivers, Texas, and then meanders its way through the scrub brush and loamy terrain to be halted at Wesley Seale Dam on Lake Corpus Christi (or as it was called in my youth, Lake Mathis). I spent one week there when I was in third grade at a Baptist youth camp on Lake Mathis. Sleeping in hell-hot tents and singing hymns were probably not any eight-year-old boy's idea of unremitting joy. The older kids tortured us with tales of nine-foot-long alligators in the water (indeed, alligators flourished there) along with nasty-looking, fangy alligator gars (which predate the Cretaceous era of over 100 million years ago and resemble every grisly minute of it). To say the least, I didn't spend a lot of time actually in the water, but I did catch my fair share of crappie and sunfish from the dock.

By the time the Nueces reaches the outskirts of Corpus at Labonte Park, right off Interstate 37—speeding traffic from San Antonio a mere arm's-throw distant—the river passes sluggishly over one final man-made weir seemingly designed to apprehend floating trees, Igloo coolers, and abandoned lawn chairs from reaching the Gulf. As the river widens and ambles toward the bay, it parallels a canal, the Corpus Christi Ship Channel, an ancient resaca of the Nueces that has been widened, deepened, and dredged numerous times. A sector of ultra-intense petrochemical fabrication, the air becomes acrid with billowing vapor, twenty-four-hour discharges of orange fumes scalding the sky, countless monolithic steel reservoirs and Escher-like tubes snaking endlessly round towers of silver-painted bewilderment. Sulfur dioxide, nitrogen oxide, carbon dioxide, carbon monoxide, methane, dioxins, hydrogen fluoride, chlorine, benzene—all a daily sampling of refinery emissions.

As the river empties its 315-mile capacity into Nueces Bay, the expansive inlet now accommodates gargantuan oil tankers, occasional fishermen, boaters, and kayakers and is bounded on both sides by monolithic refineries, lackluster palm trees, and wind turbines stretching thirty-three stories tall. On the Gulf of Mexico, the scraggly Nueces at long last evolves into a waterway fully requisite of one's attention.

The story progresses further. The Port of Corpus Christi is rapidly developing into a supertanker facility, capable of accommodating the largest oil transporters in the world, the first of its kind in the United States. Each vessel capable of hauling over 440,000 tons of crude oil (approximately two million barrels) and slinking in and out of the bay on the projected deepened and widened ship channel, two abreast, does precious little to alleviate fears of potential mishap.

Despite Nueces Bay being the fragile estuary nursery for crab, shrimp, and untold aggregates of Gulf fish, plans are proceeding to construct a one-billion-dollar anchorage facility on Harbor Island, adjacent to the tourist / fishing / spring break mecca of Port Aransas. To infer that people are at polar ends of this proposal is to suggest that it gets humid on the Gulf in summer. A similar plan was shelved decades ago as being too risky. Yet the Port of Corpus Christi is focused on revenue above all other considerations. The supertankers are on the way.

Goodbye to a river? Not hardly. The Nueces is such a beautiful, daunting, exasperating, complex, and immensely historical feature of our state, it will never be forgotten. Perhaps "gently unnoticed" would be the fitting adage for such a grand watercourse. Leave her be! She's doing fine without more dams, bait shops, tube rentals, beer joints, party boats, jet skis, factories, mines, fracking detritus, endless oil and gas exploitation, refineries, feed lots . . . and all other twenty-first century vexations.

Perhaps because the Nueces is not an "urban river," save for the tail end in Corpus. Because she's farther away from large city exodus weekends. Because virtually every foot of her is bordered by ranches, farms, and private property. Because parts of her vanish in the summer and because alligator gars are so dang gnarly—I think, I trust, I hope—the blessing of "trendy" will never be bestowed on this magnificent relic.

On one of my countless trips down to our brushy inheritance in Duval County, I pulled off the road one time, just past the Highway 16 bridge crossing the Nueces. It was late winter and brisk out, and the sun was setting, and I remember thinking, *"As many times as I've driven over this bridge, I've never once gotten out to look under it, see the river, see what's down there."* I turned and drove off on the dirt path alongside the adjacent barbwire fence and halted just at the edge of a bluff. Getting out I instantly, involuntarily felt the energy shift from "up there" on the twenty-first century highway to "down here" on the river bottom. Eerie, quiet, veiled—a million stories flowing gently past on a shallow stream of boundless memory. I remembered an old farmer telling me once that as a boy, he'd found a Mexican soldier's button at the low-water crossing on the Nueces. Made sense, as this was indeed the approximate river crossing of the Old Laredo road to San Antonio. Whose button was it? One of Santa Ana's men? A colonel, a capitán—the old dictator himself? I bowed through the slack wire fence and walked a bit farther along the banks. It felt utterly timeless. No vehicle noises of any kind came from the highway. Was it 2000, 1900, 1800 . . . when? I searched the ground, thinking for certain I'd see a medal or a sword—a ring would've been perfect! My imagination soared. How many Native Americans had stood exactly here and gazed into the future, wondering boundless, ageless thoughts brought on by solitude and sentiment? I thought about Spanish padres, some of them barely past their teens, walking into the unknown with nothing more than a Bible, a rosary, and God's forbearance to guide them. I thought about the perennial lonesome cowboy chasing a fractious steer down into the mire and cursing his bad luck. I remembered my grandmother telling me of a story once where as a girl she'd been invited to a dance at a big ranch house and the river had gotten up so high, the ranch hands had to ferry them all to the ball on lantern-lit boats.

It sounded so impossibly romantic at the time, I wondered how she avoided marrying the first cowboy she met that night.

I must've stood there for a good, long time, as I noticed it quickly getting darker. An eighteen-wheeler droned across the bridge, and I immediately snapped back from time traveling. Uncanny how the sensation arrived and departed so quickly, and yet I was definitely there for a single, boundless moment. There in a timeless place brought on by the river's reflective guise, the probing, subtle force of the Nueces.

The Lower Río Grande

in this place where children still speak and lose
        multiple tongues
  in this place where we still lose and grow
        forked tongues
    this place where white herons hunt and drink in the resacas
    this place with el río grande~bravo
        in its pipes
        in its lungs
        in our face

—Emmy Pérez, from *With the River on Our Face*

It's quiet here except for the hushed flow of the river
and the hum of bugs answered by the sharp trill of birds.
Somewhere, an ocelot growls.

I know poetry when I hear it.

—David Bowles, *The Refuge on the Ranch*

Emmy Pérez, originally from California, has lived in the Texas borderlands for more than twenty years. She was the 2020 Texas Poet Laureate and is Professor of Creative Writing at the University of Texas Río Grande Valley. From *With the River on Our Face* by Emmy Pérez. © Emmy Pérez, 2016. Reprinted by permission of the University of Arizona Press.

David Bowles is an award-winning Mexican-American author, poet, and translator who grew up on the border and teaches at the University of Texas Río Grande Valley. From *They Call Me Güero: A Border Kid's Poems* by David Bowles. Cinco Puntos Press, 2018. Published by permission of David Bowles.

Hablando y Soñando

by Norma Elia Cantú

"Me siento coma un río subterráneo entre la piel y la realidad, mis aguas son mis versos que humedecen el desierto del alma."

—Carmen Vascones

En el río muere otro hombre. Ahogado.
Por eso hemos venido hasta aquí.
Y siento un río que me instiga llanto y gemidos profundos
que me mueve hacia un fin determinado por la luna
o el sol de mediodía
desde un lado hacia el otro.
Un río. La corriente fuerte de primavera,
la sangre me hace cosquillas con sus remolinos
al correr por mis venas.

¡Lo que hemos tenido que dejar para llegar hasta aqui!

Muñecas de trapo, mi colección de LPs de los '60s, los CDs de los '90s,
    el barrio de mi niñez, las cartas, tus cartas de amor, depresión aguda
    y profunda como la noche, la solidez de la casa materna, ilusiones
    de paz, de alegría, Che Guevara, el Marxismo, mis ideas de justicia,
    la iglesia de mi niñez con sus flores de mayo, y todo lo que cargaba
    a cuestas desde la Guerra que aún no termina.

Esa Guerra.

Norma Elia Cantú is a borderlands scholar, novelist, and poet who was born in Nuevo Laredo. She is the author and editor of numerous books, a Past President of the American Folklore Society, and is the Murchison Professor in the Humanities at Trinity University in San Antonio. From *Meditación Fronteriza: Poems of Love, Life, and Labor* by Norma Elia Cantú © Norma Elia Cantú, 2019. Reprinted by permission of the University of Arizona Press.

Y hemos venido hasta aquí,
por eso que fuimos y jamás volveremos a ser.
Platicamos toda la noche de lo que no pudo ser
y lo que tal vez será.

Lo que fué: comidas en
México Tipico en Nuevo Laredo,
Rosita's en Laredo
Lhardy en Madrid
Mi Tierra en San Antonio,
paseos por el Retiro o el River Walk, da igual.

Te tomo la mano y me estremezco.
Fantasma de mi juventud.
In lak'ech: tú eres mi otro yo, "my impossible spouse."
Llegamos hasta este lugar de llanto, de escombros.
Queremos cambiarlo todo, pasear entre
jardines de suculentos verde-oscuros,
a las orillas del río, entre muros de carrizo, de hierbas.
Envueltos en silencio los árboles:
'nacahuitas, mesquites, huisaches
y algún palo verde o retama por ahí.
Los arboles sueñan, se mecen con el vaivén
del viento. Murmuran sus secretos.
Cuánto no habrán visto, testigos del dolor y del amor.
Llegamos a donde tenemos que llegar.

Aquí nos enfrentamos con él.
Me cree inútil contigo o sin ti.
Nos advierte: hay peligro.
Enumera los riesgos;
platicamos un rato.
"Los que cruzan saben bien a lo que se atienen
pero se arriesgan igual,
se cuidan unos a los otros,
pero al final cada quien viene solo."

Te miro y me hundo en tus ojos profundos
como de luto.

Tu dolor y tu ser palpable como el lodo en este río.
tus ojos me cuentan historias desconocidas, de siempre.

Hablamos de lo que fue y de lo que será
como si con el hecho de hablarlas
las palabras se convirtieran en verdad
como que probáramos ser dioses, creadores del futuro
diosas que amadran el futuro.

Te aseguro: en el río viven mundos ajenos
con dioses propios.
¿No me crees? ¿No me entiendes?

Que triste vivir sin fe,
con solo las palabras para sentirse fiel,
solo la ciencia para cerciorar la realidad,
seguir por el mundo sin mirar atrás,
sin añorar lo que fue, sin soñar con lo que podría ser.

Talking Dreaming

by Norma Elia Cantú (translated by the author)

"I feel an underground river between skin and reality, my waters are my poems that dampen the desert that is my soul."

—Carmen Vascones

In the river another man dies. Drowned.
That is why we have come.
I feel a river that impels, weeping, deep wailing
moving me toward an end set by the moon
or the noontime sun
from one side to the other.
A river. A strong spring current
the blood tickles me with its
eddies as it runs through my veins.

What we've had to leave behind to get here!

Rag dolls, my LP collection from the '60s, my CDs from the '90s,
  my childhood barrio, my letters, your love letters, acute depression
  deep as night, the solid base of my parents' home, illusions of
      peace,
  of joy, Che Guevara, Marxism, my ideas of justice, my childhood
  church with its May flowers, and all that I carried on my back since
  the War, that War that will not end. That War.

And we have come to this place
because of what we were and will never be again.
We chat all night about what can never be,
of what was and what will be, perhaps.

What was: meals at
México Tipico en Nuevo Laredo
Rosita's in Laredo
Lhardy in Madrid

Mi Tierra in San Antonio,
long walks through el Retiro
or San Antonio's River Walk, it's all the same.

I take your hand and I tremble.
Ghost of my youth.
In lak'ech. You are my other I, "mi pareja imposible."
We arrive to this place of tears, of ruins.
We want to change it all, take our walks amidst
succulent dark green gardens,
at the river's edge between walls of reeds and weeds.
Shrouded by the trees' silences:
'nacahuitas, mesquites, huisaches,
perhaps a palo verde or retama along the way—
Trees dream, they swing with the rhythm
of the wind. They whisper their secrets.
How much they have seen, witnesses to pain and love.
We arrive where we must.

We meet him.
He believes me to be useless with or without you.
He warns us: there is danger.
He lists the risks.
We talk a bit.
"Those who cross know well what they face,
but they take the risk, nonetheless.
They care for one another,
but in the end each one comes alone."

I look at you and I sink in the depths of your eyes,
eyes like mourning.
Your pain and your being as thick as the mud in the river.
Your eyes tell me unknown stories. Stories of always.
We talk about what was and what will be,
as if saying the words would make the words real,
as if we had tried at being gods, creators of the future.

I assure you: in the river live alien worlds
with their own gods.
You don't believe me? You don't understand me?

How sad it must be to live without faith,
with only words to make one feel faithful,
with only science to hold up what is reality,
to go through this world without looking back,
without yearning for what was, without dreaming of what could be.

The Tecate Journals

by Keith Bowden

Eagle Pass-Piedras Negras

On April 4, 2004, on a night in which no rain fell in Piedras Negras, the Rio Escondido, a tributary of the Río Grande, rose from a depth of eighteen inches to twenty-five feet in a matter of half an hour, due to localized downpours further up the normally tranquil riverbed. The surge of water destroyed six hundred homes in the colonia of Villa del Fuente, on the south side of Piedras Negras, and killed somewhere between thirty-five and sixty people, depending on sources . . .

The flood left its mark on the Río Grande in a peculiar and unsightly fashion, effectively covering every tree on both sides of the river with trash, giving the impression that Mother Nature had hosted a tree-decorating party of grotesque, Ripleyesque proportions. For at least fifteen miles below the confluence with the Rio Escondido, every branch of every tree within the floodplain of the Río Grande had trapped the litter from that flood, and thanks to the pricked or stickled branches of that riparian growth, no amount of subsequent wind or rain has been able to free the unsightly trash. Furthermore, a wide swath of river-bank on both sides of the Río Grande hosts a coating of litter carried in by the flood: debris from shattered homes, lawn furniture, automobile tires, children's toys, and anything else too heavy or slippery to be trapped by tree limbs. At one beach where I pulled in to stretch my legs, I found the small pocketbook, adorned with a drawing of Snoopy, of a preadolescent girl, and when I opened it, I found a tube of imitation lipstick.

It occurred to me as I paddled through this section that if I were to explore the floodplain on either side of the river, I would likely find the skeletons of cattle, fowl, and perhaps even humans. However, I found the river eerie enough already. In one tree, I spotted a soiled disposable diaper some twelve feet above the river. In another I noticed a feminine napkin. Mile after mile, the otherwise

Keith Bowden taught English at Laredo Community College for nearly thirty years. In the early 2000s, he traveled the Río Grande by bike, canoe, and raft for his book on the river. Excerpted from *The Tecate Journals: Seventy Days on the Río Grande* by Keith Bowden. Mountaineers Books, 2007. Published by permission of Keith Bowden.

pristine riparian environment was adorned with the considerable refuse of the Rio Escondido basin. I could only guess at the vast amount of trash on the river bottom.

Below Eagle Pass, the river is powerful, the current pushy, the drops frequent, and the waves large. In particular, violent crosscurrents present a formidable challenge to the canoeist. On a warmer day, I would have considered the challenges of the bigger river fun, but this day brought a chill out of the north that stoked my fear of hypothermia in the event of a tip. At every drop, I had to navigate through large cross-waves, some splashing water in my face, all of them slapping the canoe and tossing it as if it were merely Styrofoam.

By the time I reached Las Islitas—or Kingsbury Falls, as Texans call it—I was nearly overwhelmed by the elements. In addition to the trash, the cold, and the power of the river, my body struggled to meet the demands of the pace I had been keeping. I went all out every day from sunup to sundown, seldom stopping the canoe, skipping lunch breaks, paddling ceaselessly. Now finishing my seventh week, I had lost a significant amount of weight, and whatever fat stores I had begun with were long since burned away, replaced by sinewy muscle, especially in my stomach and upper back. Still, I wasn't consuming sufficient calories to fuel the incessant activity, and with the cold now entrenched, I often felt listless, driving myself more on the adrenaline rushes the tough canoeing conditions dealt than on a hearty diet.

I stopped atop Las Islitas, which, as its name suggests, is a rapid clogged with small islands of rock, many barely above the water level. The maze of channels leading down the long rapids is complex but not especially difficult if you have good command of your boat. In the nineteenth century, Las Islitas posed a barrier to riverboats. No channel is wide enough to allow the passage of a boat wider than eight feet, and with a strong current swirling in the tight lanes, any boat wider than five feet would likely pinball between the rocks. I looked at the drop for a long time, more to stretch my legs and imagine the nineteenth-century boats struggling to negotiate it than out of a need to study it carefully. The rapid offered three channels to run and wasn't technically difficult if I entered well and didn't lose my read. Another similar rapids, with rocky islands congesting the drop in the river, followed an hour later, and numerous tight and choppy lesser rapids punctuated the end of every long pool.

This section of the river also offered profuse collections of birds, more birds than I've ever seen on any river anywhere. In addition to blue and white herons, the river was thick with ducks, white pelicans, Canada geese, barn owls, kiskadees, and ravens. I found the owls and pelicans especially interesting. The pelicans would perch on rocks at the tops of rapids, typically two or three birds when I first sighted them, and as I drew to within forty yards, they would take off, seemingly too heavy to fly, propelling themselves by pushing their webbed feet against the water as their monstrous wings flapped the air. At the next rapid, I would find that the group had grown to four or five, but this time they would alight at the bottom of the drop. Just as I reached the bottom, now closer than they had allowed me to get when they sat above the rapid, the small flock would fly in a horizontal formation, perfectly spaced, landing below the next rapid. When I would arrive there, I would find the flock had increased in number again, and this process would repeat itself for miles. One flock grew to seventeen before it allowed me to pass, and another reached thirteen.

The barn owls slept in the river cane and would awaken, groggy and disoriented, upon hearing my paddle strokes just below their roost. Invariably, their fear of me would result in their dropping whitish feces in the general direction of my canoe as they struggled to flee, sometimes downriver, sometimes upriver. The ones that fled downriver typically fled three or four times before they would figure out that the only sure escape was to fly inland.

The river was always replete with birds, and teals or other ducks led me the entire way. I knew from my research that Bentsen Río Grande State Park far downriver had gained national attention as a birders' paradise, but the section of river below Kingsbury Falls had dozens of times more birds than Bentsen offered later.

The birds, the absence of human signs other than the trash, the vibrant fall colors of the forested hillsides above the river, and the challenging currents all helped keep my mind off the physical discomfort that the cold and my lack of energy were causing me. Rain fell intermittently, and I kept my rain jacket on all the time now because it was the warmest garment I had. Late in the day, I plunged the paddle into the water for yet another hard draw and suddenly felt completely drained.

Realizing I needed a rest, I stopped Mexican-side at the bottom of the next rapid, where I found a grassy access used by the local ranch for riverside picnics and fishing, and there I sawed firewood to carry to a high island I could see mid-river half a mile away. The late afternoon light reminded me of November in Canada; on such a raw day, Canadians would hustle home to a warm fireplace or woodstove, hot tea, and a good book. For the first time all trip, I felt a hint of loneliness.

Below Falcon Lake

Well aware of Starr County's reputation as a violent drug-smuggling corridor, I felt intimidated to be passing through the city of Miguel Aleman, redoubt of the

Zetas—gangs of deserters from the Mexican Army who made their livings by kidnapping, murder for hire, torture, and drug smuggling. Their reputation for barbarism had far surpassed the gruesome standards to which border residents had long since grown inured, and no one felt safe treading in their territory. The postmistress in Falcon Heights had said, "You don't even go there to fill a prescription or eat lunch in broad daylight." The Zetas, everyone warned, represented a new breed of evil that honored none of the codes of old-time narcotraficantes. For days I had nightmares about people being fed to lions.

For a half mile or so, I struggled to adapt to the new river, now a much smaller one than I had left on the other side of Falcon Lake. The water ran clear, and I could see the sandy bottom and the darting fish—mostly carp and bass and an occasional gar. For a short distance, bald cypress trees lined the shores, their drooping branches and pinnate leaves forming a feathery canopy. The river ran narrow, and the banks were steep. Above the cypress, Río Grande ash, willows, sugar hackberry, and elm concealed the fact that I was boating through an arid stretch of countryside called the Wild Horse Desert.

I had a claustrophobic, uneasy feeling as I navigated through the small canyon. I was easily startled by birds, and later by a raccoon. I passed a few homes, but I saw no people on the Texas side. On the Mexican side, I passed an empty pickup truck parked in a clearing just above the river, and a few hundred yards later, I saw two men armed with machetes walking near shore. Fighting my nerves, I angled the canoe toward them. One of them approached the bank.

"Good afternoon," the bearded man said warmly in Spanish. "Welcome to my ranch. Where are you going today?"

"I'm on a long trip. I started in Juárez, Chihuahua, and I'm going all the way to the Gulf."

"Tell me," he said, "how have we Mexicans been treating you so far?"

"Exceptionally well. Your people have been very helpful, very kind."

"Good. That makes me proud of my country. But tell me, my friend, if I made the same long trip you are making, how do you think your people would treat me?"

"Probably like a bunch of chilangos."

"That bad? Well, I would say you're lucky to have us good Mexicans living near the river."

The Roma Bluffs
Still Life with Folk

by Jan Seale

But why should love stop at the border?

—Pablo Casals

Sunday afternoon, high above the Río Grande,
we stand on a promontory rare for this delta.
Here riverboats delivered sugar, flour, salt,
returned the venturing settlers to Brownsville.
Today, the river is the only safe swimmer,
lips sealed to the media's descriptions:
drug, secure, international, illegal.

Across, a picnic family poses against mesquite.
A man tends the fire; others skim rocks.
Women chat, balance babies on hips.
Kids refuse the still life—shout, throw mud.
From the thin woods, like a cunning stray dog,
a huge sow meanders, her five piglets trailing.
The women scream, then laugh, swoop up
their toddlers hard bent on new piglet toys.

Upstream, the father of water-gatherers
has backed his pickup down an old boat landing
where five-gallon buckets form a palette:
viridian, Dutch pink, cadmium yellow, cream.
The tallest boy, braced waist-high in the eddies,

Jan Seale, the 2012 Texas Poet Laureate, is a native Texan who lives in McAllen. She is the author of more than twenty books and taught at the University of Texas-Pan American and at North Texas State University. From *The Wonder Is: New and Selected Poems, 1974–2012* by Jan Seale. Ink Brush Press, 2021. Published by permission of Jan Seale.

dips what's escaped Juarez, Big Bend, Laredo,
hands it to his brothers and cousins.

From the little town on the low horizon
drift faint accordion, *guitarrón*, *vihuela*,
announcement of a *futbol* game and *loteria*.

Brueghel the Elder would be thrilled:
gray Gulf clouds, light green of woods,
a distant bridge, Sunday calm.

Not *l'art pour l'art*, still, here's a tableau
the art lover could pause over, arms crossed,
eyes resting from modernity. This canvas
could be auctioned at Sotheby's, be precious,
collected, in its genre Rockwellian way.

While the church bell in Miguel Aleman clangs
evening vespers, the surveillance camera
high above us moves robotic, irregular, cunning.
Somewhere we appear on a screen
waving back to the Mexican children as we go.

We will carry this scene behind our eyes
and in coming days suppose families
doing things families do at river's edge:
drawing water, eating, communing.
We wish them repose. Perhaps,
there will even be harmony, perspective,
light and shade. For now, the old question
of knowing: If a landscape is out of sight . . . ?

Take a good look, we tell ourselves, and send
the same advice across the inscrutable water.
Life may imitate art, but upstream, downstream,
or across, the Great Border Wall of the Río Grande
will overpaint this riverscape forever.

Border Kid

by David Bowles

It's fun to be a border kid, to wake up early Saturdays
and cross the bridge to Mexico with my dad.

The town's like a mirror twin of our own,
with Spanish spoken everywhere just the same
but English mostly missing till it pops up
like grains of sugar on a chili pepper.

We have breakfast in our favorite restorán.
Dad sips café de olla while I drink chocolate—
then we walk down uneven sidewalks, chatting
with strangers and friends in both languages.

Later we load our car with Mexican cokes and Joya,
avocados and cheese, tasty reminders of our roots.

Waiting in line at the bridge, though, my smile fades.
The border fence stands tall and ugly, invading
the carrizo at the river's edge. Dad sees me staring,
puts his hand on my shoulder. "Don't worry, m'ijo:

"You're a border kid, a foot on either bank.
Your ancestors crossed this river a thousand times.
No wall, no matter how tall, can stop your heritage
from flowing forever, like the Río Grande itself."

David Bowles is an award-winning Mexican-American author, poet, and translator who grew up on the border and teaches at the University of Texas Río Grande Valley. From *They Call Me Güero: A Border Kid's Poems* by David Bowles. Cinco Puntos Press, 2018. Published by permission of David Bowles.

The Betrayal

by Domingo Martínez

You never really get to understand the impression a living, indifferent Titan has on your life when you and your family are born near it, depend on it for most aspects of your livelihood. It's more of a force of nature than nature itself.

As a dependent—like, say, a peasant living on a fiefdom—you tend to become inured to the good moods of your lord, frightened of his tempestuous ones, which can sweep you aside with absolutely no pause for thought or justice and would simply continue moving on with its life, headed elsewhere for more important things than understanding your troubles.

The Río Grande was like that, for us, for my family: a nourisher to start, a killer in the end.

My family home was in the farmland outside of Brownsville, headed east toward Boca Chica Beach and just a few miles from the Río Grande, maybe four or five miles away but certainly no more than ten minutes from what we understood to be our own personal access point to this landmark of American and Mexican history.

Back then, the river seemed huge to me, to us, a dangerous and living thing that provided us with much of everything we needed: food from the fish and crabs, work from the toil on its banks, meditation from the moods of the currents, and dreams from imagining what was just around the bend and what was just across the other side.

There was never a time, growing up in the farmland surrounding the easternmost side of Brownsville, when I wasn't aware of its presence, or its significance in the lives of my family. Back then, the river—to which my grandparents showed a genuine reverence by referring to it as "el Río Bravo" in a generations-old genuflection—was as central a part of our lives as the Nile would have been to a working-class Egyptian.

In our personal family mythology, the Río Grande occupied another dimension, as my real grandfather, my father's father, was a *coyote* in the 1940s and

Domingo Martínez of Brownsville is the author of the bestselling memoirs *The Boy Kings of Texas* (a finalist for the National Book Award) and *My Heart Is a Drunken Compass*. © Domingo Martínez, 2020. Published by permission of Domingo Martínez.

used this river as a highway, like the moonshiners of Appalachia, which would, in the end, write out his death warrant at the hands of the Texas Rangers. But that's another story altogether.

Then later, and in a bit less outlawish sort of terms and with another husband, my grandmother married another man who'd just returned from the Korean War and had started a business. He'd bought a couple of acres of land, cut right into the side of a large geometric field so that we were surrounded by seasonal plantings—never once giving thought to the chemistry of designer death we'd be breathing in daily, drinking in our water, washing our skin with because, well, that's just how things were then.

From the sand and rich soil of the banks of the Río Grande, my grandfather launched his business as a truck driver with a GI loan, hauling fill dirt and sand for the construction boom of South Texas, which began in the 1960s and died when Reagan took office in the 1980s. During his heyday, my step-grandfather had a total of eight working trucks, two in various states of disassembly used for parts and two John Deere tractors, upon which I would learn to drive when I was twelve at the sandpit, near the isolated safety of the river.

For those twenty years, my family carved out whole sections of earth and sand not one hundred yards from the riverbanks and sold it at $80 a truckload, and I remember spending much of my time as a child playing near the riverbanks, but never daring to get too close to the river's edge, as my father had instilled in me a real fear of the river's moods and pitfalls. In this way, it became as much my babysitter as my father's disregard for my safety, which likely laid the foundation for both my sense of independence and my fear of cliffs, no matter how small.

Recreation was another factor. On many Sunday afternoons, after church and a losing Dallas Cowboys game, it was not unusual for my father to pack the family and invite some friends or cousins to fill large coolers with Budweisers and load up their fishing poles, drive to the same spot on the river's edge and spread along the beach, build a large fire, catch some trash fish and cook it on homemade grills, usually some kind of repurposed truck parts.

In fact, so low were we on proper fishing poles and so many kids numbered in our ranks, the dads stopped even trying to cut down branches from the trees and make any attempts at a "fishing pole," would rather tie the end of a fishing line to the neck of a Budweiser longneck, loop a few yards to the body, add a lugnut for weight, tie a hook at the end, impale a piece of fajita, and boom: Bob's your uncle—you're now admitted into the land of fishermen. Now shut up and go get them.

After large downpours, the river would sometimes breach its banks and flood the working area, making the business (both farming and construction) shut down for weeks until the place dried up, the water reinvoked into the dry sand beds, the thirsty cropland nearby.

We didn't mind, could do with the time down.

As a listless, directionless teenager with limited resources or options, I often found myself exploring new trails with a few friends, wondering who'd made them or why—hunters? More fishermen? Illegal immigrants or their coyotes? The Border Patrol in search of the latter? Or maybe the Parks and Wildlife people, whom we never once saw but knew existed: while we tacitly understood one needed licenses for hunting or fishing, no one ever bothered to get one, since there was no one around to enforce the laws of the wild. Besides, we'd never catch anything but catfish or redfish, and never brought down anything other than a crow or two, maybe a few beer bottles floating downstream.

A favorite memory of the whole family was during the aftermath of a hurricane, when the river breached its banks and filled the entire place up with water, and my father had the idea to get some twine and the frozen chicken parts from the freezer, plus a few washtubs and buckets, and drive us to the sand pit.

How he knew what we'd find there amazes me still: he had us tie a knot around a frozen chicken leg or wing and then dangle it, just inside the dark, murky water, wait less than five or six seconds, then pull it out and holy shit if there were not three or four bright blue crabs crawling over themselves to get to the chicken. I remember scampering back and falling on my haunches at their violence.

All of us, in unison, howled in amazement, and what proceeded to happen can only be described as a harvest, an absolute devastation of the crab population. Seriously, we couldn't keep up with the amount of crabs we were collecting every few seconds. Quickly, we had to learn to grab them from the rear of their shells and then throw them into the washtubs, and within an hour or so, we had more crab than we knew what to do with. So off we go, back home, built a huge bonfire and boiled them alive—the whole time, I could swear I could hear them crying out, which was cruel—but then came the feast, and we fed half the barrio late into the night, with the kids staying up late and the men drinking beer, all from the bounty of the river, and for free.

A peasant's memory, sure, but it remains one of my favorites.

Later, as my horizons would start to broaden and the river's began to narrow, age began to take its toll upon my body, and many of my health issues could be traced back to that lifestyle of swimming in that unregulated water, bathing in and eating bottom-feeding fish from what was essentially a roiling Superfund site, stemming from both the lax EPA standards on the Texas side of

the border, home to far too many oil companies for its own good—art collections of bored wealthy doyennes be damned—and the nonexistent ones that
allowed heavy sludge to be dumped directly into the river from the *maquiladoras*
on the Mexican side.

But, hey: what did we know? It was a river, right? Rivers are good, demigod-
like in many mythologies, South Texas included. So we continued doing as
peasants do, which is to live and die at the behest of those who feel nothing
for the people who suffer.

Nostalgia certainly has a role to play in the tapestry of the human condition,
but it can become toxic when it outlives its purpose. When I think back on this
time, for some reason it always reminds me of that scene in *North by Northwest*,
where Cary Grant is being chased by that crop duster in that field.

What a perfect metaphor for life on the banks of the river.

See, I cannot with absolute certainty claim that it wasn't the crop dusters
that paid no mind to the families that lived on their trajectories of spraying
insecticides onto the young cotton, the early corn or grain, who were directly
responsible for the asthma I suffer today, at age forty-seven, with lungs like a
sixty-five-year-old man with pleurisy. Nor can I effectively trace it back to the
heavy metals in the river that we played in, fished from, used to water our crops,
and that sank into the water table that ran beneath the ground in Brownsville.
Not only did we cook with poisoned water, but we showered in it and drank it
from fountains.

But I suspect most of my health issues emanate from this time, and when
I describe these experiences to my doctors, I can always sense the same sort
of "Oh, you poor bastard. You don't know what's coming yet, do you?" look
that microflashes briefly across their faces before they can collect themselves.

Coming "home" after twenty-five years on the West Coast and walking across
the bridge into Matamoros one afternoon and looking down into what was
once the mighty Río Grande, I stood upon what's now a silly ritual I had as a kid
right at the line in the concrete of the bridge claiming this side to be the US,
that side to be Mexico, and in my head I remember a hundred times yelling,
"Look! I'm in two places at once!" a joke my friends never liked and I never
stopped liking.

I looked down onto what was once the Rio Bravo, the mean river, the big
river, the Río Grande, and it was now looking like a caged and starved circus
animal in chains, emaciated, eyes deadened and, if it had been a Titan and if it
had had eyes, like they were looking back at you through eyes heavily scaled
with glaucoma. It felt quite a bit like when you haven't seen your parents in that

long a time, and you see how age has caught up to them, and they've shriveled, smaller than you remember, the giants and monsters with tempers and powers of years gone by now hardly capable of a whimper, asking for your help to get out of a chair. You could bring up the years of abuse, of disease, the things they did wrong and how it was affecting you now, as an adult, but it would be pointless, and mean, because they've forgotten all about it anyway. That's what it felt like, looking down into that dying river.

And it wasn't just that it had been drained and militarized by vampires in red ties, but what deeply saddened me was that the river itself seemed to have been arrested, conquered, detained, kept in captivity in a privatized ICE facility while its future is determined by an uncaring immigration system that would have no compunction in allowing it to die under one of those Mylar blankets, holding a juice box.

This demigod of our youth, who once provided us with much of what we needed, is now withering away, left to rock itself away in a rotten La-Z-Boy in a corner of toxic nostalgia and industrial waste, losing its memory like an Alzheimer's patient in a neglected home, already forgetting its own vibrancy and past, like the rest of the generations who once knew it for the formidable force it once was, because it exists neither here nor there and simultaneously in both places and is used as a pawn in the sublimated politics of race and classism.

And no longer as the dangerous friend and benefactor I once knew and who would never again have friends like me.

The End of the River

by Jan Reid

O n a warm July afternoon, I am going to see the mouth of the Río Grande for the first time. In the sixteenth century, the bright forest of palm trees around the mouth was a landmark for navigators of the Gulf. In good years, the lowlands surrounding those groves would be marshes teeming with shellfish and minnows hunted by ibis and herons stepping sprightly in the brine. But today, as I ride eastward on Texas Highway 4, the most striking features ahead are airborne white swirls of sand and salt. Decades of clearing for agriculture and development have isolated the last native sabal palms to a small Audubon preserve outside Brownsville, and most of the wetlands have gone as dry as chalk. The sprawling river delta has been reduced to a nearly barren, eroded strip of earth, and some residents of Port Isabel are having trouble breathing because there's so much windblown grit in the air.

My guide is a pleasant man named Gilberto Rodriguez who grew up on a farm in Weslaco and now roams the lower Río Grande as a watermaster specialist for the Texas Commission on Environmental Quality (TCEQ). In layman's terms, Rodriguez is an unarmed water cop; he spends much of his time checking pump gauges on the Texas side, making sure none of its farmers are drawing more water than they're allowed. For many Río Grande Valley residents, the mere inference of such cheating sparks outrage, and Rodriguez tells me he often fears violence. "The hotter the water," he reflects, "the more hostile people become."

A dwindling supply of water is an issue for every citizen of Texas, but few residents have as desperate a case as Río Grande Valley farmers. They've suffered a dry spell in the past decade that rivals the legendary drought of the forties and the fifties that turned most of Texas into a federal disaster area. Because the groundwater is brackish, the Valley gets no help from aquifers; the Río Grande carries all the water there is.

Nowhere is this reality more clear than at the mouth of the Río Grande, which is further consumed by mats of water hyacinth and hydrilla. At the terminus

Jan Reid (1945–2020) was a journalist at *Texas Monthly* and the author of more than a dozen books of fiction and nonfiction. Two of his novels, *Comanche Sundown* (2009) and *Sins of the Younger Sons* (2017), won the Texas Institute of Letters Award for Best Fiction. Adapted from "The End of the River" by Jan Reid, *Texas Monthly*, January 2003. Published by permission of *Texas Monthly*.

of Highway 4, Rodriguez and I jostle from pavement to loose sand. It's a pretty day at the beach. The white-capped waves are bright dark blue, and squadrons of brown pelicans fold their wings and smack beak-first into the surf, trying to catch dinner. Boca Chica, which means "small mouth," has none of the glitz and development of nearby South Padre Island, but families are out fishing, splashing, building sand castles. Ahead, a portable light tower has been erected. That landmark, Rodriguez tells me, is Mexico. Parked on the beach, hood pointed toward the surf, is a green-and-white SUV marked US Border Patrol. For hours on end, two agents sit and stare at beachcombers and the Gulf.

The agents represent the increased vigilance of Homeland Security, but their presence here also marks the death of a river. The riverbank they've parked beside is now a land bridge. It is not unlike other strips of sand and shell that the tide and currents lay out in the Gulf's endless construction of beaches becoming dunes becoming barrier islands. The difference is that this sandbar has obliterated a natural frontier between nations and left the mythic Río Grande a tepid, stagnant shallow. It has too little push to cross the bar and reach the ocean.

On this day the pool trapped at Boca Chica looks blue enough, but its biological illness is indicated by crusts of salt that line the banks for hundreds of yards upstream and resemble icy slush. Freshwater inflow is an estuary's lifeblood, but these days the Río Grande has little of that to give. I watch some Mexican boys skimming the stagnant pool with fishing nets. One stands in the middle of the river, about a quarter of a mile inland, and the water comes no higher than his knees. "I have not brought you to the mouth of the river," Rodriguez says with a slight smile. "I have brought you to the end of the river."

The Río Grande has become the river that can no longer find its way to the sea.

El Río Bravo / The Río Grande

by Américo Paredes

<table>
<tr><td>

El Río Bravo

Río Bravo, Río Bravo,
que en tu cauce lento vas
con frecuentes remolinos,
cual si quieres ir atrás.

cual si quieren tus corrientes
sobre el cauce devolver
a buscar ignotas fuentes
que les dieron vida y ser,

así vas—mientras tus aguas
lloran, lloran sin cesar—
a morirte lentamente
a las márgenes del mar.

Mis pasiones y mis cuitas
en tu seno quiero ahogar;
llévate el dolor de mi alma
en tu parda inmensidad.

Que he nacido a tus orillas
y muy joven ya sentí
que hay en mi alma torbellinos,
que ella se parece a ti.

</td><td>

The Río Grande

Muddy river, muddy river,
Moving slowly down your track
With your swirls and counter-currents,
As though wanting to turn back,

As though wanting to turn back
Towards the place where you were born,
While your currents swirl and eddy,
While you whisper, whimper, and
    mourn;

So you wander down your channel
Always on, since it must be,
Till you die so very gently
By the margin of the sea.

All my pain and all my trouble
In your bosom let me hide,
Drain my soul of all its sorrow
As you drain the countryside,

For I was born beside your waters,
And since very young I knew
That my soul had hidden currents,
That my soul resembled you,

</td></tr>
</table>

Américo Paredes (1915–1999) grew up in Brownsville and became a pioneering writer, folklorist, and founding scholar of Chicano studies at the University of Texas. He challenged generations of Anglo-American mythmaking in his influential books *With His Pistol in His Hand: A Border Ballad and Its Hero* (1958) and *George Washington Gómez: A Mexico-texan Novel* (1990). © Américo Paredes, 1936. Published by permission of Alan Paredes.

Turbia, sí, de fondo obscuro,	Troubled, dark, its bottom hidden
mas el Sol le hace brillar;	While its surface mocks the sun,
con suspiros—rebeliones—	With its sighs and its rebellions,
y bregando sin cesar.	Yet compelled to travel on.
Cuando muera, cuando muera	When the soul must leave the body,
y se pudra el cuerpo ya,	When the wasted flesh must die,
mi alma, como riachuelo	I shall trickle forth to join you,
a tus aguas correrá.	In your bosom I shall lie;
Pasaremos por los campos	We shall wander through the country
que se mirarán verdear,	Where your banks in green are clad,
por jacales de rancheros,	Past the shanties of rancheros,
a las ruinas de Bagdad. . . .	By the ruins of old Baghdad,
Y tus aguas moribundas	Till at last your dying waters,
en lo azul se perderán,	Will release their hold on me,
mientras duermo dulcemente	and my soul will sleep forever
a las márgenes del mar.	By the margin of the sea.

. . . July 21, 1936

Benediction

The River

by Pat Mora

In the light is a land.
In the land is a river.
In the river is a song.
In a city flows the song.

To the river come the voices.
Stories in the voices.
Sorrows in the stories.
Longings in the sorrows.
Prayers in the longings.
Hope in the prayers.

Prayers in the hope.
Longings in the prayers.
Sorrows in the longings.
Stories in the sorrows.
Song in the stories.

Song in the river.
River in the land.
Land in the light.

Pat Mora, born and raised in El Paso, is a poet and author of books for adults, teens, and children. Her many literary honors include the Lifetime Achievement Award from the Texas Institute of Letters. She is the founder of Día / Children's Day / Book Day, a national celebration of children, families, and reading. From *Encantado: Desert Monologues* by Pat Mora. The University of Arizona Press, 2018. Published by permission of Pat Mora.

Afterword
The State of Texas Rivers Today

by Andrew Sansom

We camped on a sandbar in Santa Elena Canyon. The sheer 1,500-foot walls of the spectacular gorge on both sides of the river we Americans call the Río Grande rendered our view of the sky a narrow, winding ribbon of blue far above. At twilight a peregrine falcon swooped down between the ramparts and snatched a Mexican free-tailed bat right out of the air. After the dinner dishes were washed and put away, the ribbon over our heads deepened to a richer hue, now spangled with countless stars.

Pleasantly tired, we savored the afternoon's run. The river flowing through the canyon was challenging enough but presented no serious danger to us in our canoes. In the campfire's glow, we eagerly anticipated the day to come. The strong currents of this great river would take us through the challenging formation known as the Rockslide and ultimately out of Santa Elena and into the Chihuahuan Desert sun.

We never dreamed that the day would come when there would not be sufficient water in the river for such an adventure to be possible.

Our run was but a small stretch of one of 3,700 named streams and fifteen major rivers that wind through nearly 200,000 miles of Texas countryside. Along the way, this vast circulatory system of our state provides water for almost two hundred major reservoirs and ultimately flows into seven coastal estuaries to nourish one of the most prolific coastal ecosystems in the world.

Unfortunately, that system is threatened as never before. According to the Texas Water Plan, the population of Texas is expected to more than double between 2000 and 2060, growing from 21 million to 46 million. Although we are faced with the enormous task of proving life-giving water to all these new Texans, we have already given permission for more water to be withdrawn

Andrew Sansom, one of Texas's leading conservationists, has been Executive Director of Texas Parks and Wildlife and the Texas Nature Conservancy. He is the founding director of the Meadows Center for Water and the Environment at Texas State University. He is the author of six books and, as a series editor, has overseen the publication of dozens of titles devoted to Texas rivers and conservation leadership. © Andrew Sansom, 2020. Published by permission of Andrew Sansom.

from many of our rivers than is actually in them. To put it another way, if all the water rights permits were fully used, some of our most beautiful and important Texas rivers would actually be dry today. And that's before adding 25 million more people over the next generation.

Population growth and other factors—including the changing climate and increased groundwater pumping that threatens to dry up the springs that nourish Texas rivers—promise to strain our rivers as never before. We have already seen the mighty Río Grande with so little flow that it no longer reached the Gulf of Mexico.

In the 2000s, the Texas legislature created a nascent plan to protect the environmental flows in our rivers and streams. Unfortunately, though the process began with high hopes, the Texas Commission on Environmental Quality has never adopted the environmental flow recommendations. Even more discouraging, the Texas Water Development Board, which leads statewide water planning efforts, has never recognized the need to leave some water in the rivers to maintain aquatic habitats and ecological health.

And so . . . if you care about Texas Rivers, you need to be involved. Rivers need our help. They need our voices to speak for them before the state government. Start by contacting your state legislators and let them know you feel strongly that the flows in our rivers need to be planned for and protected. You can join and/or contribute to one of the organizations listed on the following pages or volunteer for the Texas Stream Team, which helps protect water quality. Just as important, you can visit Texas Paddling Trails and find a river to float with a youngster so that he or she will learn to enjoy being on the water and that the future of our rivers is in their hands.

Most days on the Río Grande through Santa Elena Canyon now there is so little water that you have to put in at the mouth, normally the end of the trip, and paddle upstream to the Rockslide. A still pool of water is all that remains of the river there. The canyon is still magnificent, and though it is still humbling to be back beneath the lovely ribbon of sky, the once mighty Río Grande is gone, and somehow the river has lost its soul. The Río Grande and many other Texas Rivers are threatened, but they can recover—with our help.

Appendix
River Advocacy Groups

River Conservation Groups

THE TEXAS LIVING WATERS PROJECT

A collaboration of conservation groups, including the National Wildlife Federation and the Sierra Club, working to transform the way we manage water so there will be enough for our wildlife, our economy, and our kids. texaslivingwaters.org

THE MEADOWS CENTER FOR WATER AND THE ENVIRONMENT AT TEXAS STATE UNIVERSITY

Inspiring research and leadership that ensures clean, abundant water for the environment and all humanity. Directs the Texas Stream Team, a network of trained volunteers and partner organizations that conduct scientific research and promote environmental stewardship to help understand and protect the 191,000 miles of Texas waterways. www.meadowscenter.txstate.edu

SAVE BARTON CREEK ASSOCIATION

Working to protect and conserve the watersheds so that future generations may enjoy the cool, clean waters of Barton Springs. savebartoncreek.org

BAYOU PRESERVATION ASSOCIATION

To celebrate, protect, and restore the natural richness of all our bayous and streams in the Houston area, creating a network of healthy bayous, streams, and watersheds. www.bayoupreservation.org

FRIENDS OF THE BRAZOS RIVER

Helping restore a sound ecological environment to the Brazos, especially between Lakes Possum Kingdom and Whitney. www.friendsofthebrazos.org

LOWER BRAZOS RIVERWATCH

Defending the Brazos, Waco to the Gulf. www.facebook.com/lowerbrazosriver watch.org

BUFFALO BAYOU PARTNERSHIP

Revitalizing Buffalo Bayou by creating parks and trails and acquisition of green space as well as promoting the economic and social well-being of surrounding waterfront neighborhoods. www.buffalobayou.org

COLORADO RIVER ALLIANCE

To champion the long-term vitality of the Texas Colorado River through education and engagement. coloradoriver.org

DEVILS RIVER CONSERVANCY

Committed to treasure, preserve, and protect the Devils River, its springs, and the lands within its water catchment area. www.devilsriverconservancy.org

GUADALUPE RIVER TRUST

To preserve the unique natural heritage of the Guadalupe watershed for future generations through conservation easements, education, and outreach that connects people to the water and the land. www.gbrtrust.org

LLANO RIVER WATERSHED ALLIANCE

To preserve and enhance the Llano River watershed by encouraging land and water stewardship through collaboration, education, and community participation. www.llanoriver.org

MEDINA RIVER PROTECTION FUND

To provide ongoing support for the annual river cleanup, which is necessary to conserve this valuable natural resource. www.medinariver.net

FRIENDS OF THE NECHES RIVER NATIONAL WILDLIFE REFUGE

To preserve, protect, and restore the wild and scenic Neches River to provide outdoor opportunity and enjoyment of this natural and cultural resource for present and future generations. www.facebook.com/friendsofnrnwr

NUECES RIVER PRESERVATION ASSOCIATION

To restore and preserve the natural beauty of the lower Nueces River while promoting public education and recreation. www.facebook.com/NRPACorpusChristi

RGV FISHING AREA AND WATERWAY CLEANUPS

Organizes and sponsors fishing area and waterway cleanups throughout the Río Grande Valley. www.facebook.com/RGVFAWC/

FRIENDS OF THE WILDLIFE CORRIDOR (RÍO GRANDE VALLEY)

Supports the land acquisition goals, projects, activities, and outreach plans of the Santa Ana and Lower Río Grande Valley National Wildlife Refuges. friendsofthewildlifecorridor.org

SAN ANTONIO RIVER FOUNDATION

To preserve, enhance, and transform the San Antonio River Basin as a vibrant cultural, educational, ecological, and recreational experience. sariverfound.org

FRIENDS OF THE RIVER SAN BERNARD

To restore, protect, promote, and ensure a clean, healthy, flowing San Bernard River for the sanity and enjoyment of present and future generations. www .sanbernardriver.com

SAN MARCOS RIVER FOUNDATION

Preserving and protecting the natural beauty, flow, and purity of the San Marcos River. sanmarcosriver.org

FRIENDS OF TRINITY RIVER REFUGE

To support, expand, promote, and enhance the refuge and its use for recreational, educational, and scientific research purposes. www.facebook.com/Friends-of -Trinity-River-Refuge-94940271167/

Other Conservation Organizations

THE NATURE CONSERVANCY IN TEXAS

Since 1964, we've conserved nearly one million acres of land and more than two hundred miles of rivers and streams in Texas. With your support, we'll continue working to safeguard the state's natural landscapes, preserve the Gulf of Mexico, and improve the resilience of Texas cities for future generations to enjoy. www.nature.org

TEXAS RIVERS PROTECTION ASSOCIATION

A coalition of landowners, conservationists, canoe clubs, and fishing associations dedicated to protecting the quality of our remaining natural rivers. www .txrivers.org

TEXAS CONSERVATION ALLIANCE

For more than fifty years, the Texas Conservation Alliance has successfully advocated for wildlife and wild places in Texas. We've stopped unnecessary reservoirs that drown Texas rivers, fought clear-cutting in national forests, and recruited thousands of people to conserve Texas's beautiful outdoor world. www.tcatexas.org

TEXAS PADDLING TRAILS

From Texas Parks and Wildlife: paddling access to rivers, creeks, lakes, and more! tpwd.texas.gov/fishboat/boat/paddlingtrails

BIG BEND CONSERVATION ALLIANCE

Working to conserve the living heritage and unique natural and cultural resources of the greater Big Bend region of Texas. www.bigbendconservationalliance.org

COASTAL CONSERVATION ASSOCIATION, TEXAS

Ensuring the health and conservation of our marine resources and anglers' access to them. ccatexas.org

GREATER EDWARDS AQUIFER ALLIANCE

Advocating for the protection and preservation of the Edwards Aquifer and its springs and watersheds and the Texas Hill Country that sustains it. aquiferalliance.org

HILL COUNTRY ALLIANCE

Bringing together an ever-expanding alliance of groups to preserve open spaces, water supply, water quality, and the unique character of the Texas Hill Country. www.hillcountryalliance.org

AMERICAN RIVERS

To protect wild rivers, restore damaged rivers, and conserve clean water for people and nature. www.americanrivers.org

—compiled by Kyle Davis

Acknowledgments

We thank all the writers who agreed to include their works in this book—we are truly honored to showcase so much brilliant literature. We also thank the Wittliff Collections at Texas State University for its support and leadership, particularly Director David Coleman and Director of Development Ramona Kelly. We are honored to partner with the esteemed Andrew Sansom, founding director of the Meadows Center for Water and the Environment at Texas State. (That's Andy paddling the Meadows Center canoe on the cover of this book.)

We are delighted that exceptional artist and first-class person Clemente Guzman agreed to create the cover art, which is magnificent! We are also thankful to artist and mapmaker extraordinaire Molly O'Halloran for the gorgeous maps in this book—which were inspired by working maps developed for us by Shadi Maleki and Tom Swinbank. We thank Kyle Davis for his work to create the list of river conservation groups in the appendix.

We are grateful to the following for providing publication support: the Susan Vaughan Foundation, the Jacob and Terese Hershey Foundation, the Texas Historical Foundation, Will and Pam Harte, Kathie and Ed Cox Jr. We also thank Shannon Davies, the now retired director of Texas A&M University Press, for her early and enthusiastic support for this book. We extend our gratitude to our fine partners at Texas A&M University Press, especially Thom Lemmons, Kristie Lee, Kyle Littlefield, Patricia Clabaugh, Christine Brown, Katie Duelm, Nicole duPlessis, Emily Seyl, Kathryn Lloyd, and Jay Dew. We also thank Fran Vick and Thomas Zigal for their early and helpful readings of the manuscript. We are indebted to Michael Miller and his excellent team at Scribe for their first-class copyediting and design work on this book. We salute the fine staff at the Wittliff Collections: Susannah Broyles, David Coleman, Carla Ellard, Lauren Goodley, Lyda Guz, Ramona Kelly, Hector Saldaña, Katie Salzmann, Elizabeth Skaggs, Amanda Scott, Karen Sigler, Sherry Turner-Herrmann, and Mark Willenborg. We also thank other vital people at Texas State University, including the Alkek Library's Kim Finney, President Denise Trauth, Vice President for Information Technology Ken Pierce, Associate Vice President for the University Library Joan Heath, and the staff of the Meadows Center, including Robert Mace, Susan Hankins, Carrie Thompson, and Anna Huff.

For reprint assistance we are grateful to Kathy McFarland and Carolyn Chavana at *Texas Monthly*, Louie Bond and everyone at *Texas Parks & Wildlife* magazine, and Michael Hoinski and the folks at *Texas Highways*. Thanks also to Deedy and Maggie Abernethy, Julia Balestracci, Jim Baxter, Jan Belz, Stuart Bernstein, Phoebe Bode, Sidney Brammer, Shelby Brammer, Willy Brammer, Margaret Downing, Sarah Eckhardt, Helen Graves, Jane Graves, Babette Hale, Lynn Hoggard, Sally Graves Jackson, Tomas Jaehn, Mike Kanin, Elaine Katzenberger, Sarah Gerton, McKay Keith, Daria Kelly, Mary Kinnibrughm, Michael Nye, Alan Paredes, Ben Shrake, and Liz Whitehouse.

Thanks also to our good friends who helped guide this book downstream: Bill Minutaglio, Wes Ferguson, Carmen Tafolla, W.K. Stratton, Joe Holley, Mark Busby, Joe Nick Patoski, Severo Perez, Elizabeth Crook, Cary Clack, Jeff Davis, Sergio Troncoso, Theresa Chambers Stolte, Liz Rogers, Becky Duval Reese, Ken Roberts, Walt Herbert, Kerry Russell.

Steve Davis offers much love and gratitude to his wife, Georgia Ruiz Davis; their daughters, Natalie and Lucia; and their river-loving dog, Ralfred (who agreed to model for the cover painting).

Sam Pfiester offers much love and gratitude to his wife, Rebecca Kauffman Pfiester, and to all his River Ratus Americanus companions who have floated rivers together for the past forty years.